T0163888

Karl Barth:

A Future for Postmodern

Theology?

Edited by
Geoff Thompson
&
Christiaan Mostert

Text copyright © 2000 John Webster for the following papers: 'Barth, Modernity and Postermodernity', 'The Grand Narrative of Jesus Christ: Barth's Christology' and 'Rescuing The Subject: Barth And Postmodern Anthropology'.

Text copyright © 2000 ATF for all other papers in this volume.

All rights reserved. Except for any fair dealing permitted under the Copyright Act, no part of this book may be reproduced by any means without prior permission. Inquiries should be made to the publisher.

First published April 2000

National Library of Australia
Cataloguing-in-Publication data

Karl Barth – a future for postmodern theology?

Includes index
ISBN 0 9586399 1 4

1. Barth, Karl, 1886-1968. 2. Postmodernism – Religious aspects – Christianity. 3. God – History of doctrines – 20th century. I. Mostert, Chris. II. Thompson, Geoff 1957-

231.09004

ISBN: 978-1-925612-33-2   soft
        978-1-925612-34-9   hard
        978-1-925612-35-6   epub
        978-1-925612-36-3   pdf

Published by
Australian Theological Forum
P O Box 504
Hindmarsh
SA 5007

Printed by Openbook Publishers, Adelaide, Australia

Table of Contents

iii

Part Three
Studying Barth in Postmodenity:
Emerging Themes

Part Four
Theology After Barth & Beyond Modernity

Abbreviations

CD   K Barth, *Church Dogmatics* (Edinburgh: T&T Clark 1956-1975).

CL   K Barth, *The Christian Life: Church Dogmatics IV/4: Lecture Fragments* (T&T Clark: Edinburgh, 1981).

Contributors

John Webster is Lady Margaret Professor of Divinity at the University of Oxford.

Christiaan Mostert is Professor of Systematic Theology in the Uniting Church Theological Hall, Melbourne and lecturer in the United Faculty of Theology.

John Capper is an Anglican Minister and Academic Dean at Tabor College, Sydney.

Mark Lindsay is Associate Lecturer in the Department of European Languages and Studies, University of Western Australia.

Gordon Preece is Director of the Ridley College Centre of Applied Christian Ethics, Melbourne, and Lecturer in Ethics and Practical Theology.

Nancy Victorin-Vangerud is Lecturer in Systematic Theology at Murdoch University and the Perth Theological Hall of the Uniting Church in Australia.

Geoff Thompson is the Minister of the Word in the Alphington/Fairfield congregation of the Uniting Church in Australia. He completed doctoral studies on Barth and the non-Christian religions in 1995.

Contributors

Stephen Pickard is Associate Professor and Head of the School of Theology, Charles Sturt University and Director, St Mark's National Theological Centre, Canberra.

Bruce Barber is a Minister of the Word in the Uniting Church in Australia and Dean of the United Faculty of Theology, Melbourne.

Craig Thompson is the Minister of the Word in the Narre Hampton Park Parish of the Uniting Church in Australia. His doctorate focussed on a theological analysis of George Linbeck's model of doctrine.

Trevor Hogan is a lay member of the Anglican Church and Lecturer in the School of Sociology, Politics and Anthropology at La Trobe University, Melbourne.

Neil Ormerod is Lecturer in Systematic Theology at the Catholic Institute of Sydney.

Wes Campbell is the Minister of the Word in the Essendon Congregation of the Uniting Church in Australia. His doctorate addressed Ernst Troeltsch's approach to grounding theology in history.

Introduction

Geoff Thompson and Christiaan Mostert

Deep in the footnotes of his early work on Barth, *God After God*, Robert Jenson quotes the following remark of Schubert Ogden: 'Especially through the influence of Barth's later work in *Die Kirkliche Dogmatik*, the theological task came to be received as entailing a radical separation of Christian faith and modern culture'. The response is a robust Jensonian rebuttal: 'The first step toward understanding Barth is to grasp that this is the precise and compendious opposite of the case'.[1]

This exchange crystallises much of the history of the debate that has surrounded the interpretation of Karl Barth's theology. Indeed, it is a measure of the dominance and lasting impact of liberal Protestantism's own account of the relationship between Christian faith and modern culture that Ogden's remarks would have been, even until relatively recently, widely received as self-evident and Jenson's as bordering on the incomprehensible. However, even if the limitations of liberalism's response to modernity are more evident now than they were mid-century, it is nevertheless far from clear that there is yet any consensus around the precise nature of Barth's relationship to modernity. Jenson himself, for instance, continues to press the issue that Barth's rejection of liberal theology did not amount to an evasion of the claims of modernity. Instead, Barth was involved in an alternative, christologically-focused and creative response to modernity.[2] It

---

1. R Jenson, *God After God: The God of the Past and the God of the Future, Seen in the Work of Karl Barth* (Indianapolis and New York: Bobbs-Merrill, 1969), 195. Jenson is quoting from S Ogden, *The Reality of God* (London: SCM, 1967), 5.
2. See Jenson's crisp summary of the issues in his 'Karl Barth' in D

has also been argued that we are yet fully to comprehend the exact nature of the 'modernity' with which Barth was engaging.[3] Moreover, the suggestion has been made, quite plausibly, that the interpretation of Barth's theology more generally is something that is still very much in its infancy.[4] When to these concerns is added the straightforward fact that there is no agreed definition of either postmodernism or postmodern theology, it might be thought that an exploration of the question, 'Karl Barth: A Future for Postmodern Theology?' is at least premature, if not misplaced altogether.

Yet, to explore that theme was what a group of interested academic theologians and parish ministers based in Melbourne decided to do when planning a commemoration of the thirtieth anniversary of Barth's death. The commemoration took the form of a two-day conference held on December 4-5, 1998, at Queen's College in the University of Melbourne. This volume contains the various papers that were presented at that conference which was generously sponsored by the Theological Hall of the Uniting Church in Australia (Victorian Synod), the Hotham Parish of the Uniting Church in Australia and the Melbourne College of Divinity. It became clear as the conference drew near that the organisers had tapped into a pool of interest that both surprised and delighted them: almost 100 people from five of Australia's six states, New Zealand, the

Ford (ed), *The Modern Theologians: An Introduction to Theology in the Twentieth Century* Vol 1 (Oxford: Blackwell, 1989), 23-49.

3. B McCormack, *Karl Barth's Critically Realistic Dialectical Theology: Its Genesis and Development 1909-1936* (Oxford: Clarendon, 1995), 464-467.

4   George Hunsinger, writing more than two decades after Barth had ceased (although not completed) his work on the *Church Dogmatics* claims that 'we are still in the early stages of even understanding what it was that Barth had to say' (*How To Read Karl Barth: The Shape of His Theology* [New York and Oxford: Oxford University Press, 1991], ixf).

USA and (including the keynote speaker) England assembled for what was to be a fruitful period of thought and discussion.

It is arguable that in Australia even more than usual caution should be exercised in linking Barth with postmodernity, precisely because there has been no strongly-developed tradition of Barth scholarship in the first place. Even the few individual scholars who have studied Barth closely have done so largely in isolation from each other and from the wider theological community. (It has to be said that some of the few who were studying Barth through the 1950's and 1960's also happened to be among those who were instrumental in writing the *Basis of Union* of the Uniting Church in Australia which finally came into existence in 1977. However, even in this regard, the influence of Barth was not through a direct application of his ideas, but indirectly through local scholars engaging from afar with the issues thrown up by the mid-century Barth-Bultmann debates.[5])

At most, therefore, there have been pockets of interest in Barth, but they have never consolidated into anything like a recognised corpus of Australian writings on Barth. The reasons for this are many, but the passing observations made by Richard Roberts in his study of the reception of Barth's theology in the Anglo-Saxon world are at least partly true. He writes that any such reception in Australia has been impeded, at least well into the post-Second World War period, by the restrictions placed on theological innovation by its historical entrapment in denominational issues and conflicts.[6] Nevertheless, perhaps it was the absence of a strong background of Barth scholarship

---

5   On this see M Owen, *Back to Basics: Studies in the Basis of Union of the Uniting Church in Australia* (Melbourne: Uniting Church Press, 1996), 53-60.

6   R Roberts, 'The Reception of the Theology of Karl Barth in the Anglo-Saxon World: History, Typology and Prospect' in his *A Theology on its Way? Essays on Karl Barth* (Edinburgh: T&T Clark, 1991), 136.

that opened up the possibility for a broad-based approach to the question which the conference theme posed. There were, in other words, few established axes to grind. Moreover, quite apart from these local issues, the fact remained that the question of Barth and postmodernity had become an important, if contested, issue in Barth scholarship.

The sections of this book reflect the strategy thus adopted by the conference planners to ensure, on the one hand, that the engagement with Barth was judicious and informed, and on the other hand that the agenda did, in fact, move beyond Barth into theological discussions provoked by other thinkers and movements. To this end, the scholars invited to present papers were a mixture of those whose expertise lay directly in Barth and those whose interests lay elsewhere within theology. As members of Reformed, Catholic and Anglican communities, they crossed denominational boundaries. Their papers also represent a variety of styles: exegetical, thematic and polemical.

Part One of this volume contains the three keynote addresses which were presented by John Webster of Oxford University. Webster's first paper issues in a challenge which also explains the choice of the topics pursued in the second and third: Christology and anthropology. The challenge is that any attempt to generate a 'fruitful confrontation'[7] between Barth's theology and postmodernism must begin with the explicitly dogmatic character of Barth's work. The purpose here is not just that of accurate interpretation. It is also because, in Webster's view (echoing Barth's), the dogmatic genre is the point of access to what is specifically Christian. In Barth this leads directly to Christology and anthropology because it is these dogmatic loci which bring to focus what, in his view, is central to Christianity: the identification of God in the history which takes place in the covenantal relationship between Jesus Christ and his freely responding human partners. However, as Webster goes on to demonstrate in Chapters Two and Three, where Christology

---

7.   See Webster, below, page 26.

and anthropology are determined by this covenantal relationship, the parameters of the encounter with postmodernism are immediately sharpened. Thus, in Chapter Two, Webster alerts us to the fact that a Christology whose subject matter is the grand narrative of the history of Jesus Christ in relationship with humanity inevitably confronts postmodernism's suspicion of metanarratives. In Chapter Three, we are directed to the fact that an anthropology grounded in a covenantal relationship that involves the obedient response of freely acting human subjects inevitably confronts postmodernism's denial of the subject.

Webster leaves his readers to ponder just how fruitful he thinks this confrontation ultimately is. However, what is clearly fruitful about Webster's contribution is the way in which he consistently brings to the fore the specifically Christian character of Barth's realism. Indeed, Webster claims that virtually all he wants to say in this discussion is summed up in Barth's phrase, 'It is given'.[8] As a givenness which is radically grounded in a trinitarian and christological reality, the realism which ensues is not to be equated with that realism of the Western tradition which postmodern writers have themselves made their target.[9] It is perhaps the highly idiosyncratic character of Barth's realism, tinged as it is by a certain idealist impulse without ever becoming idealist, which will continue to both attract, if also resist, the anti-realist impulse of postmodernism. If, therefore, getting the exact contours of Barth's realism right is one of the major tasks of contemporary Barth interpretation, Webster's own dogmatic exegesis is an important example of how such interpretation might proceed.

If Part One of the volume represents a sustained engagement with the conference theme, the papers in Parts Two, Three and Four are a mixture of more *ad hoc* engagements with the theme, both those which skirt around it, and those

---

[8]   See Webster, below, page 18.
[9]   See Webster, below, page 67f.

which have taken a step beyond it. The papers in Part Two are more purely dogmatic in character, dealing, respectively, with the doctrine of the Trinity and Revelation (Christiaan Mostert), Barth's treatment of the theme of Joy (John Capper) and Barth's doctrine of Israel (Mark Lindsay). Although not directly related to postmodernism, each paper raises important questions about the identity of the covenant-making God, and therefore touch on issues essential to any theology, postmodern or otherwise. The four papers in Part Three return more explicitly to Barth's relationship to postmodernism. Together they encapsulate the variety of approaches which *de facto* characterise the debate. Gordon Preece and Nancy Victorin-Vangerud with their respective papers on 'Work and Vocation' and 'The Counterpart of Others' demonstrate that the task of exegeting Barth today will inevitably be shaped by questions which emerge from the lived experience of the postmodern world. On the other hand, Geoff Thompson's paper on 'Language, Mystery and God' and Stephen Pickard's on 'Divine Simplicity' are more inclined to proceed in the other direction. Thompson traces a network of ideas throughout the *Church Dogmatics* in order to deploy some specifically theological issues as tools to counter the trend to use linguistic theory to claim Barth for a postmodern theology of the Word. Pickard (whose paper could also have been included in Part Two) offers Barth's treatment of the divine simplicity as a tool for preparing Christian disciples for the experience of variety and complexity typical of contemporary societies. The final four essays, contained in Part Four, offered the conference the opportunity to consider some already established options in postmodern theology in more detail. In most of these papers, Barth has receded into the background. Into the foreground come George Lindbeck (whose work is the focus of the papers on postliberal theology by Bruce Barber and Craig Thompson) and John Milbank (whose work is the focus of the papers by Trevor Hogan and Neil Ormerod). They provided an opportunity at the conference, and do so again in this volume, for a deeper and critical cross-fertilization of ideas between Barth and those who are consciously seeking to be postmodern theologians. Something of the debate about these issues which occurred at the conference is reflected in Wes Campbell's epilogue.

The conference did not seek, let alone attain, a definitive resolution of the question which constituted its theme. Yet the vigour and enthusiasm of the discussions and the debates over the two days seemed to suggest that the question was more than worth asking, and that it will go on being asked. As it does, the ensuing discussions are likely to continue to be characterised by debates between various interpretations of Barth's theology on the one hand, and, on the other, divergent assessments of the validity of linking Barth to postmodern theology and, indeed, of the validity of any theology that might describe itself as postmodern. In the enthusiasm and energy of such debates, we would do well to heed some remarks of Barth in his 1929 lecture, 'Fate and Idea in Theology':

> To determine whether a particular theology has as its object merely a deified concept of the living God, the first criterion might be whether the theology is conscious of its own relativity. Has it retained the patience necessary towards other theologies (which is quite compatible with posing rigorous questions) . . . ? A theology based on God's Word . . . will need to be patient as well as incisive.[10]

Lest we think that this appeal to be patient, to acknowledge our own relativity, to be incisive and to question rigorously rests on a confused combination of dogmatic toughness and social politeness, Barth quickly and predictably points us to its *theological* ground. The 'theoretical background to this practical criterion' has as its foundation the free divine election by which

---

10. K Barth 'Fate and Idea in Theology' in H Martin Rumscheidt (ed), *The Way of Theology in Karl Barth: Essays and Comments* (Allison Park: Pickwick Publications, 1986), 58.

'not only the Word's being spoken but also our reception of it is always a matter of God's free grace'.[11]

That Barth should reach *this* 'practical criterion' sustained by *this* 'theoretical background' in his own early (but, for him, seminal) response to the poles of Idealism and Realism is salutary for us who find these ancient options newly refracted in the various theological reactions to the intellectual aspirations of postmodernism. The same patience, rigour and incisiveness once advocated by Barth will need to be applied to the present task of interpreting his theology. Only then will it be possible to assess Barth's contribution to the contemporary Church's calling to speak and think of God in an age which is conveniently (if not exhaustively) described as 'postmodern'. This volume is a small contribution to those tasks.

****

The editors record their thanks to the Karl Barth Archive for permission to use the cover photograph. Thanks are also due to the Australian Theological Forum for its support of this publishing venture, to the Forum's secretary, Mr Hilary Regan, for helping to bring the book to fruition, and Ms Allie Ernst for the production of the indices.

---

11. *Ibid.*

Part One

Barth and Postmodern Theology:
A Fruitful Confrontation ?

Barth, Modernity and Postmodernity

John Webster

I

Barth would not have taken postmodernism too seriously. Though he was open to learn (and did in fact learn) from all manner of books and thinkers, and never lost his capacity to listen to the novel and unexpected, he nevertheless displayed (especially in later life) an amused and ironic view of solemn theory, especially if it seemed faddish or inflated. In letters from the 1960s, he sometimes spoke in comical terms of the hermeneutical goings-on in Ebeling's Zürich as a farrago of nonsense,[1] and we may perhaps conjecture that he would view at least some postmodern theology in the same light. Certainly, it would not bother him excessively; he would be unimpressed by its solemnities, irritated by its vanity, and, though he would be appreciative of its anti-ideological impulse, its relativism would be deeply foreign to his temper, spiritual, intellectual and cultural.

In thinking about Barth in relation to postmodernism, it is important, therefore, not to take postmodernism too seriously (that is, with the wrong kind of seriousness), and also to do Barth the courtesy of taking his theology seriously, but, once again, not *too* seriously. What Barth expected of his readers (and, as he grew in stature and fame, he insisted on the point with some vigour) was that they should take with ultimate seriousness, with a kind of joyful earnestness, not what he himself had to say, but rather the object of his testimony, which was none other than the name of Jesus Christ, the sum and

---

1   See, for example, the letter to Paul Tillich in *Letters 1961-1968* (Edinburgh: T&T Clark, 1981), 142.

1

substance of the gospel, the beginning and end of the works and ways of God.

Our task in what follows is not to use Barth's work to show either that postmodernism is to be repudiated, or that postmodernism is the prolegomena to any future Christian thought. Both Barth and postmodernism are far too complex to be caught within any such simplified, oppositional schema. Nor is it our job to be preoccupied with the question: How is the future of Christian theology determined by the 'postmodern condition'? To that question, Barth would simply reply that no cultural or intellectual context is a fate, and that, if we allow context to take on the character of necessity, we quickly lose our grasp of the real *theological* determinants of theology's nature and tasks. Rather than pursuing these questions, then, I want us to explore a much more interesting and theologically fruitful issue, namely, the resources which Barth's theological testimony may point us towards as we try to discern the church's current theological responsibilities towards the gospel. Giving our attention to that issue will, I hope, prevent us from cultural capitulation, and from mere uncritical reverence for a Christian thinker of undoubted classical stature (neither of which errors Barth would approve). And it may also help us to look both at Barth's work and our own situation with the right sort of cheerfully relative attitude, and, therefore, with the right kind of seriousness.

In this first section, I want to introduce the theme by offering some broad but not, I hope, vacuous characterisations of Barth's relationship to modernity and postmodernity; from there I want to try to articulate some working principles which will help us find a route through the questions before us, and to begin the task of indicating the sorts of lines of reflection which Barth's work invites us to follow. But, before all that, I will make a few (mercifully brief) remarks about the 'p' word, postmodernism.

I shall not be using the term 'postmodernism' simply to identify an historical epoch (that which chronologically succeeds modernity), but to draw attention to a diverse set of cultural representations, particularly as they are expressed in some currently fashionable theoretical texts of a broadly philosophical nature. As what has been called a 'fluid cultural field',[2] postmodernism is by its nature eclectic, not amenable to either systematic statement or crisp definition: 'in the Zeitgeist of postmodernity, there can only be postmodernisms'.[3] But as cultural and intellectual ambience (and as a not-so-minor academic industry) postmodernism can best be characterised descriptively. One recent survey puts it thus:

> Postmodernity is a style of thought which is suspicious of classical notions of truth, reason, identity and objectivity, of the idea of universal progress or emancipation, of single frameworks, grand narratives or ultimate grounds of explanation. Against these Enlightenment norms, it sees the world as contingent, ungrounded, diverse, unstable, indeterminate, a set of disunified cultures or interpretations which breed a degree of scepticism about the objectivity of truth, history and norms, the givenness of norms and the coherence of identities.[4]

Three characteristic postmodern preoccupations are especially germane to the themes that we will be pursuing. First, a turn from 'the given'—most sharply, of course, from the metaphysics of substance or 'presence' (whose corruption lies both in its systematic exclusion of 'the Other' and in its refusal to rest content with surfaces), but also, along with that, a turn from such supposed corollaries of substance metaphysics as representational accounts of language, theories of universal reason, and the longing for 'form', whether in art, morals, politics or philosophy. Second, a turn from 'history',

---

2   P Lakeland, *Postmodernity: Christian Identity in a Fragmented Age* (Minneapolis: Fortress Press, 1997), xiii.

3.   G Ward, 'Postmodern Theology' in D Ford (ed), *The Modern Theologians* (Oxford: Blackwell, 1997), 586.

4.   T Eagleton, *The Illusions of Postmodernism* (Oxford: Blackwell, 1996), vii.

3

understood as a comprehensively ordered whole of which we may speak in teleological terms. Talk of time and human action in time as having some sort of *telos* inevitably means closure, and directional schemes sustain their universality only by forgetting that there *is* no depth and progression, but simply an unmappable tangle of differences. Third, a turn from the humane. No longer 'placed' within a metaphysical region or an overarching temporal scheme, the 'self' (if such there be) no longer has an identity, whether as one playing a rôle in a premodern 'order of things', or as the modern bestower of order, meaning and value through representing and working on the world. Identity is repudiated in favour of indeterminacy; as Zygmunt Bauman puts it: 'Well-sewn and durable identity is no more an asset; increasingly and ever more evidently, it becomes a liability. *The hub of postmodern life strategy is not making identity stand*—but the avoidance of being fixed'.[5]

Such, in skeletal form, is the 'postmodern condition'. Whether these turns from being, time and selfhood are in fact a condition or simply a construct is not clear—and I am not sure a postmodern thinker would think it a worthwhile question to pursue: Is there anything other than construction? What is clear, however, is that the intellectual and moral temper which the term 'postmodernism' gestures towards has come to have quite considerable prestige in the academy and its subcultures, and is regarded by many to have some demonstrable explanatory power.

What of postmodern theology? If the term 'postmodernism' is pretty porous when used to talk of culture and philosophy, it is an absolute sponge when applied to contemporary theological work. If we try to impose a bit of order on the terminological confusion, there seem to be at least three ways of deploying the term. First, there are those who employ it simply as a chronological indicator, equivalent to 'contemporary':

---

5. Z Bauman, *Postmodernity and Its Discontents* (Cambridge: Polity Press, 1997), 89.

postmodern theology on this account is simply all theology done in the present era, the era after modernity has drawn to a close. Quite apart from the question of whether modernity has, in fact, drawn to a close, this seems too loose a deployment of the term 'postmodern' to be of much use to us. Others want to reserve the term for those theologies which have decisively turned from modernity, understood as the Enlightenment project of the application of critical reason to *inter alia* Christian orthodoxy, and which propose the reconfiguration of church and theology around the specifics of lived Christian culture. Along with one of the major voices of this viewpoint, George Lindbeck, I prefer to call this strand of contemporary theology 'postliberal', largely because one of its defining characteristics is a desire to move beyond the liberal compact with the historicist idealism of the critical tradition. I would prefer, therefore, to retain the term 'postmodern' for those theologies which analyse the cultural situation of Christianity through the turns from substance-oriented accounts of being, time and selfhood characteristic of postmodern philosophy, and which articulate Christian beliefs in terms of such accounts. It is to these theologies—those, that is, which share the 'severe postmodern vision'[6]—that I want us to direct our attention as we put our questions to Barth. And I suggest that we make this our focus, not because I am persuaded that such work offers a fruitful avenue for theology—in fact, it seems to me in important respects little more than a cul-de-sac—nor because I think such work genuinely leaves modernity behind—in fact, it seems to me too close a cousin of modernity's idealism to effect a radical rupture with the past. Rather, I suggest that we focus here because postmodern theology of this kind has sponsored some important readings of Barth which will help us both to raise

---

6.   W A Beardslee, 'Christ and the Postmodern Age: Reflections Inspired by Jean-François Lyotard' in D R Griffin et al, *Varieties of Postmodern Theology* (Albany: SUNY Press, 1989), 63.

5

questions about how to place his work, and to ponder our own responsibilities before the theological task.

II

Barth has been variously placed with regard to modernity. He is sometimes read, particularly by revisionist theologians who tend to be tone-deaf to what Barth is doing and find him merely irritating, as if he were a pre-modern thinker beached on the shores of modernity, seeking (perhaps in some measure even succeeding) to repristinate a pre-critical mode of theological activity by ignoring, subverting or changing the rules of reasoned discourse. Such accounts, rightly identifying Barth's polemic against 'modernist' dogmatics and morals and their foundations, tend to be beguiled into thinking of Barth as a classical Christian thinker of the stature of Augustine, Anselm or Calvin who happened to find himself in the wrong historical epoch. Yet it was Barth himself who, near the end of his life, said: 'I am a child of the nineteenth century'.[7] That is, the sensibilities which Barth brought to the theological task, the issues which continued to trouble and fascinate him, emerged from a collision between post-Enlightenment Protestant thought and his construal of the biblical message. Without the heritage of the nineteenth century, Barth simply would not have been the thinker that he was. It is not just that the rebel took on the lineaments of that against which he rebelled, but that the rebellion consisted in thinking through from the very foundations some of the most major preoccupations of the modern traditions of Christian theology.

Does this, therefore, mean that Barth is to be seen as a fundamentally modern thinker—that, for all his repudiation of modernity, he nevertheless remained trapped within its

---

7.   H Stoevesandt (ed), *A Late Friendship: The Letters of Karl Barth and Carl Zuckmayer* (Grand Rapids: Eerdmans, 1982), 3.

religious or philosophical idioms and was not able finally to
shake himself free? Certainly this case has been argued from a
number of angles. Lutheran critics of Barth have persistently
urged that his emphasis on revelation transposes Christian
doctrine out of a salvific into an epistemological idiom, so that
he takes knowledge of God rather than righteousness before
God to be the organising theme of dogmatics.[8] Something of the
same line of critique has been pursued against Barth's doctrine
of the Trinity, which some readers believe to be dominated by
the logic of a self-manifesting, monadic divine ego, with the
result not only that Barth consistently underplays the theme of
divine community, but also that he tends to make revelation a
matter of epistemology rather than of participation in the divine
life.[9] This reading of Barth is connected with another account
(associated above all with Trutz Rendtorff), according to which
Barth's inability to wrest himself free of modernity can be seen
in his understanding of divine selfhood. For Rendtorff, the
idiom of Barth's understanding of divine sovereignty is
determined by his transposition onto God of modern notions of
absolute subjectivity: God is a kind of transcendental Fichtean

---

8. Classically made by G Wingren in *Theology in Conflict: Nygren-Barth-Bultmann* (Philadelphia: Muhlenberg Press, 1958), the
   argument surfaces many times in the literature. See, for example,
   A E McGrath, 'Karl Barth and the *Articulus Iustificationis'*,
   Theologische Zeitschrift 39 (1983): 349-61; *idem*, 'Karl Barth als
   Aufklärer?' *Kerygma und Dogma* 30 (1984): 273-83; *idem*, *The
   Making of Modern German Christology* (Oxford: Blackwell, 1986); K
   Tanner, 'Jesus Christ' in C Gunton (ed), *The Cambridge Companion
   to Christian Doctrine* (Cambridge: Cambridge University Press,
   1997), 264-8.
9. See, most recently, A Torrance, *Persons in Communion: An Essay on
   Trinitarian Description and Human Participation, with Special
   Reference to Volume One of Karl Barth's Church Dogmatics*
   (Edinburgh: T&T Clark, 1996).

ego, a magnified image of modern anthropology.[10] Others, again, have argued that Barth's theology, far from effecting any kind of breach in modernity, in fact trades on a capitulation to modernity, in conceding the force of Kant's restrictions, cordoning theology off as a special sphere of inquiry and so dodging the real task of mounting a theological critique of modern reason and its claims to omnicompetence.

> [B]y refusing all 'mediations' through other spheres of knowledge and culture, Barthianism tended to assume a positive autonomy for theology, which rendered philosophical concerns a matter of indifference. Yet this itself was to remain captive to a modern—even liberal—duality of reason and revelation, and ran the risk of allowing worldly knowledge an unquestioned validity within its own sphere.[11]

To pursue these critiques in any detail and undertake any kind of full critical evaluation would take us far from our theme. But it is worth noting that the most satisfying accounts of the issues have been those which exercise considerable care in handling Barth's texts, taking the time to establish with some precision those strands of modernity with which Barth interacted, and tracing the ways in which his thinking developed over the course of such interactions.[12] Such care has been pretty rare;

---

10. See, for example, T Rendtorff, 'Der Ethische Sinn der Dogmatik' in *idem* (ed), *Die Realisierung der Freiheit* (Gütersloh: Mohn, 1975), 119-34, and J Macken, *The Autonomy Theme in the Church Dogmatics: Karl Barth and His Critics* (Cambridge: Cambridge University Press, 1990).

11. 'Introduction. Suspending the material: the turn of radical orthodoxy' in J Milbank *et al, Radical Orthodoxy: A New Theology* (London: Routledge, 1999), 2: the argument is curiously reminiscent (though more effective than) Pannenberg's rather flat-footed criticism of Barth's response to Feuerbach.

12. By far the best example is B McCormack, *Karl Barth's Critically Realistic Dialectical Theology: Its Genesis and Development 1909-1936*

more often than not, accounts of the topic have been directed by polemical concerns (usually a desire to deflate Barth or Barth's disciples by showing that—despite all claims to the contrary—he is as enmeshed in modern presuppositions as those whom he opposed). And, more often than not, the presentation consists of an alarmingly impressionistic picture of parallels between themes in Barth's writing (revelation, divine subjectivity, and so forth) and putative trends in modern thought.

None of this, of course, is to suggest that it is illegitimate to try to locate Barth in modernity, but simply to advertise the difficulty of the project. The notion of 'modernity' is itself a complex evaluative construct, and Barth's writings are far too varied, intricate and ramified to allow schematic presentations to succeed.

Many of the same problems attend the discussion of Barth and postmodernity (this time exacerbated by the labyrinthine character of postmodern thought). In this case, there is the added difficulty that, in placing Barth in modernity, we are placing him by reference to his past, in processes of which he was in many respects fully aware; whereas with questions of postmodernity, we are about the much more speculative business of asking what Barth might have said, or perhaps, of trying to discern whether what Barth did say was as it were some kind of 'pre-postmodernism'.

The literature which has so far addressed Barth in relation to postmodern thought has generally presented one or more of three features. First, it has often proceeded by offering a thematic comparison of some aspect of Barth's work and the work of a representative postmodern thinker—'the Other', givenness, totalities, negative theology, the determinacy of

---

(Oxford: Clarendon Press, 1995). McCormack's work is notable above all for the care with which he does not allow polemical issues about the utility of Barth's work to intrude into genetic-historical questions about his relation to modernity.

texts, the crisis of representation are the themes, and Derrida,
Levinas, Irigaray are the thinkers.[13] As I shall try to show in a
bit more detail later in this lecture, such thematic comparisons
are usually less than successful, since almost inevitably they
have to abstract certain ideas or patterns of argument from their
proper context in Barth's work and translate them into
something more generic, less Christianly specific, in order to
allow the conversation to proceed. One of Barth's basic rules of
thought—*Latet periculum in generalibus!*—is thereby lost, and
what starts as a conversation quickly becomes a matter of
adjusting Barth to a conceptual scheme quite foreign to his
convictions.

A second feature of the literature is that of interpreting
Barth's theology—especially in its so-called dialectical phase
associated with the second commentary on Romans—as
emerging from or representative of the sea-change in Western
culture which we think of as the break-up of modernity and the
rise of postmodernism. For example, it has been argued that

---

13. On Barth and Derrida, see I Andrews, *Deconstructing Barth: A
Study of the Complementary Methods in Karl Barth and Jacques
Derrida* (Frankfurt/M: Lang, 1996); G Ward, *Barth, Derrida and the
Language of Theology* (Cambridge: Cambridge University Press,
1995); W Lowe, *Theology and Difference: The Wound of Reason*
(Bloomington: Indiana University Press, 1993); M Lafargue, 'Are
Texts Determinate? Barth, Derrida and the Role of the Biblical
Scholar', *Harvard Theological Review* 81 (1988): 341-57. On Barth
and Levinas, see S G Smith, *The Argument to the Other: Reason
beyond Reason in the Thought of Karl Barth and Emmanuel Levinas*
(Chico, CA: Scholar's Press, 1983) and J F Goud, *Levinas en Barth:
een godsdienstwijsgerige en etische vergelijking* (Amsterdam: Rodopi,
1984). On Barth and Irigaray, see S Jones, 'This God Which Is Not
One: Irigaray and Barth on the Divine' in C W Maggie Kim *et al*
(ed), *Transfigurations: Theology and the French Feminists*
(Minneapolis: Fortress Press, 1993), 109-41. More generally, see W
S Johnson, *The Mystery of God: Karl Barth and the Postmodern
Foundations of Theology* (Louisville: WJKP, 1997).

Barth's early rhetoric of crisis is an indication that his work is to be understood against the background of a wider 'crisis of representation at the end of modernity'.[14] From this, it is sometimes suggested that the second Romans commentary offers perhaps the greatest example this century of a 'necessary atheology' in the postmodern situation[15]—even though the pathos of Barth's later work is that he turns back from the brink and returns to a 'strident theological rhetoric of the "real"'.[16] Whether these generalisations about the epoch of the 1920s are anything other than impressionistic, and whether Barth's own denials[17] that his early theology is driven by the mood of European high culture after the Great War are enough to overturn this interpretation, are open questions. But, as we shall again come to see, it is very difficult to be persuaded by an interpretation of his work which routinely passes over the *theological* character of Barth's convictions, making his theology a simple register of cultural trends. Barth was a theologian from the beginning; what he stumbled into when he stumbled into Romans in the summer of 1916 was a reality possessed of a unique, incomparable character which simply cannot be assimilated to anything else: the world of God.

A third feature of postmodern readings of Barth has been their strong interest in harnessing Barth to proposals about how Christian theology is to be undertaken in the present; Barth, for

---

14. Besides G Ward, see D E Klemm, 'Toward a Rhetoric of Postmodern Theology: Through Barth and Heidegger', *Journal of the American Academy of Religion* 55 (1987): 443-69; S H Webb, *Refiguring Theology: The Rhetoric of Karl Barth* (Albany: SUNY Press, 1991); R H Roberts, 'Barth and the Rhetoric of Weimar: A Theology on Its Way?' in *idem*, *A Theology on Its Way? Essays on Karl Barth* (Edinburgh: T&T Clark, 1991), 169-199.
15. Roberts, *op cit*, 197.
16. *Ibid*, 196.
17. Such as in the 1922 lecture on 'The Problem of Ethics Today' in *The Word of God and the Word of Man* (London: Hodder and Stoughton, 1928), 150.

instance, can be read as an instance of genuinely theological transcendence of 'ontotheology', of a reserve towards representation of God which qualifies him as a negative theologian. In itself, of course, this is not an improper approach: unless one is reading great theological texts simply out of antiquarian interests, it is impossible not to have one's reading directed by constructive interests (and it is doubtful if even antiquarianism can avoid this). The crucial question, however, is: What constitutes the shape and the limits of the 'use' of a theologian's work? As with (for example) Aquinas and Calvin, so with Barth: the interpretation of a corpus of such range and depth is particularly exposed to being skewed by selection and partiality (so that Aquinas and Calvin are routinely read as if their biblical commentaries were not germane to the interpretation of their work), and to making all-too-ready constructive use of ill-digested accounts of some or other of their preoccupations. It is all-important, then, in exploring the question of the resources which Barth's work offers for 'postmodern' theological work, that we do not trade away respect for the details of what he wrote. Such respect is not born of uncritical, slavish or deferential reverence for Barth; it is simply a safeguard against the tendency to annex Barth to other projects by providing only the most impressionistic readings of his work. More than anything else, it is vitally important that we keep alert to the theological character of Barth's work, and do not allow ourselves to fall into the sort of interpretation which takes from him a certain ambience or tone, or relates some of his patterns of thought or characteristic turns of phrase to reconstructions of the highly-strung culture of Weimar, or perhaps, of today. If we once neglect Barth's 'particularism',[18] his strict insistence that the traffic always proceed from the particular to the general and not vice-versa, then Barth quickly

---

18. See G Hunsinger, *How to Read Karl Barth: The Shape of His Theology* (Oxford: Oxford University Press, 1991), 32-5.

12

will become a mere token of a project of our own, and we would do well both for his sake and ours to leave him behind.

We can best sidestep these dangers, I suggest, by observing two rules as we think about Barth in relation to our own theological situation. First, we need to take seriously Barth's *theological* construal of the situation of theology; second, we need, accordingly, to focus on dogmatics. I want to spend the rest of our time in this first chapter exploring these two rules and their ramifications.

III

First, one pivotal way in which Barth may be of service to us in thinking about current theological tasks is by helping us to acquire some distance from and perspective upon the present, above all by teaching us how to map our situation through the categories of the Christian faith. One of Barth's chief legacies is that he offers an example of one who told the history of thought and culture, and, therefore, the history (including the present history) of theology from the perspective of gospel, church and faith. Because Barth mapped the situation of theology in the projection of the Christian gospel, and not by reference to any supposed 'givens' of intellectual culture, he was able to demonstrate a calmness and confidence in the face of the demands of the context in which he undertook his theological responsibilities. Barth was always about the business of 'doing theology as if nothing had happened'[19]—whether 'what had happened' was National Socialism, Christian existentialism, the new hermeneutic, the death of God, or even postmodernism. What Barth may help us discern is that our history and the immediate context of our theological work is not a fate, an iron necessity which requires us to recast the nature of our task; we

---

19. K Barth, *Theological Existence Today! A Plea for Theological Freedom* (London: Hodder and Stoughton, 1933), 9.

need to learn that theological confidence requires, amongst other things, a properly cheerful sense of the relativity of context when viewed from the vantage-point of the gospel.

A great deal is to be learned in these matters from Barth's own way of reading the history of Christian theology (a topic, incidentally, largely unexplored). Barth was deeply interested in, and deeply knowledgeable about, the history of the various branches of Christian theology, especially dogmatics, and demonstrated a considerable facility with the history of modern philosophy, in what are some brilliant (and partial) readings of classic modern texts, both theological and philosophical (the partiality of the readings is one of the things which makes for their brilliance). Moreover, from his early days as a theological professor, Barth was strongly gripped by a need to place himself vis-à-vis the history of modern theology, deeply conscious as he was that his work involved a rethinking and reconstructing of many of the established conventions of modern Protestantism and its place in the intellectual traditions of Western Europe since the eighteenth century. In trying to distinguish himself in this way, Barth had something in common with other seminal thinkers of the earlier part of the century: a sense of being at the pivot of intellectual change, and therefore of having to undertake a genealogical task in order to extract himself from the representations of modern life and thought which he was leaving behind by giving an account of them and displaying them as no longer axiomatic. Nevertheless, Barth's account had a certain uniqueness which is germane to our theme.

The kinds of judgments which Barth reached about the context of theology derive from a very particular understanding of theology's content. As he moved into the writing of Christian dogmatics beginning in the mid-1920s, he discovered in a deeper way a manner of thinking and speaking about God which was not wholly consumed by notions of cultural, intellectual or moral crisis. As he came to invest more and more in his chosen medium, and as his thought world came to be peopled by strong texts of the exegetical and doctrinal traditions of Christianity, his work increasingly took on a feature which he noted in his study of Anselm: a 'characteristic' absence of crisis.[20] Given the prominence of the term 'crisis' in Barth's earlier occasional writings and in the second Romans commentary, it is hard not to feel the force of Barth's commendation of a theological attitude in which crisis—even if it is not sublated—is nevertheless not assigned a foundational role. This (relative) absence of crisis is, of course, a signal of the fact that, in discovering dogmatics, Barth came across the possibility of a properly 'positive' theology—that is, a theology whose referents and procedures are given by the nature and free activity of the object of theology. The precise character of this givenness is quite crucial to understanding what Barth is about as he tries to read his own context. In essence, Barth developed over the course of the latter half of the 1920s and the early 1930s a specific theological and Christological construal of the givenness of revelation to church and faith, and therefore to theology, which furnished the basis of a confidently theological evaluation of the contexts of theology, past and present.

Much of the material which seeks to relate Barth to postmodernism has often lost its way here, both by failing to grasp Barth as 'positive' church theologian, and by failing to see how this churchly positivity drove his interpretation of theology's contexts. A couple of examples may suffice at this point. First, in her comparison of Barth and Derrida, Isolde Andrews argues that, for both Barth and Derrida, 'the reality we apprehend (to do with God or the world) cannot be conceived as a functioning system which may be comprehended once a suitable hermeneutic device is found with which to unlock it'.[21] Though she is in one sense quite correct to stress Barth's resistance to rational control of reality,

---

20. K Barth, *Anselm: Fides Quaerens Intellectum* (London: SCM, 1960), 26.

21. Andrews, *op cit*, 29.

her attempted defence of the point from Barth's writings leads her to misconstrue him in a quite fundamental way. Barth's refusal to espouse a 'standpoint', his repudiation of 'systematic' or 'totalising' theology (which Andrews calls 'Barth's "no view" of God')[22] is not rooted in any general principle of indeterminacy, or any abstract refusal of logocentrism: it is simply a massive foreshortening of the issues to speak of Barth's work as 'evidently a theology of the "flux"',[23] or to align Barth with the principle that 'thought of God must be in terms of non-meaning or else it is caught up in a human system that interprets itself'.[24] Certainly Barth rejects the wrong kind of positivity, but does so, not in order to ensure 'non-meaning', but in order to retain the freedom of God's self-manifestation, a freedom in which God really is present. In rejecting systematisation, Barth is not rejecting God's 'givenness' but specifying it, and thereby turning from the theological vanity which seeks to appropriate that givenness and annex it to projects of the theologian's own choosing.

The trap here is one of allowing Barth's criticism of the wrong sort of realism to beguile us into thinking of him as an idealist.[25] It is a trap which a second, much more acute, commentator on Barth and postmodernism generally avoids in what is to date the best survey of the area, Stacy Johnson's *The Mystery of God*. Johnson rightly identifies Barth's aversion to 'any theology that tries to prop itself up according to ready-made foundations somehow "given" in advance and presumed to be self-evident or beyond revision',[26] and so proposes that one clue to Barth's theology is the principle that, 'in order to "center" on God, one must effect a "de-centering" of

---

22. *Ibid*, 45.
23. *Ibid*, 76.
24. *Ibid*, 158.
25. Only a very careless reading of the two lectures *Fate and Idea in Theology* could lead us to think of him in this way.
26. W Stacy Johnson, *op cit*, 3.

theology'.[27] Whether Johnson is correct that Barth is here companionable or formally parallel to Derrida is an open question; but what is clear is that Johnson has to press a rather strained reading of Barth, one which tends to magnify the anti-systematic impulse in his work (focused for Johnson by the term 'mystery') and minimize Barth's insistence on the presence of the Word in the church and its acts of confession of the *Credo*.[28] Johnson concludes:

> Christian theology does have a 'center' or 'foundation' it wishes to know and proclaim, for it believes in the living God. Nevertheless, this God cannot be reduced to a foundation located in human experience or tradition or anywhere else. In one sense God alone is the foundation of theology; but God is never reducible to a simple 'given' or 'presence'. Rather than proclaiming the absence of a 'center', therefore, Barthian theology insists that it is the divine center *itself* that infuses the postmodern intellectual task with all its instability and risk.[29]

There is a valuable half-truth there, one which certainly has not always been registered in Barth scholarship; and, moreover, Johnson has the good sense to draw back from excessive and bold claims about Barth as a deconstructionist *avant la lettre*. But more needs to be said. For Barth, the divine 'centre' of theology means not only instability and risk; it also means permission, call and order, making possible a theology from which the right kind of positivity is by no means absent.[30]

---

27. *Ibid*, 14.
28. Johnson's account of Barth's Anselm book is particularly questionable at this point: see *e.g.* 35.
29. *Ibid*, 184f.
30. If Johnson's account fails to convince, it is in large part because he tends to make rather too clear a separation between the Christocentric and theocentric 'melodies' (1) in Barth's work, and then tries to redress the interpretative imbalance by giving

John Webster

Barth gave many depictions of the right kind of positivity from the *Göttingen Dogmatics* onwards. Discussing the doctrine of verbal inspiration with his Göttingen students, Barth objected that that doctrine historicizes revelation by transforming it into 'an open and directly given revelation'.[31] By contrast, Barth asserts: 'The holy that is obvious, the sacral, is never the true holy. The true holy is spirit, not thing. The *Deus dixit* is revelation, not revealedness.'[32] But that this is by no means a rejection of revelation as a 'given' reality can be seen from Barth's statement a page or two later: 'Nowhere and never is the *Deus dixit* a reality except in God's own most proper reality'.[33] It is that 'except' which Barth expands, in his discussion of the divine hiddenness later in the lecture cycle, for the proper understanding of which, as Barth says, 'everything hinges on his covering his inaccessible divine I-ness with a human I-ness as with a veil so that we can grasp him as a person'.[34] It is this Christological construal of the dialectic of 'givenness' and 'non-givenness' which is so often absent in accounts of Barth's apparent proximity to postmodernism. The principle which Barth enunciated at Göttingen lay behind the many discussions of the relation of dogmatics to its given norm in the *Church Dogmatics*, all of which focus on the unique character of God's objectivity in revelation. That objectivity, God's freely taking form in the incarnation of the Son, bestows upon Christian dogmatics a specific kind of positivity. Right at the beginning of the *Church Dogmatics*, Barth puts matters thus:

> [Dogmatics] does not have to begin by finding or inventing the standard by which it measures. It sees and recognises that this is given with the Church. It is

---

renewed attention to the theocentric, 'the side that incessantly underscores the hiddenness of God' (*ibid*).

31. K Barth, *The Göttingen Dogmatics: Instruction in the Christian Religion*, Vol 1 (Grand Rapids: Eerdmans, 1991), 59.
32. *Ibid*.
33. *Ibid*, 62.
34. *Ibid*, 136.

18

given in its own peculiar way, as Jesus Christ is given,
as God in His revelation gives Himself to faith. But it
is given (*CD* I/1, 12).

'It is given': virtually the whole of what I want to say about Barth's relation to postmodernism is summed up in those three words. Construed through trinitarian and incarnational categories as the free, self-manifesting majesty of God's presence, that 'givenness' for Barth made possible a kind of theological activity whose primary concern was not with questions of its own feasibility in a culture in disarray, but with the sheer actuality of God's act of revelation, which as it were had already set theology on its path, thereby requiring the theologian to follow its given—spiritually given, but nevertheless given—presence and movement. The direction of that movement, he came to see, is towards the church, appointed by God as the sphere in which revelation meets the recognition of faith. Hence Barth's 'positive' dogmatics is a church dogmatics, making confident use of the language of the church, above all as found in its textual deposit. Unlike much postmodern theology, Barth did not feel the need to maintain a suspicious bearing towards the church and its traditions of speech. He could castigate it for its idolatries and its capacity to convert God into an ecclesiastical ornament; but his account of the church was too deeply grounded in dogmatic principles to allow him to be fundamentally ironic or distant in his attitude. The ecclesial character of the positivity of Barth's theology was particularly manifest in his style of writing, which was never simply clever, sophisticated or—one has to say—mannered and hermetic in the style of a great deal of postmodern theology. And, moreover, he had a clear sense of responsibility to a determinate field of inquiry: where much postmodern theology is deliberately eclectic, dodging around in social and cultural studies, literary criticism, aesthetics, philosophy and religion, Barth is no *bricoleur*, but—in short—a positive theologian of the church of Jesus Christ.

19

John Webster

From here, we may go on to note a further lesson which we may take from Barth, one which ought to guide us in our reading both of him and of our present situation. His particular construal of the *positum* of Christian theology, his confidence in the spiritual presence of the object of theology in its gracious self-bestowal, enabled Barth to read the context of his theological activity through theological categories. Part of what makes Barth so foreign is his abiding sense that the difficulties which attend theological work are not solely or even primarily problems which have to do with cultural or historical or intellectual context; they are *spiritual*. For Barth, the real history of Christian theology is not only the history of its struggle to articulate the Christian gospel in a variety of cultures, borrowing more or less serviceable tools and enjoying greater or lesser degrees of success in retaining a sense of its own distinctive substance. Viewed at its deepest level, the history of Christian theology is a series of episodes in the wider history of God and humanity, and, if we are properly to read the history of theology and our own responsibility for continuing that history in our situation, we must read it theologically.

It is this argument which Barth outlines in the opening chapter of his *Protestant Theology in the Nineteenth Century*. 'To describe and understand the history of Protestant theology from the time of Schleiermacher onwards,' he writes,

> is a *theological* task. Even as an object of historical consideration, theology demands theological perception, theological thought and theological involvement. Of course, there is no method, not even a theological one, by means of which we can be certain of catching sight of theology . . . Nevertheless, it is a *conditio sine qua non* of the success of our undertaking that it should be approached theologically, in accordance with its subject-matter.[35]

---

35. K Barth, *Protestant Theology in the Nineteenth Century: Its Background and History* (London: SCM, 1972), 15.

Barth's point is not simply that to do historical theology well we need a 'special participation in its subject-matter',[36] and so cannot adopt the stance of the 'idle onlooker',[37] but something rather deeper. We are to read the history of theology as taking place in the sphere of the church—that is, not simply as a cultural activity, as an *exercise* or *discipline* participating in the general history of human inquiry. Rather,

> [e]very *period* of the Church does in fact want to be
> understood as a period of the *Church*, that is, as a time
> of revelation, knowledge and confession of the one
> Christian faith, indeed, as a special time, as *this* time
> of such revelation, knowledge and confession.[38]

Barth is deadly serious here: when we try to reflect on the history of Christian theology, we are firmly in the sphere of the one, holy, catholic and apostolic church. And, if that is so, then two important consequences are to be noted. One is that we may not pretend to the kind of assurance in which we set ourselves up as critics of the past of theology, as if we in our situation had somehow transcended church and faith, or been granted a clearer, more comprehensive grasp of theology than was granted to our forebearers in the church.[39] 'History writing cannot be a proclamation of judgment'[40]—a point rather easily overlooked in some postmodern writing about the changed conditions under which theology today must operate. A second consequence is that it may not be inappropriate for us to reflect seriously on our own situation and responsibilities in the same light; to ask ourselves whether—with all the differences

---

36. *Ibid.*

37. *Ibid*, 16.

38. *Ibid*, 27.

39. Barth probably had in mind the over-eager students who first heard his lectures on historical theology and who looked to him to provide reasons for not taking the nineteenth century seriously. See also K Barth, *The Theology of Schleiermacher* (Grand Rapids: Eerdmans 1982), xvi.

40. *Protestant Theology*, 23.

between pre-modern, modern and postmodern—we should not also see ourselves as participants in the same history, facing the same demands, placed under the same requirements, offered the same opportunities. '[O]ver and above the differences,' Barth wrote, 'a unity can continually be seen, a unity of perplexity and disquiet, but also a unity of richness and hope, which in the end binds us to the theologians of the past'.[41]

This is—emphatically—not to suggest that theological responsibility in our current situation means simply repeating what Barth or any other classical theologian has said. It is rather to suggest that we need to learn how to understand that all contexts are relative to the ways of God with humanity, which are made known in the spiritual reality of the church of Jesus Christ. That reality—for which we need the language of God, Christ, Spirit, revelation, faith—is the condition of theology. Whether there is also alongside that a 'postmodern' condition, I am not sure; on the whole, I am disposed to think that, if there is such a condition, it is only one of a number of conditions in which we find ourselves. Apocalyptic readings of our cultural history which describe it as having reached a definitively new stage may identify some significant matters to which we must give our attention; but, in the end, they quickly become historically specious,[42] intellectually vain, and politically unwise. Our condition, if it is anything, is definitively theological, describable through the gospel of reconciliation.

Again, this is not a matter of claiming that Barth's work encourages theology simply to carry on business as usual, if by 'usual' business we mean doing exactly what past generations

---

41. *Ibid*, 27.
42. On the whole, I tend to agree with Charles Taylor's judgment that postmodernism is 'an overelaborated boost for the first spiritual profile of modernism, in the name of unrestricted freedom': C Taylor, *Sources of the Self: The Making of Modern Identity* (Cambridge, Mass: Harvard University Press, 1989), 490; cf 590, n90.

attempted, pretending that our situation is theirs. We are where we are. But where we are is in the history of the church, in the history of revelation and repentance, confession and hope, and it is that history which is to be allowed to shape our definitions of who we are as theologians and which of the many possible tasks of Christian theology are to engage our efforts.

IV

So far, I have tried to suggest that we will not make much headway in understanding either his work or its relevance for our own situation unless we follow the rule of construing both him and our situation theologically. This leads to a second rule: that in trying to understand what Barth may offer to us in the present, our focus must be on dogmatic issues. Where does the real work need to be done? Nearly all the literature on theology and postmodernism is either implicitly or explicitly apologetic. Towards the end of his instructive introduction to postmodernism, Paul Lakeland proposes that

> the postmodern theological agenda is apologetic in its true purpose if not always in conscious content. This theological work will be found somewhere between philosophy of religion and fundamental or philosophical theology, not principally in the domain of systematic theology . . . But to do its work adequately, apologetical theology must embrace—sometimes critically and sometimes appreciatively—the spirit of the age and the sometimes unthematized convictions that ground it.[43]

Over against this, I suggest that we are more likely to advance in our discussion of the issues if our focus is not apologetics but dogmatics.

Neglect of the dogmatic character of Barth's work (that is, its character as the church's reflective inquiry into its coherence

---

43. P Lakeland, *op cit*, 86.

with its divinely-given basis) has led to some distorted pictures of Barth in the literature on Barth and postmodernism. Extracting certain themes from Barth and setting them alongside similar-sounding themes in one or other postmodern thinker, the result has often been precisely the sort of *mixophilosophicotheologia* which Barth so deplored,[44] and which is of very little use in establishing the real nature of his project, which was dogmatic to the core.[45]

One consequence of Barth's focus on dogmatics was that he was unafraid to field dogmatic convictions when engaging and criticising philosophical ideas; indeed, his most characteristic response to the philosophers whom he engaged (not only in

---

44. K Barth, *Evangelical Theology: An Introduction* (London: Weidenfeld and Nicolson, 1963), iii.

45. Despite the reservations expressed above, Stacy Johnson's work *The Mystery of God* is a refreshing counter-example. In addition, attention should also be drawn to two Christian theological responses to postmodernism which have attempted to retain a focus on doctrinal issues. In *The Trespass of the Sign: Deconstruction, Theology and Philosophy* (Cambridge: Cambridge University Press, 1989), Kevin Hart proposes that attention to deconstructive thinkers may enable the development of an authentically Christian theology; whatever judgments may be made of the historical or doctrinal content of the analysis, Hart is surely correct to make these themes his concern. A second work (heavily critical of Hart), Brian Ingraffia's *Postmodern Theory and Biblical Theology: Vanquishing God's Shadow* (Cambridge: Cambridge University Press, 1995), similarly argues that the central point at issue is the concept of God which is rejected in postmodern critiques of Christian theology, since postmodernism rejects a bastard form of Christian faith which had made its truce with ontotheology. Again, it may not be easy to share Ingraffia's confidence in being able to isolate a 'pure' form of Christian faith and theology uncontaminated by philosophy (see *e.g.* 235); but, nevertheless, the book sets us in the right direction.

Protestant Theology but also in the *Church Dogmatics*)[46] was to ask after their adequacy in the light of the God confessed in Christian faith. He did not set them alongside Christian faith as equal sources for theological reflection; still less did he think of philosophy as affording us a better vantage-point from which theology could be criticised. Rather, his accounts of philosophers show him concerned—with his usual mix of curiosity and determination—both to be addressed by philosophy and to respond with the only language available to him, namely, that of the Christian confession. Barth did not think that engagement in conversation with philosophical texts and ideas could proceed only by temporarily abandoning or suspending the specific concerns and thought patterns of Christian dogmatics. Nor did he think that refusing (sometimes stubbornly) to abandon or suspend those concerns spelled the end of any conversation; indeed, it was precisely at this point that the real debate began.

What are we to make of this? It is not, I think, to be seen as Barth's obstinate reluctance to come out of his lair and talk to the rest of the world; quite the contrary: in writing, as in life, Barth showed remarkable openness to all manner of ideas, provided he was allowed to exercise Christian nonconformity. Nor is it a matter of Barth making a claim to have achieved a proper, fully sanctified, 'theological' way of thinking about and articulating the Christian faith unmixed with philosophy. On a number of occasions, Barth argued pretty firmly against 'the method of isolation'[47] in which theology confidently asserts its 'Christianness' over against philosophy. 'The Christianity of theology does not in any way rest upon itself but upon the revelation that is its theme.'[48] Nor, again—*contra* Pannenberg—is it a matter of Barth irrationally claiming an

---

46. For example, Descartes (*CD* III/1, 350-63) or Leibniz, Heidegger and Sartre (*CD* III/3, 316-49).
47. K Barth, *Ethics* (Edinburgh: T&T Clark, 1981), 24.
48. *Ibid*, 34.

exemption clause for Christianity by arguing that it is immune from such criticisms of religion as those offered by Feuerbach. Over against all these interpretations, what Barth is doing and what we may learn from him is that whatever interesting and helpful things Christian theology has to say in conversation with philosophy will derive from what it has learned as it has tried to attend to the gospel. And, furthermore, we may also learn here that philosophical criticism of Christian faith must engage genuinely Christian claims in all their specificity, rather than simply making do with whatever approximations to or substitutes for them are propounded, whether in philosophy or Christian theology itself.

If this is the case, then it underscores the centrality of dogmatic issues if we are to move beyond the rather easy co-ordinations of Barth and postmodernism, to a more fruitful confrontation. In the two papers which follow, I want to identify and think through two such dogmatic themes as at least an indication of where the work might best be done: the theme of Christology (and especially Barth's claims about Jesus' history as embracing and founding the true history of humanity), and the theme of anthropology (and especially the question of the human self as agent). Two considerations lie behind taking up these specific concerns.

First, both take us into central issues in postmodernism and postmodern theology. Postmodernism is characteristically acutely suspicious of overarching narrative schemes which bestow shape, coherence and direction on human history and experience. This resistance to both protology and teleology, and to the placing of the present as an episode in a structure of time is an assertion of the sheerly contingent, plural character of temporality, and a negation of totality as a metaphysical construct. What does it mean, we may therefore ask, to talk of God's history with creation, and of humanity as having a history: elect, providentially ordered, consummated in Jesus Christ, whose history is as it were the innermost circle surrounded by all other human histories and acts? Is the church's talk of Jesus Christ simply one more grand narrative which—like those of release from tutelage or emancipation from alienation—has to be surrendered? Again, postmodernism has characteristically proposed that the picture of the substantial self—the self as performer in a drama, or as unique point of consciousness and responsibility—is to be abandoned, and that being human is to be extracted from the pretences of self-identity. Again, what does it mean, we may ask, to talk of the gospel as the proclamation of God's history *with humanity*, of salvation as our liberation from self-wrought death and our liberation for responsible selfhood? Are the anthropology and ethics of Christian theology thereby further casualties of the dissolution of the metaphysics and morals of coherence and the institutions which have been their bearers?

Second, beyond their centrality for any Christian theological reflection on postmodernism, Christology and anthropology are the points at which we need to work if we are really to get inside Barth's work. At the heart of Barth's theological vision is a construal of Christianity in which the triune God who is manifest in creation, reconciliation and redemption is God in covenant with humanity, and therefore the ways of this God are identical with (and therefore identifiable from) the history which he makes with humanity in Jesus Christ, who was and is and is to come. Supremely in the *Church Dogmatics* (but by no means exclusively so, for Barth began to lay the very deep foundations of this construal of Christianity in the early days after his break from theological liberalism) Barth thought of the gospel as a uniquely truthful and compelling account of reality, in which God in Jesus Christ cannot be understood in abstraction from his determination of humanity as grateful, active partners in covenant.

> Just as [God's] oneness consists in the unity of his life
> as Father, Son, and Holy Spirit, so in relation to the
> reality distinct from him he is free . . . to be the God of
> *man*. He exists neither *next to* man nor merely *above*
> him, but rather *with* him, *by* him and, most important

27

> of all, *for* him. He is *man's* God not only as Lord but
> also as father, brother, friend; and this relationship
> implies neither a diminution nor in any way a denial,
> but, instead, a confirmation and display of his divine
> essence.[49]

Attention to Barth's work, both in its grand lines and in some of its details, is crucial to identify the gap between what Barth actually thought and the representations of him in some postmodern accounts of his work, as well as to shift our own conversation with postmodernism away from specious generalisations like 'ontotheology', 'grand narratives' and 'the death of the subject' into something more Christianly (and humanly) specific. When we do this, I suggest, then our anxieties that current intellectual or cultural crises may sweep the ground from under our feet can be dealt a kindly but firm reminder that 'God for us' is not the church's invention, but a gift which really is given, something which, because we may trust it, we must trust. By way of conclusion, we may ponder some words from Barth's late lectures on evangelical theology:

> The 'place' of theology . . . will be determined by the
> impetus which it receives from within its own domain
> and from its own *object*. Its object—the philanthropic
> God Himself—is the law which must be the continual
> starting point of theology. It is, as the military might
> say, the post that the theologian must take and keep,
> whether or not it suits him or any other of his fellow
> creatures. The theologian has to hold this post at all
> costs, whether at the university or in the catacombs, if
> he does not wish to be imprisoned for dereliction of
> duty.[50]

---

49. Barth, *Evangelical Theology*, 10f.
50. *Ibid*, 16.

The Grand Narrative of Jesus Christ: Barth's Christology

John Webster

I

The severe postmodern vision involves dismantling the idea that there is any essence to history. 'History' is both mutable and multiple, without direction or form, literally inconsequential, what Mark Taylor calls an 'eternally fooling, maddening, clowning, jesting, tricking . . . field of force'.[1] As such, it is simply not narratable: to attempt to give history some sort of plot, to see it as in some sense more than erratic, is mere fiction, rendering substantial a set of differential relations which can never be organised into a coherent pattern of roles, purposes or goals. The distinctive animus of postmodern rejection of 'grand narratives' can quickly be grasped by contrasting it with 'modern' repudiations of the metaphysics of history. Modern suspicion is anti-ideological in intent. But postmodern suspicion is not simply turned against those narratives whose satisfyingly coherent schemes of history serve the interest of legitimation, by eliding the conflicts and suppressions which are involved in the production of such a narrative.[2] The 'modern' critic of narrated ideology customarily mounts a protest in order to establish a *better* account of human

---

1. M Taylor, *Erring: A Postmodern A/Theology* (Chicago: University of Chicago Press, 1984), 137.

2. See the work of J P Faye, *Langages totalitaires: critique de la raison narrative, critique de l'économie narrative* (Paris: Herman, 1972), and J Thompson's essay on Faye, 'Narratives of National Socialism' in *Studies in the Theory of Ideology* (Cambridge: Polity Press, 1984), 205-31.

history, one whose telling would be emancipatory rather than repressive or deceptive. A classic thumb-nail sketch of such a narrative can be found in Kant's *What Is Enlightenment?*, which plots the story of thought and morals as one of 'escape from self-incurred tutelage' into 'an age of enlightenment'.[3] For the postmodern, however, narrative conspires not only with ideology but also with teleology. Thus, for example, Jean-François Lyotard, who famously defined postmodernism as 'incredulity toward metanarratives', offers a critique of the Enlightenment narrative of rational emancipation, that story in which 'the hero of knowledge works towards a good ethico-political end'.[4] But a critique such as Lyotard's is not made against the background of a search for better rational practice: rational order and history alike are dissolved into 'a pragmatics of language particles'. All that can be said about the history of rational activity as of any other history is that 'there are many different language games—a heterogeneity of elements'.[5] Thereby, destiny simply dissolves.

Whether that kind of historical atomism, lacking in *longue durée*, can sustain serious art, politics or intellectual practice is a question we cannot here pursue. Christian theology has characteristically responded to postmodern dispersals of history in one of two ways. Some (Mark Taylor's *Erring* is an obvious example) have considered themselves required to abandon *historia* as a ruined category, since what we have is (in David Tracy's nice phrase) not a *status quo* but a *fluxus quo*.[6] Others (one of the most thoughtful of whom is Peter Hodgson

---

3.   I Kant, 'What Is Enlightenment?' in *On History* (New York: Macmillan, 1973), 8.

4.   J-F Lyotard, *The Postmodern Condition: A Report on Knowledge* (Manchester: Manchester University Press, 1984), xxiv.

5.   *Ibid.*

6.   D Tracy, 'On Naming the Present' in *On Naming the Present: God, Hermeneutics and Church* (Maryknoll: Orbis, 1994), 16.

in *God in History*[7]) have checked the renunciation of any narrational coherence by suggesting that the notion of history needs to be both chastened and diversified.

> Recognizing the many foci of creativity need not imply the renunciation of orienting narrative . . . The severe postmoderns are too preoccupied with the break-up of the single-thread story to contemplate the possibilities of another kind of story. A story can be open, multiplex, and indeterminate.[8]

What instruction might we take from Barth over these matters? My suggestion is along the following lines. An attentive and, if I may say so, leisurely reading of some central passages from Barth will help us see that the 'grand narratives' which are the object of postmodern negation are bastardized versions of authentically Christian claims about the nature of historical destiny, and this at two levels. First, Barth routinely insists that faith's apprehension of history as a coherent, ordered and purposive whole, assembled around a centre in the history of Jesus Christ, does not permit conversion into a manipulable scheme. The history of Jesus Christ which gathers creation, providence and the final ends of human history into itself simply cannot be instrumentalised, whether politically or conceptually. Second, and in a closely related way, when Barth reflects on the way in which faith apprehends historical meaning and purpose, he lays some emphasis on the irreducibly spiritual character of that apprehension. Such apprehension is a receptive rather than a straightforwardly constructive form of knowing. In short: Barth may help us see that what Christian faith says about history is properly not a 'grand narrative', not a 'world picture'.

The point here is not simply that Barth is rather more modest in his claims than the totalising historical maps which

---

7. P Hodgson, *God in History: Shapes of Freedom* (Nashville: Abingdon Press, 1989).

8. W A Beardslee, 'Christ and the Postmodern Age' in D R Griffin *et al*, *Varieties of Postmodern Theology* (Albany: SUNY Press, 1989), 69.

the postmodernist criticises, or that he is more 'open' than his less attentive critics are wont to allege. Barth in fact has something of critical importance to indicate to us here. He demonstrates how imperative it is that, in responding to its critics, Christian theology should not (whether out of carelessness or out of ignorance) tacitly consent to the shabby versions of Christian beliefs which critics propound, and then trim its sails accordingly. And thereby he also demonstrates the necessity for Christian theology to exercise constant vigilance lest its own self-articulations put forward versions of Christian faith which are uncorrected by the gospel—versions which all too quickly acquire public currency and make hostile criticism devastatingly effective. This strategy—which Barth developed to considerable effect in his reading of Feuerbach and to which he returns many times in later writings—can be formulated by the following rule: one of the necessary conditions for apologetic success is an alert dogmatic conscience. With that in mind, we proceed to look at what Barth may have to offer by way of advice.

II

It would be easy enough to present Barth as a grand narrativist of Christianity *par excellence*. Certainly the *Church Dogmatics* appears to present an 'awesome story'[9]—made all the more extraordinary by the fact that it involves a counter-intuitive set of claims: that God, not the human person in history, is the primordially temporal being; that our temporality is accordingly derivative; that the human present is not constituted by temporal self-awareness but by the presence of the risen Jesus. Already in the first volume of the *Church Dogmatics* Barth develops an account of the 'special time' (*CD*

---

9. F Kerr, *Immortal Longings: Versions of Transcending Humanity* (London: SPCK, 1997), 45.

32

1/2, 45) of revelation as one of a number of strategies for establishing that the self-manifesting being-in-act of God is not to be confused with some mere modulation of the history of the world. The time of God's covenant, the work of special divine goodness, is what he calls 'the new, the third time' (*CD* I/2, 49): neither time created with the original ordering of creation, nor fallen time, but a time which is the site of God's incomparable presence and activity. Barth's refusal here to be caught within the modern problem of faith and history (*CD* I/2, 56ff) is only one trace of what the later volumes of the *Church Dogmatics* will show to be a quite staggering claim that 'real time' is God's time with us. Again, at a number of points in *Church Dogmatics* III, Barth tries to map out some of the implications here. Thus 'human history' is essentially, not just accidentally, 'the sequence of events in which God concludes and executes this covenant with man . . . This history is from the theological standpoint *the* history' (*CD* III/1, 59). From the anthropological angle, the culmination of the presentation is the lengthy treatment of temporality in *Church Dogmatics* III/2, whose focus is the assertion that 'the existence of the man Jesus in time is our guarantee that time as the form of human existence is in any case willed and created by God, is given by God to man, and is therefore real' (*CD* III/2, 520). However, the most extended treatment of this Christological construal of history is, of course, the presentation of Christ's person and work in *Church Dogmatics* IV, that history which for Barth is 'the most actual thing, the sum and substance of God's time with us and our time for God' (*CD* IV/1, 83).

What shocks a modern reader like Wilhelm Dantine here is Barth's boldness in making such a 'massive assertion',[10] one which derives the 'essence, sense and significance of history

---

10. W Dantine, 'Der Welt-Bezug des Glaubens' in W Dantine, K Lüthi (ed), *Theologie zwischen Gestern und Morgen* (Munich: Kaiser, 1968), 269.

from the events of covenant and revelation'.[11] Such a move is what Dantine calls a 'christologising pipe-dream',[12] which simply bypasses the realities of history as human action and suffering. A modern instinctively reads Barth as an idealist or ideologist, subversive of the modern narrative of intellectual and political liberation. For a postmodern reader, by contrast, the problem is not that Barth tells the wrong story or fails to coordinate his story with the wider history of freedom, but that he tells a story at all. Thus Richard Roberts can only lament Barth's move into positive dogmatics as a turn from the 'atheology' of the second edition of *Romans* in which Barth gave expression to the dissolution of history. The *Church Dogmatics* on this account institutes a (tragic) return to the security of a closed narrative scheme whose cogency is dependent upon an increasingly authoritarian rhetoric of 'the real'.[13]

Is this what Barth is about? Is his work (along with von Balthasar's *Theodramatik*) one of the last great attempts in Western theology to propound a theology which retains the dramatic apparatus of role, plot and purpose abandoned by postmodern thinking? The answers to those questions can only be sought inductively and therefore exegetically, by close attention to what Barth says (rather than what his critics say he says or by what he himself can be pressed to imply), and here I try to offer at least the beginnings of an exegesis which points in the direction of an answer. But, by way of preparation, a couple of prefatory remarks.

First, in getting our minds round Barth's presentation of the 'awesome' story of Jesus, we must resist the temptation to simplify. Barth's work can and has been reduced to a few quasi-totalitarian assertions which make him pretty easy to dismiss. What such schematisation fails to catch is the manner in which

---

11. *Ibid*, 270.
12. *Ibid*, 273.
13. R H Roberts, *A Theology on Its Way? Essays on Karl Barth* (Edinburgh: T&T Clark, 1991).

Barth presents his case. Anyone who has tried to read Barth seriously will know that his modes of argument sometimes seem extraordinarily laborious and repetitive ways of getting across a point which could, in fact, be expressed in a much leaner, more spartan, fashion. But, if we persevere with our reading, we come to see that Barth's arguments are deliberately not linear or simply sequential; they proceed by setting out a complex set of variations or modulations. It is not just that Barth has a great deal to say and has to be heard at length; it is also, and more importantly, that, especially in the *Church Dogmatics*, no one stage of Barth's argument is ever definitive of the whole. Each stage, therefore, must be read in coordination with and counterpoint to its neighbours, and not extracted and used as the key to unlock the whole.

Second, in this context it is important to be clear that Barth is not best categorised as a 'narrative theologian'. It is certainly true that one of the major factors behind recent renewal of interest in Barth's work has been attention to his handling of biblical narrative; equally, it is true that appreciation of the 'storied' character of aspects of the Christology in *Church Dogmatics* IV has yielded valuable insight into his way of understanding the identity of the incarnate One.[14] But Barth was interested in God, not narratives, however grand. What he sought to recover was not Christian textuality, or even the 'strange new world' within the Bible as an item in and of itself, but rather the perfect, utterly sufficient, being and action of the triune God to which that textual world bears witness. If narrative attracted his theological imagination, it was because its presence in the apostolic testimony articulated the identity between the sovereign purpose of God and the career of the man Jesus. But Barth was far too magisterial a thinker to be

---

14. That being said, the wider applicability of 'narrative' to Barth's exegetical work is very doubtful: see P McGlasson, *Jesus and Judas: Biblical Exegesis in Barth* (Atlanta: Scholars Press, 1990).

35

attracted by simple devices which purport to solve all problems; and so 'narrativity' as such was not his concern.

The question before us, then, is whether his 'dramatic' (a term much to be preferred to 'narrative') account of God's dealings with humanity in Christ is just the kind of grand narrative which postmodernism counsels us to reject. By way of answer, I want to look in a little more detail at what Barth has to say about providence in *Church Dogmatics* III, and then at some aspects of the Christology in volume IV.

Barth's account of divine providence (set out chiefly in *Church Dogmatics* III/3, but also in IV/3, 695ff) is undergirded by the basic principle which he announced in *Church Dogmatics* II/1: 'The world has meaning as it acquires meaning from Him who alone has and is meaning' (*CD* II/1, 427). This statement occurs towards the end of Barth's discussion of the relation between divine patience and divine wisdom. God's wisdom, he argues, is God's self-attestation to the world, God's glorious self-demonstration, God himself as 'the truth and clarity which justifies, confirms and attests itself' (*CD* II/1, 427). It is God's 'holy and righteous, gracious and merciful meaning, to lead us to penitence, and therefore to make our own lives meaningful'. Meaning, we note, is not established so much as *acquired*; and, strictly speaking, it is not communicable (God alone, Barth tells us, has meaning). And so, whilst God's wisdom is, indeed, 'the philosophy of the created universe and the philosophy of human life', nevertheless it is 'not to be derived from reflection upon the universe or the being of man. It can be appreciated only by the bearing of God's own Word which as such gives us the right philosophy of the universe and our own human life' (*CD* II/1, 432). At the outset, then, it is crucial to note Barth's separation of a true apprehension of the divine wisdom from the processes of inventing, schematising or otherwise bestowing meaning upon the world. 'The divine wisdom,' Barth says, correcting a statement from Schleiermacher, 'is the divine self-communication ordering and determining the world for itself' (*CD* II/1, 433).

It is this which lies behind two important statements early in the presentation of providence in *Church Dogmatics* III/3. First, the content of providence is God's continuing fellowship with the creation over which he is Lord: 'in the act of creation the Creator as such has associated Himself with his creature as such as the Lord of its history, and is faithful to it as such' (*CD* III/3, 12). Second, belief in providence so defined is 'the practical recognition that things are as we have said'; that is to say 'it is the joy of the confidence and the willingness of the obedience grounded in this reality and its perception' (*CD* III/3, 14). From the very beginning, in other words, Barth refuses any kind of idealism in Christian talk of providence. We would simply not be talking of the providence of the God of Israel, nor of *Christian* belief in that providential God, if we thought that we were dealing with some projected historical totality. Barth clearly wants to ensure that the point does not elude his readers, and offers three 'sharp delimitations' of the nature of Christian belief in providence.

First, 'the Christian belief in providence is faith in the strict sense of the term, and this means . . . that it is a hearing and receiving of the Word of God' (*CD* III/3, 15). Belief in providence is not consent to a narrative projection. It is not 'an opinion, postulate or hypothesis concerning God, the world, man, and other things, an attempt at interpretation, exposition and explanation based upon all kinds of impressions and needs, carried through in the form of a systematic construction' (*CD* III/3, 16). And it is not this because the movement which the doctrine states begins with God. 'We can and must understand that the knowledge of this lordship of God can be compared only to the category of axiomatic knowledge, and that even in relation to this knowledge it forms a class apart . . . It consists in a realisation of the possibility which God gives to man' (*CD* III/3, 16). In sum: in belief in providence we do not have to do with 'a so called world view, even a Christian world view. For a world view is an opinion, postulate and hypothesis even when it pretends to be Christian' (*CD* III/3, 18).

Second, therefore, the content of belief in divine providence is strictly theological, depending 'on God and God alone' (*CD* III/3, 19). Crucially, this means that Barth distinguishes belief in providence from the unavoidable human activity of making sense of life by plotting a course of the cosmic process and one's own place in it. 'Man makes such conceptions. It is inevitable that he should do so, for otherwise he would not be capable of any practical orientation and decision' (*CD* III/3, 20). Barth's point is not that we can dispense with all and any such constructs, but that they should not be allowed to step beyond their limits, replacing the Word of God by some 'little booklet of history' (*CD* III/3, 22). Belief in providence 'is faith in God and his dominion and judgement to which all history, even that of the Spirit, even that of human conceptions of history, is holy subject. It cannot, then, become belief in a human system of history invented by man' (*CD* III/3, 21). From the beginning, then, Barth takes some care to differentiate faith in providence from totalising historical schemes.

> Our attempts to orientate ourselves in the dark, in the great movement of the masks of God which we call history, are necessary, right and good. But when it is a matter of receiving and having light in this darkness . . . we are forced back upon the Word of God, and this alone is to be received (*CD* III/3, 23f).

This in turn entails Barth's rejection of any over-belief at this point. The fact that Christian knowledge of providence is 'true and thoughtful and courageous' does not exclude the fact that it is also 'relative, provisional and modest' (*CD* III/3, 23). Faith is not blind; but nor is it all-seeing; rather, it is a seeing which is given ever afresh by the Spirit.

> The establishment of a fixed Christian view, of a lasting picture of the relationship between the Creator and creature, would necessarily mean that in taking today the insight given him today man hardens himself against receiving a new and better one tomorrow . . . The knowledge received in

enlightening and empowering by the Holy Ghost will
never be closed but always open (*CD* III/3, 56).

A third delimitation crowns the whole discussion, grounding
what has been established in the first two. 'In its substance the
Christian belief in providence is Christian faith, *i.e.*, faith in
Christ' (*CD* III/3 26). Providence is not the outer court where
Christian faith mixes with all manner of other accounts of God
and the world; it is not one species of a genus of belief in
historical order. On the contrary: belief in providence bears the
name 'Father, the name of the one manifest in Jesus Christ as
God for us, and it is this one of whom we speak when we speak
of providence'. Belief in providence therefore 'looks to the
history of the covenant which is fulfilled in the mission, in the
person and work of the incarnate Son, of the "God for us". And
through and beyond this it looks to the divine election of grace'
(*CD* III/3, 29).

How does all this relate to postmodernism's critique of
grand narratives? Two lines of reflection are worth pursuing.

On the one hand, throughout the entire discussion Barth is
at pains to be Christianly specific. He accords priority to the
particular content of Christian belief in providence, confident
that these aspects are of far greater significance for theological
talk about God's providential activity than any formal features
which a Christian account undoubtedly shares with, for
example, a philosophy of history. For Barth, attention to this
particular content is sufficient to establish the uniqueness of
Christian faith and its theology. He returns to this argument
many times in the course of the discussion. Thus the thrust of
the three lengthy depictions of *conservatio, concursus* and
gubernatio in *Church Dogmatics* paragraph 49 is, by a series of
theological meditations on Scripture, to try and display the
particular character of providence as these acts undertaken by
this God for these ends. However much a Christian account of
providence may appear to be merely one more master-story,
what establishes its difference is the identity of its divine
subject.

> The rule of God as opposed to the control and
> outworking of a natural or spiritual cosmic principle

is characterised by the fact that it is here in these particular events attested in the Old and New Testaments, in the 'I am' spoken and actualised by the King of Israel, in the covenant of free grace instituted and executed, promised and fulfilled by Him, that it has the centre which controls and is normative for everything else (*CD* III/3, 183).

In sum: 'the Subject who speaks and actualises the "I am" in these events, the King of Israel, is the God who rules the world' (*CD* III/3, 177). Such a narrative is, we might say, non-degradable; it will not permit any quiet removal of its central subject, so that the King of Israel could be smuggled off the stage and yet the story would somehow continue to perform its task of ordering history into a coherent scheme. The biblical story of God's providential activity is not just a 'grand narrative' any more than the *Aeneid* is just a long poem. We may treat it as such, of course, and criticise it as such; but to do so is to let its real character slip through our fingers.

This leads to a second comment. Barth emphasises the uniqueness, not only of the content of a Christian doctrine of providence, but also of the manner in which providence is apprehended. What he has to say here reinforces what we have already seen of the anti-constructive nature of Barth's account of Christian belief in providence. Postmodernism is instinctively idealist or nominalist in seeing so-called historical order as the attempt to impose depth, structure and sequence where there is only randomness. For Barth, by contrast, to believe in providence is not to shape the scatter of the world's history but to confess the existence of a 'formative economy', a disposition of all things by the God of the gospel, on the basis of which 'occurrence acquires the character of a motivated history . . . [T]he individual thing receives its particular dignity and value on the basis of a formative economy which assigns to all things a place and time and function' (*CD* III/3, 192f). But form, we note, is acknowledged, not imposed. And so, in a memorable statement Barth suggests a reversal of epistemological direction, in which we are answerable to the reality which it is given to us to perceive:

> [W]e cannot treat of the perception and
> understanding of the superiority of the divine work
> in the same way as we can of a human opinion, or as
> indeed we must of even the most serious of human
> suggestions. In other words, we are not in any
> position to treat of this perception and understanding
> as though they were open to discussion. Naturally,
> our own comprehension and formulation of them are
> always open to discussion. By its very nature the
> matter is one which demands constantly a better
> formulation. But as it does so, it remains outside and
> above the sphere in which it itself can be called into
> question. It is a matter which questions us. Our
> relation to it can consist only in our rendering an
> account *to* it rather than *of* it (*CD* III/3, 109).

And this, in the end, is why the condition for a correct
perception of providence is spiritual; we are out of the region of
technical reason. To see providence, we have to become certain
sorts of persons, those from whom the Spirit has taken away
both fear and vanity, those who are set free to *see*.

If this rather detailed reminder of some features of Barth's
thought is necessary, it is because what is rejected in much
postmodern writing (or sometimes affirmed in postmodern
theology) is scarcely recognisable as authentically Christian
faith and practice. Perhaps what we may learn most of all from
Barth is that our response to postmodernism need not lead us to
abandon Christian specificity or to relativise it into one strand
of religious or cultural discourse: the most urgent need is for
attention to Christian claims, renewed attention to both their
particular content and the kind of dispositions which they
require for their correct understanding. Both Barth's
'personalism' (his referring of all theological statements to the
personal reality of Jesus Christ) and his 'actualism' (his
insistence that faith's knowledge is 'event' not 'deposit') make it
hard to see his doctrine of providence as a grand narrative.
And, of course, at the heart of what he has to say here is a
Christological affirmation:

> Jesus Christ is a living human person who comes and
> speaks and acts with the claim and authority of God,

and in relation to whom there can be no question whatever of controlling and using Him to grasp or master this or that even in the sphere of thought . . . What is there here to see and fix, to be the object of speculation and disposition? The grace of God addressed to the world in Jesus Christ is that which exists supremely, but quite uniquely, only as on the basis of God's eternal love and election and faithfulness it was and is and will be event, inaccessible to all human or even Christian *hybris*, recognisable only in gratitude for the fact that it is real and true, and in prayer for ever new recognition of its reality and truth (*CD* IV/3, 706f).

III

Following from here, then, I offer some briefer remarks on some features of Barth's explicit Christology in *Church Dogmatics* IV (though of course what we have been examining in the doctrine of providence is no less Christological in orientation). The stone of offence for the postmodern reader of *Dogmatics* IV is the sheer grandeur of Barth's doctrine of reconciliation. The scale of the design and the cogency of the rhetoric through which it is accomplished may indeed be sufficient to persuade us that here, if anywhere in twentieth century theology, grand narrative and teleology make a bid for power. By way of reflection, a number of things might be said.

First, we must not allow worries about the universal scope which Barth claims for the history of Jesus to crowd out the fact that the most basic function of his presentation is to stress Jesus' *particularity* before his cosmic pertinence. The theme of the doctrine of reconciliation is *solus Christus*; but it is this, not in the sense that Jesus Christ's reality is celebrated *at the expense of* other history, but in the sense that Jesus Christ's reality must be seen for what it is, possessed of an irreducible *Istigkeit*. Christology is concerned with 'a definite story . . . a unique event' (*CD* IV/1, 70; cf 73; *CD* IV/3, 165-8, 179-81), what Barth calls 'the concrete and unique story of Jesus Christ' (*CD* IV/1, 75). It was amongst Barth's most substantial achievements that he resisted the Christological nominalism of post-Kantian Protestantism, refusing both to turn Jesus into a cipher for some state of affairs or truth (moral, existential, political) and to abstract Jesus' 'meaning' from the apostolic evangelical history of his life-act. To think and speak well of Jesus Christ, we must simply indicate his specificity as the one who lived, surrendered and took up again this life:

> It came to pass, we have just said; as we do when we tell the story of something that happened in the world at a definite place and a definite point of time. To think the matter out further and to understand it in detail, all that remains actually for us to do is simply to recount it in the manner of a story which has come to pass . . . to bring it before ourselves as something which has objectively happened. There and then, in the existence of the man Jesus of Nazareth, who was the Son of God, this event came to pass in the kingly freedom of God who is holy and righteous in His faithfulness and mercy . . . Before there is any consideration of its significance, it can and must be taken as that which is significant in its significance, and therefore in and for itself as the history of Jesus Christ as it took place there and then, and as it can be and is recounted: That is how it happened for us (*CD* IV/1, 232).

Second, problems arise for the postmodern reader because Barth affirms not only that Jesus has an irreducibly particular identity but also that that identity is the unique point of conjunction between, on the one hand, the sovereign freedom of God and, on the other, the fate of humanity as a whole. In this single history, in this simple 'It came to pass', there takes place that which gives shape and destiny to all other occurrence. The history of reconciliation which Jesus is 'rules and controls' all the dimensions of time in whose limits the world and the

Webster

John Webster

human race exist. It is that turning from the lie to the truth, *i.e.*, from the unfaithfulness of man to his faithfulness, and therefore from death to life, which is the basis of all world occurrence, and in a hidden but supremely true sense the purpose and measure of all contemporary occurrence, and also its goal, enclosing it on every side in order to direct it and set it right (*CD* IV/1, 76). Or again, in the treatment of 'Jesus is Victor' in IV/3, Barth proposes that the history of Jesus is 'the "specific fact" in relation to the whole world and in the face of all other facts' (*CD* IV/3, 224). The conflict and victory which here takes place *is* human destiny, 'the arrival, advent, manifestation and incursion of a new, complex but unitary reality of human thought and speech, abstention and action, *i.e.*, the presence of a new man' (*CD* IV/3, 246). It is that 'unitary character' which is the object of postmodern critique: does not this assertion about Jesus inevitably raise the spectre of history as a single line, traceable to a unique source or locus of agency, and fail to grasp that what we call 'history' is, in fact, a field of negotiations or differences which cannot be resolved into a totality? When the atoning history of Jesus is distinguished 'from every purely contingent event' (*CD* IV/1, 50; cf IV/2, 31), when it comes to be a 'necessary happening' (*CD* IV/1, 48), then do we not inevitably drift into a Christological metaphysics of history in which one fragment acquires 'unconditional validity and scope and binding force' (*CD* IV/1, 48) and which can then be read and expounded as if it were 'a definitely given text'? (*CD* IV/1, 122) In short: do we not here have a bad case of ontotheology?

Such questions raise themselves with particular force against Barth's theology because of the sheer range and purposiveness of his exposition. But they are questions for any Christian theology which tries to ponder the decline of teleology in postmodernity. What sort of answer might be offered? If we take seriously the rule I indicated earlier—that one necessary condition for good apologetics is an alert dogmatic conscience—then we will adopt a quite specific procedure at this point, consisting of two parallel paths of argument.

44

The first line of response will be to follow the logic of faith's confession of the gospel, allowing that confession to indicate the direction which Christian doctrine is to take at this point. If Christian theology is inescapably teleological in its exposition of the mystery of salvation, it is because that mystery itself is teleological. Christian theology tells a story because a story is there to be told. Put differently: theology does not decide to speak teleologically; it is commanded, and therefore authorised and enabled to speak of the orderly, narratable character of that which is given to faith—the 'it came to pass' which, in all its ramifications for the unitary story of humanity, is given in and with faith's confession. Thus Christian theology will not invest too heavily in establishing on extra-theological grounds the possibility or reality of teleology in general. Certainly it will observe with interest the work of those who try to show the philosophical implausibility or the injurious moral and political effects of postmodern denial of any identity to history, and it will quietly offer its encouragement and applause. But it cannot wait anxiously on the success of such work, holding its breath in the hope that the arguments will work in its favour and it will be given permission to proceed. And it need not wait, because its concern is not with teleology in general, but with this given history of the manifestation of the ways of God.

Alongside this Christian theology will develop a second set of arguments. The aim here is to respond to criticism by clarifying and correcting misunderstandings, demonstrating that they rest on misconstruals of the Christian confession, whether perpetrated by its supporters or its detractors. Once again, the aim is not a principled apologetic, but an occasional polemic and defence, directed towards the end of displaying the proper content of Christian faith against mangled or incomplete representations of it.

Both responses are 'dogmatic', that is, within the sphere of the church and of faith's confession of the gospel. We have already seen in some detail that Barth adopts the first procedure in his doctrine of providence and his account of the story of

Jesus: teleology is not so much argued for as received and described. The second procedure can also be found throughout the *Church Dogmatics*. We have already seen something of it in Barth's insistence that Christian belief in providence is not a 'world picture'. And we fittingly close this account of Barth's Christology by seeing how it is used there also.

Barth's Christology is sometimes read as a unitary narrative which, as they say, 'absorbs the world'. At one level this is obviously untrue: it is certainly not the case that Barth suggested that the story of Jesus *as text* absorbs the world. Barth was not an 'intratextual theologian', for the simple reason that he understood the New Testament story of Jesus as apostolic testimony, appointed by God to bear witness to his presence and activity, but not itself a cultural condensation of the gospel. Nor is it a matter of Barth saying that the lived story of Jesus is a single, mythic totality which swallows everything else into itself. This latter point is singularly important in clearing up a misunderstanding of Barth's Christology. He makes the point on a number of occasions in a couple of ways.

On the one hand, Barth is adamant that Jesus' history is the history in which the covenant between God and humanity is brought to fulfilment. As such, it sustains other histories, directing them to their true end but by no means obliterating them. Covenant history is differential history—something I want to explore at length in the next chapter, on Barth's anthropology. On the other hand, Barth displays a rather deliberate reserve in what he has to say about the universal scope of Jesus in the course of the Christology. He is careful to protect it from becoming some kind of controllable principle of knowledge or explanation or world view. Partly this comes across in the manner of Barth's presentation, which we might describe as one of indication. He seeks simply to set the story of Jesus before his readers in its own integrity, without extrapolating or schematising. Indeed, one has hardly begun to grasp the nature of Barth's doctrine of reconciliation unless one senses the *modesty* of the undertaking. Partly, again, Barth's reserve is expressed in his insistence that the story of Jesus is *strange*, that is, something which cannot be appropriated. Thus, writing of the history of atonement as justification, Barth stresses its puzzling character. Certainly,

> we are participants in this great drama. This history is
> in fact our history. We have to say indeed that it is
> our true history, in an incomparably more direct and
> intimate way than anything that might present itself
> as our history in our own subjective experience, than
> anything which we might try to represent as our
> history in explanation of our own self-understanding
> (*CD* IV/1, 547).

But even in this directness and immediacy 'our real today, the today of true and actual transition from wrong to right, from death to life, and therefore the today of the judgment which falls upon us by the righteousness and grace of God, is always a strange today' (*CD* IV/1, 548). The point is crucial. Jesus' history is no ideological 'grand narrative', because his history, for all that it includes us, is *his* history, full, perfect, sufficient, and only because of that catholic. The story of Jesus, the 'today' of Jesus Christ' which is also our 'today', cannot be made an instrument for historical computation (*CD* IV/1, 548). The *doctrinal* safeguard against 'grand narrative' is thus in part Christological (the incommunicability of Jesus' identity as Lord and Saviour) and in part pneumatological (Jesus' self-communication is his own act in the operation of his Spirit). Or, as he puts it, the transition from Christ's time to ours is the Spirit's work:

> The witness of the Holy Spirit . . . opens up the whole
> history within which the world flies like an arrow
> from its origin in the will and decree of God to the
> goal and end already set and declared for it in the
> history of Jesus Christ. The witness of the Holy Spirit
> brings about this transition—the transition of the self-
> witness of Jesus Christ into Church history, into the
> history of individual lives, into world history (*CD*
> IV/2, 135).

We may draw matters to a close by drawing attention to two things. The first is this: Barth's theology is far too modest, cheerful and good humoured to be described as a grim ontotheology cased in a narrative mould. Its heart is not a scheme, but a name, a set of actions, and the corresponding free actions of those who find that name supremely worthy and delightful. The second is this: If Christianity has a teleology, it is of a very distinct kind—once again, not a scheme, but a name and a set of actions, the name and activity of the man Jesus, in and as whom God enables all things to attain their true end. Only a fearful person, a person strange to faith, would think of those things as other than matters for praise. Perhaps we need also to learn that here, too, Christian perception is spiritual, and that the knowledge of the axioms of Christian faith is vouchsafed, as Calvin said, to 'quiet and composed minds ready to learn'.[15]

---

15. J Calvin, *Institutes* (London: SCM, 1960) I xvii.1.

Rescuing the Subject:
Barth and Postmodern Anthropology

John Webster

I

Let me begin with three quotations.

> The world always looks outward, I turn my gaze
> inward; there I fix it, and there I keep it busy.
> Everyone looks before him; I look within. I have no
> business but with myself, I unceasingly consider,
> examine, and analyse myself. Others, if they will
> but see, are always going elsewhere; they are
> always going forward, *nemo in sese tendat
> descendere*. But I revolve within myself.[1]

> One thing in any case is certain: man is neither
> the oldest nor the most constant problem that has
> been posed for human knowledge . . . It is not
> around him and his secrets that knowledge
> prowled so long in the darkness . . . As the
> archaeology of our thought easily shows, man is
> an invention of recent date. And one perhaps
> nearing its end.[2]

> We define God's patience as His will, deep-
> rooted in His essence and constituting His divine
> being and action, to allow another—for the sake of
> His own grace and mercy and in the affirmation of

---

1. Montaigne, 'On Presumption', *Essays* II 17 (Harmondsworth:
    Penguin, 1958), 219f.
2. M Foucault, *The Order of Things: An Archaeology of the Human
    Sciences* (London: Tavistock, 1970), 386f.

His holiness and justice—space and time for the
development of its own existence, thus conceding
to this existence a reality side by side with His
own, and fulfilling His will towards this other in
such a way that He does not suspend and destroy
it as this other but accompanies and sustains it and
allows it to develop in freedom (*CD* II/1, 490f).

Both in philosophy and theology, the anthropological axioms
of modernity have ceased to command immediate assent. To
answer why this is so, we would need to point to a number of
factors. In philosophy, we might highlight the prominence of
a number of stylish and comprehensive critical readings of the
so-called turn to the subject; the rise of neo-Aristotelian
virtue-oriented moral and political theory; the return from the
wilderness of the notion of tradition; the replacement of the
thin moral psychology of both analytic and existentialist
ethics by something more historically and humanly robust
and rounded. At least some styles of theology have similarly
witnessed a parallel turn from the subject. It would be
premature to announce the demise of subject-oriented
theological anthropologies, since they retain some vigour,
especially in the revisionist theologies which remain indebted
to Tillich and (on some interpretation) to Rahner.
Nevertheless, the force of a good deal of recent work has been
to disentangle Christian anthropology from the
phenomenology of the transcendental experiencing subject,
and instead expand it more directly through such doctrinal
themes as trinity, incarnation or church. Both in philosophy
and theology, we might say the metaphysics of subjectivity
has been chastened, by placing it within a shapely economy of
being which transcends it but which it does not transcend.

For the severe postmodern, this critique of modernity
simply misses the point. Something far more radical is
required: not the chastening of subjectivity but its exposure as
an illusion. The postmodern might tell a story which would
run something like this. The history of modernity is the

50

history of the invention of the self. *Modernity* tells that history as an emancipation of cognitive and moral selfhood from the encompassing orders of gods, societies, customs and texts, and all their attendant officials. In the course of this emancipation, the modern story goes, the self finally emerges into the light as that which is axiomatically real, true and good. Postmodernism announces that this history of emancipation is mere pretence. The transcendent subject is simply a fictive conglomeration of fragments. And so Kant's lonely, severely rational and utterly responsible agent becomes Musil's 'man without qualities'—either an empty space played upon by systems of differences, or an anarchic trickster figure lacking in form or definition. Whereas modernity stands under Montaigne's rubric, 'I look within', postmodernism more characteristically says: '[E]ach of us knows that our self does not amount to much'.[3]

Like all such stories, the cogency of the postmodern version of the history of anthropology depends on not being too worried about the details and on being harnessed to a strong proposal in the light of which it acquires plausibility. This strong proposal—the so-called 'death of the subject'—is well described by Calvin Schrag at the beginning of the very best study of the topic, *The Self after Postmodernity*:

> For the most part, questions about the self, and
> particularly questions about the self *as subject*, are
> deemed anathema. As there is no longer a need for
> the unification of the diverse culture-spheres, so the
> problem of the self, at least as traditionally
> formulated, is seen to evaporate. Questions about
> self-identity, the unity of consciousness and
> centralized and goal-directed activity has been
> displaced in the aftermath of the dissolution of the
> subject. If one cannot rid oneself of the vocabulary

---

3. J-F Lyotard, *The Postmodern Condition: A Report on Knowledge* (Manchester: Manchester University Press, 1984), 15.

of self, subject, and mind, the most that can be
asserted is that the self is multiplicity,
heterogeneity, difference, and ceaseless becoming,
bereft of origin and purpose. Such is the manifesto
of postmodernity on matters of the human subject
as self and mind.[4]

Tracing the background to the demise of the transparent, reflexive, original self of modernity would take us away from our central concern here. But it is worth at least noting an ambiguity. In so far as it involves a repudiation of all form or shape to selfhood, postmodern dissolution of the subject often follows something of the same trajectory as modernity, which it supposedly rejects, by making 'unrestricted freedom' basic to its account of human life.[5] There are no doubt important differences between modern and postmodern accounts of liberty: unlike modernity, postmodernity is unconcerned to locate this liberty in an understanding of human nature, and, lacking a sense of the teleological, liberty is often construed in quasi-anarchic rather than in political or moral terms. But it is nevertheless true that postmodernism can often present itself as simply 'the intensification of modernity's quest for autonomy—freedom without terminus or telos'.[6] Charles Taylor's judgment on Derrida has, I think, wide application:

A philosophy which supposedly negates
subjectivity, self-possession and full presence and
which sees thought as perpetually dispersed and
'deferred' in a field of infinite substitutions also
exalts the indefinite freedom of play, and presents

4. C O Schrag, *The Self after Postmodernity* (New Haven: Yale University Press, 1997), 8.

5. C Taylor, *Sources of the Self: The Making of Modern Identity* (Cambridge, Mass.: Harvard University Press, 1989), 490.

6. F C Bauerschmidt, 'Aesthetics. The Theological Sublime' in J Milbank *et al* (ed), *Radical Orthodoxy: A New Theology* (London: Routledge, 1999), 202.

itself as a liberating doctrine. Engulfment and
extreme subjectivism come together.[7]

How might Christian theology begin to engage these
anthropological issues? One—serious—option is to articulate
a fully postmodern theological account of human selfhood.
Such an account would stress the connection of ontotheology
and subjectivity. In the Western tradition of metaphysics and
theology, so the argument goes, God the supreme being is
equally the supreme subject, the monadic, substantial, self-
possessing bearer of a name. 'From a monotheistic
perspective,' Mark Taylor writes, 'to be is to be one. In order
to be one, the subject cannot err and must always remain
proper. By following the straight and narrow course, the self
hopes to gain its most precious possession—itself'.[8]
Subjectivity is thus the replication of divine self-possession:
'The self-presence of the self-conscious subject reflects the self-
presence of absolute subjectivity'.[9] Whether Taylor is correct
in discerning a single historical trajectory of this sort from
Augustine to Hegel is, of course, an open question. Moreover,
one could certainly argue that Taylor's pretty monochrome
portrait of the Western theological tradition succeeds only by
maximizing certain doctrinal aspects (divine absoluteness,
mentalist accounts of human nature) and minimizing other
corrective features within the tradition, such as the doctrine of
trinitarian relations, or those traditions of ascetical theology
which have given weight to dispossession (both spiritual and
social) as a mode of authentic humanity. Indeed, to target the
whole tradition as resting on 'the repressive logic of identity',
or 'the "logic" of oneness [which] implies an economy of

---

7.   C Taylor, *op cit*, 590, n 90; cf here L Dupré, *Passage to Modernity:
     An Essay in the Hermeneutics of Nature and Culture* (New Haven:
     Yale University Press, 1993), 6.

8.   M Taylor, *Erring: A Postmodern A/Theology* (Chicago: University
     of Chicago Press, 1984), 41f.

9.   *Ibid*, 42.

ownership',[10] is to offer nothing more than a crude pastiche. What it serves, however, is a proposal for a differential structure of human selfhood, which 'subverts the exclusive logic of identity' by seeing the self as 'a function of the intersection of structures and the crossing of forces'.[11] '*Desubstantialized*' and deindividualized the self is '*co-relative*' and '*co-dependent*'[12]: not the centre of a set of given structures, but a trace, a point at which fluid lines of force play against one another (the link between postmodern theology and process theology is not incidental). 'Fabricated from transecting acentric structures, the deindividualized subject is never centred in itself'.[13]

In effect, then, this severe postmodern theological anthropology[14] uses deconstructive philosophy as a purgative, scouring out ontotheology and enabling the emergence of a post-metaphysical, non-subjective account of human existence. Others take a different theological tack, mounting an imminent critique of postmodern anthropology, and often appealing to a metaphysical theory which is hostile to deconstruction. Such arguments frequently lay some stress on the apparent inability of postmodern anthropology to generate anything like an adequate ethics of politics. Lacking any teleology to moral action, and viewing the self merely as a point in a mobile, differential field of force, postmodernism finds it acutely hard to articulate an account of resistance or courage, since to talk in such terms seems to require a sense of durable subjectivity which postmodern theory cannot

---

10. *Ibid*, 130.

11. *Ibid*, 134.

12. *Ibid*, 135.

13. *Ibid*, 139.

14. For further representative works here, see R P Scharlemann, *The Reason of Following: Christology and the Ecstatic I* (Chicago: University of Chicago Press, 1991), and C E Winquist, *Desiring Theology* (Chicago: University of Chicago Press, 1995), 99-126.

support. In particular, ethics and politics—if they are to be more than merely arbitrary, occasional concrescences, temporary alliances or short-term projects—require the regularities and directions which we articulate by talking of human life and activity as involving the assumption of roles, the formation of character, the following of a plot. In effect, the postmodern de-substantialised self is too slender and porous to be a narrative subject: the postmodern subject does not *perform*.[15]

When we try to place Barth on the map of competing possibilities, matters become rather difficult. In one sense, he clearly is not 'modern', at least to the extent that he can often write as the determined foe of a certain kind of construal of autonomy and self-realisation which he associates with the intellectual and spiritual traditions of modernity. His anthropology is neither foundational nor transcendental; he is antipathetic to allowing reflexive subjectivity to function as a basic anthropological datum, whether in epistemology or morals. But, if this makes Barth seem companionable to at least some aspects of postmodern de-centring of the self, other features of his work point in a quite different direction. Above all, he insists that human life and history are derivative, and what he says about them is thus consequential upon the trinitarian, incarnational and pneumatological materials which he expounds at such length and with such intense joy, and which constitute the 'formative economy' of the human self. Hardly postmodern, and hardly modern. Yet again, from another point of view, there is a distinctly modern strand to

---

15. See Schrag, *The Self after Postmodernity*, and A C Thiselton, *Interpreting God and the Postmodern Self* (Edinburgh: T&T Clark, 1995), both of whom make much use of P Ricoeur, *Oneself as Another* (Chicago: University of Chicago Press); D Tracy, 'On Naming the Present'; R Williams, 'Hegel and the Gods of Modernity' in P Berry, A Wernick (ed), *Shadow of Spirit: Religion and Postmodernism* (London: Routledge, 1992).

55

Barth's anthropology. He regularly appeals to a rather robust sense of human selfhood, which he clearly believes to be a basic ingredient of a proper construal of Christianity. Without that substantial anthropology and its corresponding emphasis on the realisation of selfhood through action, Barth's understanding of covenant, and his consistent stress on the moral character of human response to God, would be simply unthinkable. What such features suggest is that Barth is, in important respects, a (rather rebellious) child, if not of Kant, then at least of the refractions of Kant in the modernist moral dogmatics of the nineteenth century.

Barth's anthropology can be (and has been) read as pre-modern, modern and postmodern. The reason for this is not, I think, a fundamental incoherence in his work at this point, but something like the following. In the course of what he has to say about humanity, Barth says things that are formally and sometimes materially similar to what is said by others: pre-moderns, moderns and postmoderns. The apparent 'occasionalism' which troubles many critics in his moral anthropology—that is, his rejection of an 'ethics of being'[16]—sounds postmodern, as does his generally hostile stance towards interiority; his stress on self-realisation sounds modern. But, as always in Barth, the full force of the argument is not conveyed by any one statement, but by a layered, or perhaps cumulative, effect. Poor readers of Barth extract one layer, make it stand for the whole, and then find it a relatively simple matter to annex Barth to another scheme or project. Good readers endure the perplexity for longer, but in the end are afforded a rather more complex (and ultimately satisfying) account of the matter.

What, then, would a 'good reading' of Barth on these matters look like? Two initial comments before I offer a sketch. First: it is only a sketch—a few suggestive lines, but

---

16   K Barth, *Ethics* (Edinburgh: T&T Clark, 1981), 80.

nothing like a finished picture, which would require a thorough treatment not only of the *Church Dogmatics* but also of, for example, Barth's political writings and, indeed, the political activity which accompanied most of his career from Safenwil onwards. Second, and more importantly, it is crucial to understand that Barth's anthropology is non-theoretical and non-utopian. He is not about the business of expounding an anthropological ideal, for to do so would simply repeat the error of thinking that human beings are at liberty to constitute themselves in ways of their own choosing. His aim is *descriptive*, namely the portrayal of the human person as one with a specific set of contours, a specific identity which comes from participation in the history of Jesus Christ, which is the culmination of God's covenant with humanity. Barth's hostility to abstraction is nowhere more evident than in his anthropology: 'There is no abstract humanity and therefore no correspondingly abstract human self-understanding. Man is no more, and no less, no other than what he is through and with and for Jesus Christ' (CL, 19). It is this which gives Barth's work here not only its Christological specificity but also its humane quality and its descriptive depth. With that in mind, then, we turn to what Barth has to say.

II

Barth's theology is the-anthropology; it is a theology which is concerned with the depiction of the covenant between God and humanity, and which is therefore not single but twofold in theme. To present Barth's theology, as many have done, as a bleak, even morbid, exposition of the logic of divine sovereignty in antithesis to human freedom and flourishing is not even to begin to grasp what Barth is about: the joyful affirmation of God's partnership with those whom he has made and remade in Jesus Christ.

57

This the-anthropology is often thought to be a 'late move' in Barth (partly because it was expressed in most available form in lectures from the 1950s:

> 'Theology' in the literal sense, means the science and doctrine of God. A very precise definition of the Christian endeavour in this respect would really require the more complex term 'the-anthropology'. For an abstract doctrine of God has no place in the Christian realm, only a 'doctrine of God and of man', a doctrine of the commerce and communion between God and man.[17]

What is expressed in these later texts (and in the sustained statements of the same theme in the volumes of the doctrine of reconciliation which Barth was writing at the same time) was not, however, simply the fruit of a mature spirit now ready to concede that earlier negations and antitheses were too sharp. Rather, the later writings simply re-articulate something which was ingredient within the *Church Dogmatics* from the beginning, and which, indeed, predates the start of the *Church Dogmatics* by more than a decade. From the earliest days of his turn from liberalism, and his alliance with a theology driven by Scripture and its derivative confessions, Barth did not lose sight of the fact that anthropology is an intrinsic element of any adequate account of Christian faith. What finds expression, therefore, in the explicit the-anthropology of the later *Church Dogmatics* is a set of instincts formed in the early days of Barth's engagement with the classical traditions of Christianity—most of all, perhaps, with the soteriology, pneumatology and theology of the Christian life which Barth found in Calvin and the Reformed confessional writings. Even in the midst of his early denials of any *independent* anthropology and ethics and his attacks upon the moralising of Christianity which threatened to engulf any

---

17. K Barth, 'The Humanity of God' in *The Humanity of God* (London: Collins, 1961), 11.

genuine disturbance of cultural complacency by the sovereignty of God, Barth was already a *moral* theologian. That is, he was a theologian—as he put it in his early lectures on Calvin at Göttingen—of the horizontal as well as of the vertical or—perhaps better—of the horizontal because he was a theologian of the vertical.[18]

Grasping the continuity of Barth's thinking at this point is important not just for making correct judgments about the genetic and developmental questions which have attracted recent attention. It is also vitally important for understanding the overall design of his thought. Barth's theology was never one in which anthropology had, as it were, to struggle to the surface from underneath the crushing weight of assertions about absolute divine subjectivity. Even less was it a theology in which human subjectivity and agency were so radically taken apart that no sense of human substance remained. It was a theology which spoke of God and humanity: only because and precisely because it spoke of God—Israel's God, the God and Father of our Lord Jesus Christ—it also spoke of the human creature and the creature's world.

An early text from Barth will help us to see this particularly well, precisely because it is to the early writings that postmodern interpreters of Barth most often are drawn. The famous 1919 Tambach lecture on 'The Christian's Place in Society' is sometimes read as an unmitigated attack on the socio-ethical realm, as Barth rejected to the uttermost the ethics of society and culture which had so deeply impregnated German liberal Protestantism. And many of Barth's rallying cries certainly give initial credence to a postmodern reading of the lecture as polemic against anthropological or ethical *form*. 'Keep your distance!' Barth warned his no doubt astonished hearers; 'No mental

---

18   On what follows, see J Webster, *Barth's Moral Theology* (Edinburgh: T&T Clark, 1998).

apprehension of the *form* of this truth'.[19] Or again: 'We must return to that reserve maintained by the divine over against the human'.[20] But, in a crucial move, Barth goes on to assert that 'the separation of the two cannot be ultimate, for then God would not be God. There *must still* be a way from there to here. And with this "must" and this "still" we confess the miracle of the *revelation* of God'.[21] One is tempted to say that the whole of Barth's *Church Dogmatics* can be found in that statement, for what is the *Dogmatics* if not one long, astonished testimony to the fact that God—because he is the self-revealing God—has blazed a path from there to here, for his own glory and our eternal well-being? Furthermore, already at Tambach the anthropological and ethical consequences are indicated. Neither the moralism which identifies God's kingdom with the order of human society, nor 'radical and absolute opposition'[22]—we might say: neither modernity's 'yes' nor postmodernity's 'no'—are adequate to the reality of the gospel, which Barth here, as often in earlier writings, identifies as the gospel of the resurrection. Rather, 'the *resurrection* of Jesus Christ from the dead is the power that moves the world and us, *because* it is the appearance in our corporeality of a *totaliter aliter* constituted corporeality'.[23] That new corporeality is no straightforward extension of the kingdom of nature. But nor is it the denial of that kingdom, its erasure through eschatology or its dissolution into sheer contingency. No: 'We need not be apprehensive of any pessimistic discrediting of our life here and of activity in our life here, *if* we conclude with Calvin to

---

19. K Barth, 'The Christian's Place in Society' in *The Word of God and the Word of Man* (London: Hodder and Stoughton, 1928), 286.
20. *Ibid*, 287.
21. *Ibid*.
22. *Ibid*, 320.
23. *Ibid*, 323.

fix the place of the Christian in society within the *spes futurae vitae*.[24] Even at its most deconstructive, in other words, Barth's theology is anthropological, moral and political, and clearly disallows any ultimate irony about the world of human history and action.

What Barth expresses more instinctively in this early text gradually acquires more strictly dogmatic expression as he moves into academic work and adopts the genre of the lecture. The commitment to an account of the divine majesty which grounds rather than annihilates the human can already be found in the very early lectures on Calvin from 1922, and steadily acquires force over the 1920s. It is already firmly in place by the time of the Münster ethics lectures, which themselves provided draft material for large tracts of the ethical discussions in the *Church Dogmatics*. Within the *Church Dogmatics* itself, the the-anthropological shape of Barth's thinking leads to a simultaneous development of two lines of argument, one concerned with the doctrine of God proper, the other with anthropology.

With regard to the doctrine of God proper, Barth is insistent that a judicious Christian anthropology and ethics can only be rooted in trinitarian doctrine: in election, Christology and soteriology, and their pneumatological realisation and application. More than anything, Barth wants to shake anthropology free from the assumptions that 'being in Christ' is merely one modulation of something more humanly basic, and that human history and activity can be understood without direct and immediate reference to the history and activity of Jesus Christ. It is, Barth says, 'the creature and not the Creator of whom we are not certain' (*CD* III/1, 6). But the force of Barth's statement is not to leave the creature as it were hanging in contingency. Sovereign grace does not entail some doctrine of continuous creation in which

---

24   *Ibid*, 324.

61

the created realm has no substance of its own, but is at every moment dependent on a fresh act of God to make it be, or to prevent it from plunging into sheer chaos. Though Barth is uniformly hostile to any idea of the absolute autonomy of the creature and the creature's world, he does not allow this to trap him into denying their substance. Grace—that is, God's covenant history with us in Jesus Christ—evokes and sustains the active life of the creature, establishing us as God's partners in the ordered moral fellowship of Father and child.

It is this ordered, moral fellowship established by divine grace which is the subject of Barth's second line of argument in the *Church Dogmatics*. Anthropology and ethics are ingredient within dogmatics, not as a separate theme, or as a concession to the need to establish meaningfulness or relevance, but precisely because of the identity of the one confessed in Christian faith as 'God for us'. Thus, in the overall structure of Barth's treatment of divine election, he is emphatic that election carries with it an anthropological entailment.

> To be truly Christian, the doctrine of God must carry forward and complete the definition and exposition of the Subject God. It must do this in such a way that . . . it makes the Subject known as One which in virtue of its innermost being, willing and nature does not stand outside all relationships, but stands in a definite relationship *ad extra* to another (*CD* II/2, 5f).

And so, '[a]ccording to the Christian perception the true God is what He is only in this movement, in the movement towards this man [Jesus], and in Him and through Him towards all other men in their unity as His people' (*CD* II/2, 7). Moreover, this anthropological entailment does not simply mean that God's self-fulfilment brings humanity into being as an essentially passive reality, elected simply to wait upon the divine self-glorification. Election is election to a certain kind of

62

activity. Predestination is not simply a matter of determination of status or final end. No:

> In it there begins the history, encounter and decision between [God] and man. For the fulfilment of the election involves the affirmation of the existence of elected man and its counterpart in man's election, in which God's election evokes and awakens faith, and meets and answers that faith as human decision . . . There is . . . a simple but comprehensive autonomy of the creature which is constituted originally by the act of eternal divine election and which has in this act its ultimate reality (*CD* II/2, 177).

Barth's point is not only that he refuses to work with competitive accounts of divine and human freedom, in which God's autonomy and our own are inversely proportional. It is also that—as he puts it later—'the grace of God . . . has teleological power . . . Grace is the movement and direction of man in accordance with his determination' (*CD* II/2, 566f). This teleological character of grace is expressed structurally in the fact that Chapter 7 of the *Church Dogmatics* ('The Election of God') is followed by Chapter 8 ('The Command of God')—a simple fact which seems to elude many commentators, for whom Barth's ethics is something either to be ignored or to be wondered at as having no logical place in his dogmatics. But command—ethos, human action, responsibility—is ingredient within the divine election because election is the self-election of God to be God with, and not just over, humanity. '[T]he being and essence and activity of God as the Lord of the covenant between Himself and man include a relationship to the being and essence and activity of man. It is as He makes Himself responsible for man that God makes man, too, responsible. Ruling grace is commanding grace' (*CD* II/2, 511).

This twofold pattern of argument, affirming simultaneously the utter freedom of God and the directedness

63

of that freedom to human life, history and activity, is repeated many times throughout the *Church Dogmatics*: in his treatment of self-determination as humanly basic; in his repeated claim that dogmatics and ethics are inseparable; in his account of gospel and law; in the linkages between creation and covenant; in the haunting discussions of 'the unique opportunity' and 'vocation' in *Church Dogmatics* III/4; in the late denials of sacramental status to water baptism, precisely so that water baptism can be seen as the first great step of human obedience. But it is stated with particular penetration in Barth's discussions of prayer in the *Church Dogmatics*. For Barth, Christian existence is at its heart invocation, what he calls 'the humble and resolute, the frightened and joyful *invocation* of the gracious God in gratitude, praise and, above all, petition' (*CL*, 43). Invocation of God, going to God and beseeching him in petition, is the essence of the Christian life because the Christian life is a life of covenant mutuality with God. The covenant is the expression of the miracle of grace, in which there is a proper order in the relation of God to the world. God is the eternally gracious initiator, the one who goes before us in all our ways; we are those whom God's grace creates and establishes and sustains.

This means, first, that invocation is *made possible* by God. Prayer is thus a matter of God's permission, a permission which not only allows us to pray but also equips us so to do. Prayer is not based on our endowments, but in our being set free by God to perform this work. As God commands 'Call upon me', so we become those who can and must call upon him. 'The real basis of prayer,' Barth writes, 'is man's freedom before God, the God-given permission to pray which, because it is given by God, becomes a command and an order and therefore a necessity' (*CD* III/4, 93). Moreover, at the heart of prayer is supplication, petition. And supplication means that the goal of prayer, that towards which prayer is directed, is not our action but God's: we cry to God that God may act.

64

Our crying, our invoking of God, is done out of sheer emptiness, sheer need. '[E]mpty hands are necessary when human hands are to be spread out before God and filled by him' (CD III/4, 97). All of this is the first, 'theocentric' line of argument noted above. Yet, second, the fact that we are the creatures of God's grace, the fact that God is before us in all our doings, does not entail that helpless passivity. On the contrary: electing grace evokes gratitude, and gratitude is expressed in action. Undertaking his own most proper, incommunicable work, God commissions us to our own sphere of life and activity, at the centre of which lies prayer.

> What God the Father wills with us and for us . . . is
> more than a solid but stationary relation or a firm
> but passive connection. He is the living Father of his
> living children. What he wills with and for these
> children is therefore . . . living dealings between
> himself and them . . . They too have to enter into
> these dealings on their side. They have to actualize
> the partnership in this history (CL, 85).

And the way we do this—the way in which we make real our partnership with God in the covenant—is by invoking God in prayer. In prayer, Barth writes, 'we stand before the innermost centre of the covenant between God and man' (CD III/4, 93). Invocation of God, asking, pleading with God, is that basic activity which expresses the situation in which we have been placed by God. The electing God has called us; and what that God has called us *to* is, very simply, to be those who go to God in prayer. It was for this act that the covenant was established; it was, indeed, to make possible this act that God himself took flesh and lived and died and rose again. Here, in the invocation of God, we have the fulfilment of our relation to God; here we are most truly human in the way which God in his eternal mercy has appointed us to be human.

Yet invocation is never quiescent. To pray 'Thy kingdom come' is not only to appeal for the act of another, divine agent, but also to enter into revolt against the disorder and unrighteousness which deface human life. Christians

> *wait* and *hasten* toward the dawn of God's day, the appearing of his righteousness, the parousia of Jesus Christ . . . They not only wait but also hasten. They wait by hastening. Their waiting takes place in the hastening. Aiming at God's kingdom, established on its coming and not on the status quo, they do not just look toward it but run toward it as fast as their feet will carry them. This is inevitable if in their hearts and on their lips the petition 'Thy kingdom come' is not an indolent and despondent prayer but one that is zealous and brave (CD III/4, 263).

Hence, of course, Barth's basic rule *lex orandi lex agendi*: a rule which summarises an entire vision of the ethico-political character of the life of prayer, and the prayerful determination of ethical and political action.

III

What does all this suggest about theological anthropology in the present context? Two closing points can be made. The first is that the Christian gospel is humane: it concerns that action or history of God whose goal is our great and endless comfort. Christian theology cannot therefore readily accede to the 'death of the subject', precisely because what theology traces as it is taken up into the history of God is God's establishment of new humanity in Christ. The humanism of the Christian gospel is, of course, quite different from the humanism of the modern traditions of subjectivity. Where modernity speaks of interiority, Christianity speaks of faith; where modernity speaks of conscience, Christianity speaks of command and obedience; where modernity speaks of self-fulfilment, Christianity speaks of fellowship with Christ and of heaven.

In short: 'the Christian message is the humanism of God'.[25] Without its anthropology, Christian faith would not be itself.

Second, in the conversation between Christian theology and postmodernism over anthropology, special attention needs to be paid to the particular content of Christian faith, lest it be assimilated (whether by detractors or apologists) to some sub-Christian ontotheology, or perhaps to a philosophical celebration of pure contingency. In anthropology, as in any other field of theological inquiry, patient attention to the substance of the Christian confession is the prerequisite of real engagement with conversation partners. In particular, Barth may help us see that postmodern proposals for a Christian anthropology beyond substance and agency fail to catch the coinherence of Christology, spirituality and the ethical-political sphere which is, on Barth's reading, so basic to the humanism of Christian faith. If that humanism is strange to modernity and postmodernity alike, then it is because of the fact that 'with the Christian message it is not a case of a classical humanism nor of a new humanism which is to be rediscovered today, but rather of the humanism of God'.[26]

In closing, some rather more wide-ranging remarks on the situation of theology and the kinds of responsibilities which are before us.

First: I am unconvinced that Christian theology can long survive after we have silenced the questions which arise from the impulse which I would call metaphysical. That is, Christian theology involves claims about the substance of the world, its givenness and its purpose or character. Nominalism or pure idealism serve Christian theology no better than the

---

25   K Barth, 'The Christian Message and the New Humanism' in *Against the Stream: Shorter Post-War Writings 1946-52* (London: SCM, 1954), 184.

26   *Ibid.*

wrong sort of realism, which postmodern thinkers have been quick to identify as the corruption of the Western theological tradition. Christian realism will have some strongly determinative features which will not allow it to dovetail neatly with other kinds of realism—features which are derived from the kinds of claims made by Christian faith about the nature and purposes of the self-manifesting God and the modes of his activity in the world. But, if these features teach us caution about being over fluent in our speech of God's reality, they do not counsel pure irony, or the kind of silence before God which is all too easily an empty space to be filled in by all manner of projections. Seeing, knowing, speaking are intrinsic to Christian faith, and without them neither its dogmatics nor its ethics would have any real bulwark against the riot of the imagination.[27]

Second: Christian theology works well when it emerges from slow, patient, deliberate reading of the canon of Christian text—above all, the scriptural canon, and then by derivation the family of commentary traditions which Scripture has evoked and nourished. In their introduction, the editors of *Radical Orthodoxy* note that Barthianism 'can tend to the ploddingly exegetical'[28]—the implication being that the intellectually stylish theology of the future is to take the form of some sort of their own collage of 'exegesis, cultural reflection and philosophy'.[29] But: the future of Christian theology is exegesis, plodding or otherwise. Particularly in the current context, exegesis is our necessary first task because we are so little acquainted with the Christian faith as it

---

[27]   In a recent article, S F Du Toit distinguishes Barth from Mark Taylor in that Barth's understanding of revelation allows for '*the occurrence of genuine and proper reference between God and his revelation in our words*': S F Du Toit, 'Revelation or Reveilation? Barth and Postmodernism', *Heythrop Journal* 40 (1999): 12.

[28]   J Milbank et al (ed), *Radical Orthodoxy*, 2.

[29]   *Ibid.*

encounters us in the prophetic and apostolic witness and as it has been received in the reading and teaching of the people of God. This is—emphatically—not to issue a call that the future of Christian theology is or lies in a renewal of 'textuality'. It is rather to say that theology derives from attention to God, and attention is directed to God by obedient listening to Holy Scripture. Exegesis is never a finished business; there is no exegetical capital on which we may rely. And so, a theology which takes seriously its specificity—its requirement to attend to this one, here, now—will be particularly vigilant lest the primacy of the exegetical task be lost in a great wash of cultural theory insufficiently disciplined by the gospel.

Third: The future of Christian theology is simply a matter of doing theology: calmly, cheerfully and humbly, with astonishment, repentence, vigilance, hope and joy. Nothing has happened to compel us to do otherwise. The demands of our context are no more stringent or compelling than those which faced church thinkers who sought to make sense of Aristotle, nominalism, Cartesianism or Kant: indeed, I am inclined to think the demands of postmodernism rather less stringent. If the history of Christian thought teaches us anything it is that, behind the church's intellectual recapitulation in the face of philosophy, there usually lies a *theological* mistake: a misperception or misconstrual of or loss of interest in the habits of mind of the gospel. Not the least of what we may learn from Barth is that good, fruitful and edifying theology is theological theology, done as if nothing had happened.

Part Two

Studying Barth after Modernity: Persistent Issues

Barth and Pannenberg on Method, Revelation and Trinity[1]

Christiaan Mostert

Introduction

It has been said of both Barth and Pannenberg that they started a new way of doing theology, Barth in the second decade of this century and Pannenberg in the sixth. This is not to suggest that Pannenberg's theological achievement is (or will be seen to be) the equal of Barth's, but it is formidable nonetheless. Comparisons of rank are of no great interest. But comparisons of theological issues and themes, including the nature of the theological enterprise itself, may be both interesting and instructive. A study of Barth and Pannenberg on three important theological issues is, in my view, of particular interest.

Pannenberg was a student of Barth in Basel for a term in 1949. Much later he wrote, 'I had read through all the volumes of Karl Barth's *Church Dogmatics* that had been published up to then. I greatly admired Barth and I never ceased to do so, but in Basel already I was dissatisfied by the lack of philosophical rigour in his thought.'[2] Whatever one may think of it now, Barth is unlikely to have been very troubled by such a judgment. He was not concerned with the question of the

---

1.   This essay is a modified version of what was presented at the conference. I am indebted in particular to Professor John Webster for his constructive criticism of the original paper.

2.   W Pannenberg, 'An Autobiographical Sketch', in C E Braaten & P Clayton (eds), *The Theology of Wolfhart Pannenberg* (Minneapolis: Augsburg, 1988), 14.

Christiaan Mostert

philosophically grounded *possibility* of knowing God; he began with the *actual* knowledge of God given by Godself.[3] The Word has been spoken! Thus the knowledge of the Word of God is essentially its acknowledgment (*CD* I/1, 187ff).

Barth was a theologian of the Word of God. He was its passionate, prophetic servant. It is as true that he was a theological poet as that he was a systematic theologian. His prose strikes the reader even now as unusually rich and powerful in its use of metaphor. The complex Germanic style of writing is used to probe and analyse arguments and to construct careful counter-arguments, but the language of narrative runs like a deep stream within it, and it is not accidental that a large part of the *Church Dogmatics* is a commentary on the narratives of the Bible.[4] Unquestionably, such language, not the precise language of philosophy, is the more powerful, and arguably the more fundamental language. Language rich in symbol and metaphor is primary, arguably more 'truth-ful' and more disclosive of how things really are in the world than the language of metaphysics and the empirical sciences.[5] Iris Murdoch wrote more novels than philosophical

---

3. George Hunsinger lists Barth's 'actualism' as the first of six major motifs in his theology. It is present, he suggests, 'whenever Barth speaks, as he constantly does, in the language of occurrence, happening, event, history, decisions and act'. Closely related to this is Barth's 'particularism', *i.e.* Barth's determination to move always from the particular to the general, rather than the reverse. See G Hunsinger, *How to Read Karl Barth: The Shape of his Theology* (New York: Oxford University Press, 1991), 30, 32.

4. William Stacy Johnson notes that Christian theology is, in Barth's view, essentially about God's 'turning toward humanity', which is 'enacted in the dramatic unfolding of a story'. He adds that it might better be called a 'metanarrative'. W S Johnson, *The Mystery of God: Karl Barth and the Postmodern Foundations of Theology* (Louisville: Westminster John Knox Press, 1997), 46f.

5. I acknowledge my indebtedness at this point to some ideas of my colleague, Dr Dorothy Lee.

treatises, though she was good at both.[6] Can Barth be expected to meet Pannenberg's requirement of philosophical rigour in theological writing? In answering this question, a good deal depends on how one sees the nature and task of theology. This brings us to a first point of comparison between the two.

The Nature and Task of Theology

For Barth theology is the human work of thinking and speaking about God in accordance with the way in which God has given Godself to be known by humankind. It is not simply a human work, but it is a work of the Christian church. The church must speak about God, and it has 'the further task of criticising and revising its speech about God' (*CD* I/1, 3). It must do so always in the light of the revelation of God; indeed, theology stands in the service of God's self-revelation. Moreover, according to Barth, theology is under no requirement, imposed on it from outside, to be 'scientific' (*i.e. wissenschaftlich,* having to do with real knowledge in any field of enquiry). If it is, as a matter of fact, 'scientific', this is only because it recognises a definite object of its enquiry and proceeds by clear and consistent ways toward the understanding of this object (*CD* I/1, 7f).[7] Scientific status *per se* matters not at all; nor, by extension, does

---

6. Peregrine Horden, commenting on Murdoch's work, observes that 'the novel is wholly different from the philosophical treatise'. 'Philosophical Fictions', Introduction to P Horden (ed), *The Novelist as Philosopher* (Oxford: All Souls College, 1983), xi; quoted by D F Ford, 'System, Story, Performance: A Proposal about the Role of Narrative in Christian systematic theology', in S Hauerwas & L G Jones (eds), *Why Narrative? Readings in Narrative Theology* (Grand Rapids: Eerdmans, 1989), 192.

7. Barth had no particular concern with Heinrich Scholz's question, 'Wie ist eine evangelische Theologie als Wissenschaft möglich?' Cf also *CD* I/1, 275ff, especially 283.

philosophical status. What matters is its rigorous attention to the self-revelation of God attested to in Holy Scripture.

For Pannenberg, too, theology is concerned above all with God; God is its 'single, all-embracing object'.[8] In the foreword of his *Systematic Theology* he regards the subject matter of theology as 'the unfolding of the Christian idea of God'.[9] Theology is and must be 'scientific'; it is nothing less than a *Gotteswissenchaft*. This was a major contention of his earlier work, the title of which was rather misleadingly translated as *Theology and the Philosophy of Science*.[10] '. . . [T]heology, as it appears in the history of Christian theology, can be adequately understood only as a science of God.'[11] To this point, formally at least, Barth would have no quarrel with Pannenberg. But their paths soon diverge. For Barth, theology as *Gotteswissenschaft* stands opposed to the idea of theology as *Religionswissenschaft*, the study of religion. Speaking about God is different altogether from speaking about humankind 'in a loud voice', even (and especially) humankind in its religious interests and experience. For Pannenberg, however, theology as *Gotteswissenschaft* can only be done as *Religionswissenschaft*. The reason for this view is that the reality of God is only given in and with other things; it is *'co-given* to experience in other objects' and is therefore 'accessible to theological reflection not directly but only indirectly'.[12] We shall return in the next section to the question whether Barth saw the self-revelation of God in Jesus Christ as direct or indirect. But there is no question

8. Pannenberg, *Systematic Theology*, Vol 1 (Grand Rapids: Eerdmans, 1991), 4.

9. *Ibid*, x.

10. Philadelphia: Westminster, 1976; a translation of *Wissenschaft-theorie und Theologie* (Frankfurt/M: Suhrkamp Verlag, 1973). See especially Chapter 5. (Perhaps 'Theology and Theories of Knowledge' would have been a more accurate title for the English translation.)

11. *Ibid*, 297.

12. *Ibid*, 301.

for Barth of confusing the self-revelation of God with human experience, religious or not. This is nothing better than an indirect Christian Cartesianism, in which human beings might try to become certain about God from certainty about themselves (*CD* I/1, 214)![13]

This, however, is not Pannenberg's point; there is no way of arriving at certainty about God before the eschatological demonstration of God's glory in all things.[14] Pannenberg regards anthropology as a fruitful field from which to build up speech about God, but he does not imagine that there is any obvious, direct way from anthropology to theology, from human experience to true speech about God. Nor does he overlook the fact that the decision about the truth of human attempts to speak truly about God 'rests with God himself'.[15] The provisionality of all theological affirmations is as strongly affirmed by Pannenberg as by Barth. The point of seeing a coincidence (but not an identity) of *Gotteswissenschaft* and *Religionswissenschaft*—of the theological and the anthropological nature of religion—is quite different. The point argued by Pannenberg is that the concept of religion includes the idea of God (or of gods), and that the truth of a religion depends fundamentally on the truth of what it claims about God.[16]

---

13   Barth recognises no 'anthropological centres as the basis of the possibility of human experience of God's Word'; see also *CD* I/1, 203.

14   'The knowledge of Christian theology is always partial in comparison to the definitive revelation of God in the future of his kingdom (1 Cor 13:12)' (Pannenberg, *Systematic Theology*, Vol 1, 55).

15   *Ibid*, 56.

16   *Ibid*, 172ff. This is not to ignore the plurality of ideas of God, nor the existence of religions which do not (or no longer) have a view of God. In an extended discussion Pannenberg argues that religion cannot be considered merely from an anthropological point of view but involves the idea of a relation with a divine power, regardless of how this divine reality is understood. The

Religions require above all to be studied *theologically*, not merely anthropologically, since God, not human beings, is their true object.[17] To study religion theologically is to wrestle with the question of the truth of what is believed about God. If God is the creator of all things, the question of God's being and nature may in principle be asked in any field of human enquiry, even (though it does not now typically happen) in the natural sciences; after all, very many scientists do actually believe in God! But it is in the religions that the question about God's being and God's action is properly thematised, and for this reason the study of religion cannot in principle be irrelevant to the study of God. This view is not without its difficulties, and Barth's warning against confusing human ideas about God with the divine self-attestation are a necessary element in the discussion of the truth of human thoughts about God. But in Pannenberg's discussion 'the primacy of divine reality and its self-declaration over all human worship of God'[18] is no less critical. Methodologically, what is at issue between Barth and Pannenberg is whether this 'primacy of the divine reality' can be advanced directly. For Barth there is no other way; for Pannenberg the fear of advancing theological ideas simply by assertion requires an indirect approach. This raises the question of the place of faith in theological work.

For Barth, theology presupposes faith. It is not the task of theology to establish the credentials of the self-revelation of God. Barth clarified this point in his study of Anselm's *Proslogion*. The understanding for which faith yearns presupposes the certainty of faith.[19] Theology has its place within the obedience of faith.[20] To put it bluntly, theology is not permitted

---

question of the truth of this idea is a distinct but related matter. See also 136-151, especially 142.

17.   *Ibid*, 136-151.
18.   *Ibid*, 127.
19.   Barth, *Anselm: Fides Quaerens Intellectum* (London: SCM, 1960), 21.
20.   *Ibid*, 35. It is 'grounded on the obedience of faith'.

to ask the question whether the Word of God is true. For Pannenberg the question of truth—the truth of the Christian proclamation, the truth of the church's doctrine—has irrevocably become part of the agenda of systematic theology. The opening chapter of the *Systematic Theology* is entitled, 'The Truth of Christian Doctrine as the Theme of Systematic Theology'. Pannenberg defends the view that doctrines are assertorial; they assert something, and in the modern world the truth of what they assert can neither be enforced, nor assumed, nor avoided. He appeals to that tradition in theology in which both the content and the truth of the church's teaching is at issue. With Barth, he rejects the pietistic appeal to subjective experience—the 'retreat to commitment', as he calls it[21]—which characterises a good deal of theological and religious discussion at the present time. But unlike Barth, he will not make the givenness of revelation the unquestioned basis for theology. He writes,

> [D]ogmatics may not presuppose the divine truth which the Christian doctrinal tradition claims. Theology has to present, test, and if possible confirm the claim. It must treat it, however, as an open question and not decide it in advance. Its concern must be that in the course of all its thinking and arguments the rightness of the claim is at issue.[22]

For Pannenberg the certainty of faith does not make the 'theological ascertainment of the truth' superfluous. Not only is this view in conflict with Barth's view of the task of theology, but it also leads Pannenberg to question whether Barth's theology is sufficiently a *Gotteswissenschaft*, despite its patent intention to be so. He argues that 'dialectical theology . . . remained *in practice* a prisoner of nineteenth-century positivism because even Karl Barth could practise a science of God only as

---

21. Pannenberg, *Systematic Theology*, Vol 1, 47f, citing W W Bartley, *The Retreat to Commitment*, 1961.

22 *Ibid*, 50.

a science of faith'.[23] What Pannenberg aims to do is to reformulate the way in which theology must be said to be a science of God. Although God must, as a matter of definition, be held to be the reality that determines everything—'the all-determining power'[24]—the idea of God remains hypothetical, even in theology. The question of God's reality remains open in the secularised climate of much of today's world. The unavoidable consequence for theology, in Pannenberg's view, is that although God is 'the thematic point of reference for all [theology's] investigations', God is the object of theology 'first as a problem'.[25] The reason for such a conclusion, however, is not simply cultural; it is grounded in God's being and nature, in God's debatability, and in the eschatological nature of God's self-disclosure. This brings us to a second point of comparison.

The Nature of Revelation

Barth's decision to introduce the doctrine of the Trinity at the outset of the *Church Dogmatics* emphasises that the revelation of God is in fact the revelation of the triune God, whom the church addresses as Father, Son and Holy Spirit. The doctrine of the Trinity and the doctrine of God's self-revelation are not to be

---

23 Pannenberg, *Theology and the Philosophy of Science*, 298 (emphasis added).

24 Pannenberg adopted this phrase as a nominal (and incomplete) definition of God, for reasons explained in his relatively early *Theology and the Philosophy of Science*, 302. In English the term will always raise suspicions of determinism, but Pannenberg strongly denies that he is a 'determinist'. The main reason for using it is the conviction, shared by Jewish monotheism and Greek philosophical monotheism, that everything that exists (including all the contingencies of nature and history) has its being by virtue of this power and must ultimately be unintelligible except in relation to it.

25 *Ibid*, 299.

confused, but they are closely connected.[26] It is clear that for Barth the Word of God is 'the material of dogmatics' (*CD* I/1, 47), no less than it is the concern of church proclamation. The Word of God, in the form of Holy Scripture, rules over the church magisterially, and the task of theology is to test the church's proclamation for faithfulness to this Word. The Word of God is God's own speech and act. Humankind is addressed by this Word, listens and makes its decision about the claim of this Word.

Pannenberg is no less serious than Barth was about revelation—understood as the self-revelation of God. He writes, 'whether inside the Christian church or outside it, and even in the so-called natural knowledge of God, no knowledge of God and no theology are conceivable that do not proceed from God and are not due to the working of his Spirit'.[27] In *Revelation as History* Pannenberg agrees that 'revelation' must mean 'the self-revelation of God', a point in which he is entirely at one with Barth.[28] However, at several points Pannenberg's views diverge from Barth's. He does not accept that in the Bible the notion of the 'Word of God' has God, *i.e.* the essence of God's being, 'as its content in any unmediated way'.[29] This has several consequences, each major in its significance. First, Pannenberg is unwilling to make the category of the Word of God the central category that it is for Barth. For him the acts of God in

---

26 Pannenberg criticises Barth for grounding the doctrine of the Trinity not in the historical revelation of God but 'from the formal concept of revelation as self-revelation' (*Systematic Theology*, Vol 1, 296). Barth does leave himself open to such a charge, but sharply denies the suggestion (specifically in relation to his use of the formula, *Deus dixit*) that he was deriving the doctrine of the Trinity 'from the general truth of such a formula' (*CD* I/1, 296).

27 Pannenberg, *Systematic Theology*, Vol 1, 2.

28 Pannenberg *et al*, *Revelation as History* (London: Collier-Macmillan, 1968), 4.

29 *Ibid*, 10.

history are the basis for theological speech about revelation. As he says in an important essay,

> History is the most comprehensive horizon of Christian theology. All theological questions and answers are meaningful only within the framework of the history which God has with humanity and through humanity with his whole creation—the history moving toward a future still hidden from the world but already revealed in Jesus Christ.[30]

The category of 'the word' is connected with that of 'history' in terms of understanding, hope and remembrance. In his seventh Thesis on revelation he writes, 'The Word relates itself to Revelation as foretelling, forthtelling, and report'.[31] Pannenberg argues (specifically against G Ebeling) that in the Old Testament a special importance is attached to 'the prophetic word of demonstration', but the key element in this word is 'the knowledge of God as the goal of the *events* which are announced'.[32] In the New Testament the key element of the word is the Word of God as kerygma, the word of apostolic proclamation. Again, this word makes clear the meaning of the *events* of which it speaks. The point is that in Pannenberg's view the word—whether of foretelling or reporting—only becomes revelatory in virtue of its historical content, 'the events in which God demonstrates his deity'.[33] The same is true again in relation to the word which announces an eschatological consummation of all things, the transformation of the creation and the resurrection of the dead; it is these final events that will reveal the nature of God's being and the glory of God. Pannenberg's theology is clearly not one in which the Word plays no part; his quarrel is with 'the simple and naive

---

30. Pannenberg, 'Redemptive Event and History', in *Basic Questions in Theology*, Vol 1 (Philadelphia: Westminster, 1983), 15.
31. Pannenberg, *Revelation as History*, 152. See also *Systematic Theology*, Vol 1, 250ff.
32. Pannenberg, *Systematic Theology*, Vol 1, 239. My emphasis.
33. Pannenberg, *Revelation as History*, 155.

understanding of God's self-revelation as the Word of God'.[34] The heart of his difficulty with the centrality of the Word of God in Barth's theology—and the variations on this theme in other theologies—is that, in his view, the various biblical ideas about the Word of God 'do not directly treat God himself as the content of the Word'.[35] It may be natural to suppose that God's self-revelation to humankind will be 'in the mode of word and speech', but Pannenberg cautions against undue anthropocentrism, and maintains that the biblical concept of the Word of God 'does not have the function of direct self-revelation'.[36] The stress on events goes hand in hand with an emphasis on the action of God in history, understood in the broadest terms. To quote one more time from his discussion,

> When we think of God's self-revelation we have to
> think of it as mediated by his action, for that is always
> the content of biblical ideas of the Word of God,
> whether it be God's action in creation, his historical
> action as it was intimated in the prophetic word, or
> the action in Jesus of Nazareth to which the primitive
> Christian kerygma made reference.[37]

This brings us to the second consequence of Pannenberg's reservations about the uncritical use of the category of the Word in connection with revelation, namely his insistence on the indirectness of revelation. According to his first Thesis on revelation, 'The self-revelation of God in the biblical witnesses is not of a direct type in the sense of a theophany, but is indirect and brought about by means of the historical acts of God'.[38] There is a history of the divine action which has as its goal the achievement of the knowledge of God by all people (not just Israel). The events that comprise the divine action constitute 'the one all-embracing event of self-revelation'; it is God's

---

34. Pannenberg, *Systematic Theology*, Vol 1, 241f.
35. *Ibid*, 243.
36. *Ibid*, 241.
37. *Ibid*, 243.
38. Pannenberg, *Revelation as History*, 125.

action, but it conveys the essence of God's being only indirectly.[39] The immediate content of the events that can be seen retrospectively to be God-revealing is not explicitly theological or religious; it lies in the field of natural event, or socio-political action. Its theological nature can be easily missed and easily misconstrued. It is tempting to see here a simple contrast between Pannenberg and Barth, with Pannenberg the advocate of an indirect self-revelation of God in history and Barth the champion of a direct self-revelation of God in the divine Word. The truth, however, is more complex.

There can be no doubt about the christological concentration of Barth's doctrine of revelation. The truth about God is mediated to humankind by Jesus Christ; Barth has a hundred ways of making this point! God takes form in the world of human experience in the humanity of Jesus Christ. Only in him is the ontological divide between God and the creation crossed. What is to be known about God can be known in him alone. Here God becomes an object of our knowledge. Barth's doctrine of revelation is a clear example of the 'objectivism' of his thought in general.[40] But the clarity of the noetic focus is only one side of the coin; there is another.[41] Barth also has a passionate concern to respect the freedom and the mystery of God. In the act of self-revelation, God does not relinquish God's freedom, nor completely unveil God's nature. The divine hiddenness is not dissolved in the unveiling. God is object to human knowledge in a different way from which God is object

---

39. Pannenberg, *Systematic Theology*, Vol 1, 243f.

40. The point is well made by G Hunsinger, *How to Read Karl Barth* (Oxford: Oxford University Press, 1991), 35ff & 76ff.

41. Hunsinger issues a salutary warning to the reader of Barth's theology. No single statement ever captures the complexity of Barth's position. 'Nothing is more likely to lead the reader of the *Church Dogmatics* astray than a nondialectical imagination. One must never fail to ask about the dialectical conceptual counterparts to the position Barth happens to be developing at any particular moment' (Hunsinger, *op cit*, ix).

to Godself (*CD* II/1, 10, 16f). The objectivity and truth of the knowledge of God are never compromised, but whereas God is 'objectively immediate to Himself' (since the Father is object to the Son and the Son to the Father, without mediation, 'to us [God] is objectively mediate'(*CD* II/1, 16). Three brief remarks must suffice to make the point that Barth takes great care to avoid an unequivocal account of revelation as direct.

First, it is enormously important to Barth to safeguard the mystery of God, even as he asserts with all possible vigour the divine will to convey the truth of God's being to humankind. God remains impenetrable mystery to us; revelation does not dispel this mystery, but discloses it. If, in making the divine being an object for us, there is a real 'givenness' about God, there is also an ineradicable 'non-givenness' about God.[42] Second, the knowledge of God that results from God's self-disclosure, is not at the disposal of humankind. In its very objectivity for us it retains its own freedom and subjectivity. The knowledge of God is always a matter of grace, not a matter of an innate human capacity. The priority remains with God, not the human subject of the knowledge of God.[43] In this respect, God is unlike all other objects. It is always the case that God is ready to give the knowledge of Godself, but humankind is not ready to know God unless God grants the possibility, objectively and subjectively. Third, even the human life of Jesus Christ, the place of God's self-revelation, is not something from which the knowledge of God can be simply 'read off' without

---

42 W S Johnson comments that 'for Barth the divine non-givenness itself is part of the very "reality" with which theology must contend'. Theological realism must be open to its dialectical counterpart, a sense of 'the apprehension and unsettledness before the non-givenness of this God' (Johnson, *op cit*, 28).

43 'There cannot be allowed here any precedence of man which can entitle his subsequence . . . to ascribe to itself a right of disposal over the object, to make use of a power of disposal over it—as man does continually and obviously in regard to all other objects' (*CD* II/1, 21f).

further ado. Here above all it is necessary to think dialectically; here especially the 'givenness' of God's revelation has its unavoidable counterpart in God's 'non-givenness'. Jesus Christ, the Logos made flesh, is for Barth the sign or instrument of God's self-revelation.[44] Revelation is not an automatic consequence of looking at the life of Jesus. The life, death and resurrection of Jesus are a sign which points to revelation; they are instruments by which the Word of God seeks to become a word of revelation and salvation for humankind (*CD* I/2, 223f). They are not a guarantee that the event of revelation will inevitably take place in any given situation. Of course, this raises deeper questions about Barth's christology, but Johnson is surely right when he says that 'the significance of Jesus Christ . . . is that in his life there occurs a coincidence, though not an identity, of divine and human action'.[45] It is clear from these considerations that, in his view of revelation, Barth cannot be simply contrasted with Pannenberg. Barth's account of revelation is more differentiated; revelation is both direct and indirect, although, unlike Pannenberg, he does not make an issue of this point as such.[46] What is important for Barth is the nature of God, in particular God's grace, God's freedom and God's mystery. Pannenberg's discussion is more focussed on the nature of revelation as such. Since he regards the revelation of God as taking place in the whole sweep of historical events, and since the action of God in history is not obvious, it is more central to his concern to emphasise the indirectness of God's

---

44. This is the proper place at which, in Barth's view, one should speak of 'sacrament'; *CD* I/2, 228ff, especially 231f. See also Johnson, *op cit*, 106.
45. *Ibid*, 101.
46. Barth rarely refers explicitly to the matter. When he does so, he speaks of our knowledge of God as a knowledge of faith. As such, 'it is indirect and mediate, not immediate knowledge'. *CD* II/1, 57.

revelation. In discussing God's self-revelation, Pannenberg accentuates more God's debatability than God's mystery.[47]

In an indirect way, all revelatory events, regardless of which part of the Bible refers to them, make their distinctive contribution to the totality of events that disclose God's nature, a totality not yet arrived at but already, in an anticipatory way, present. The Christian claim of a definitive revelation of God in the history of Jesus—his life, work, proclamation, death and resurrection—can be justified only if this history is understood as essentially of one piece with the manifestation of God's nature 'at the end of the age', indeed as its proleptic appearance. Pannenberg emphasises the eschatological character of revelation. Already in his second Thesis on revelation he said, 'Revelation is not comprehended completely in the beginning, but at the end of the revealing history'.[48] Only at the end will it become unambiguously clear what God's nature and purpose truly are. The revelation of God in Jesus Christ is 'an anticipatory revelation . . . of the deity of God that in the future of his kingdom will be manifest to every eye'.[49] In giving his doctrine of revelation a characteristically eschatological shape, Pannenberg has made explicit what normally remains implicit in theology. The eschatological structure of *salvation/redemption* is normal in theology. Barth gives it a triadic form: it begins with creation and ends with redemption, and between the two there is the divine work of reconciliation, with its focus on the humanity of Jesus Christ.[50] In a quite distinctive way, Pannenberg constructs his doctrine of

---

47. Pannenberg, *Systematic Theology*, Vol 1, especially 49f, 58f. This does not mean that Pannenberg has no place for the concept of 'mystery', but he uses it in respect of the 'mystery' of God's plan of salvation, following NT usage; see *Systematic Theology*, Vol 1, 211, 235f, 332.

48. Pannenberg, *Revelation as History*, 131ff.

49. Pannenberg, *Systematic Theology*, Vol 1, 247.

50. See Johnson, *op cit*, 100-103.

revelation in a similarly eschatological way. It begins with God's creation of the cosmos and ends with the incontestable manifestation of God's glory in the whole creation, and between them—parallel to the scheme of salvation—there is the revelation of God in the person of Jesus Christ.

Another point at which the ideas of Barth and Pannenberg on revelation diverge is in respect of its relation to religion, a point already alluded to. In terms of the knowledge of God, Barth gave few credit points to the religions of the world, the Christian religion *qua* religion included. The early Barth thundered against the presumption of religion to know the truth. Instead, 'the truth has encountered us from a frontier we have never crossed'.[51] Religion is undoubtedly holy, righteous and good, but it has a 'dangerous ambiguity' about it. It has the possibility of mistaking death for life.[52] Barth did not lose the Kierkegaardian hostility to the idea that *homo capax verbi Dei* (*CD* I/1, 212f). Pannenberg, however, sees the religions as 'the place in which experience of the self-revelation of God or of divine reality in general is articulated in the totality of the reality of the world'.[53] Religions are therefore to be searched for evidence of the self-communication of God.[54] Acknowledging that he speaks from within the framework of monotheism, Pannenberg argues that 'where belief in the one God proved to be true in the experience of adherents, we can speak not only of an interpretative achievement on the part of believers but also, even if only provisionally, of God's own demonstration of his deity to them'.[55] History, including the history of the religions, is the sphere of the self-demonstration of God's deity. It is likely that such a view of religion will have greater appeal in today's

---

51. Barth, *The Epistle to the Romans*, 6th ed (London: Oxford University Press, 1933, 1968), 238.
52. *Ibid*, 254.
53. Pannenberg, *Theology and the Philosophy of Science*, 313.
54. *Ibid*, 315.
55. Pannenberg, *Systematic Theology*, Vol 1, 170.

world than Barth's view. More important, it avoids the sharp division between religion and revelation asserted by Barth, a position eminently understandable against the background of issues facing Europe in Barth's time but requiring now to be held in tension with other aspects of the phenomenon of religion. God's revelation and the history of religion cannot be seen simply as polar opposites; their relation requires a more differentiated statement.

The Doctrine of the Trinity

A final point of theological divergence between Barth and Pannenberg is in relation to the doctrine of the Trinity. Both theologians are as strongly trinitarian in their theology as any that one could name. The recovery of the doctrine of the Trinity in the twentieth century after its low ebb in the nineteenth is due pre-eminently to Barth. Ted Peters describes the important developments in trinitarian theology in the present time as the blossoming of Barthian shoots.[56] Corresponding to the threefold form of the Word of God, the revelation of God also has a triadic structure, which provides the basis for the trinitarian ontology of God for which Barth is so well known. As God reveals God's lordship it becomes clear that, 'in unimpaired unity yet also in unimpaired distinction', God is Revealer, Revelation, and Revealedness (*CD* I/1, 295). God, the Revealer, is 'identical with His act in revelation and also identical with its effects' (*CD* I/1, 296). God is Father, Son, and Holy Spirit, three modes of being in one God. Moreover, on the grounds that God must be what God reveals Godself to be, Barth understands the Trinity as the *immanent* Trinity, not just the *economic* Trinity (*CD* I/1, 333).

---

[56]   T Peters, *God as Trinity* (Louisville: Westminster/John Knox, 1993), 82.

Quite early in his career, Pannenberg also determined to be thoroughly trinitarian in his doctrine of God. In an article in *The Christian Century* he expressed the view that his doctrine of God would be 'more thoroughly trinitarian than any other he knew of'.[57] The theological basis for the doctrine of the Trinity is the revelation of God in Jesus Christ. Pannenberg's approach to the doctrine of the Trinity is christological and soteriological, an approach shared with other contemporary writers. In summary, Catherine LaCugna speaks of 'an *essential* connection between the threefold pattern of salvation history and the eternal being and identity of God'.[58] The combination of Jesus' oneness with the God whom he called Father and his self-differentiation from this God provided the impetus for the doctrine of the Trinity. The Spirit's work of linking believers with the fellowship between the Father and the Son was the other major catalyst for the doctrine of the Trinity.

On the face of it, there is little to suggest disagreement between Barth and Pannenberg in their trinitarian theology. However, there are three points in particular at which Pannenberg finds himself at odds with Barth's view of the doctrine of the Trinity. First, the common appeal to revelation conceals a significant difference between them. Although few theologians have written more eloquently than Barth on the economy of salvation, in Pannenberg's view this does not turn out to be the basis for his doctrine of the Trinity. Instead, it is the *concept* of revelation that provides the essential stimulus for this doctrine.[59] He writes,

> the *Church Dogmatics* does not develop the doctrine of
> the trinitarian God from the data of the historical
> revelation of God as Father, Son, and Spirit, but from
> the formal concept of revelation as self-revelation,
> which, as Barth sees it, entails a subject of revelation,

---

57. *The Christian Century*, 11 March 1981.
58 C M LaCugna, *God for Us* (Harper: San Francisco, 1991), 23.
59. See note 26 above for an earlier reference to this point.

an object, and revelation itself, all of which are one and the same.[60]

Barth does say that 'we arrive at the doctrine of the Trinity by no other way than that of an analysis of the concept of revelation (*CD* I/1, 312),' and thus (as suggested earlier) invites criticism of this kind. Barth's intensive and extensive treatment of the concept of revelation, together with his placement of the doctrine of the Trinity within the discussion of revelation, provides some support for Pannenberg's contention. However, Pannenberg does not discuss the point at length. He notes Barth's rejection of such a criticism but insists that Barth's grounding of the doctrine of the Trinity is more conceptual than historical.[61] Pannenberg certainly has a point, and the criticism that Barth's appeal to the actual *history* of revelation is ambiguous is not new. At the very least, Pannenberg's own understanding of the basis for the doctrine of the Trinity is unambiguously clear.

> To find a basis for the doctrine of the Trinity we must begin with the way in which Father, Son, and Spirit come on the scene and relate to one another in the event of revelation. Here lies the material justification for the demand that the doctrine of the Trinity must be based on the biblical witness to revelation or on the economy of salvation.[62]

To the extent that there is indeed a substantial difference here between the approaches of Barth and Pannenberg to the doctrine of the Trinity, the reason is likely to be found in their respective orientation to the Western and Eastern emphases in trinitarian doctrine. The point will be made more explicit presently. It is a difference which is also reflected in a second criticism which Pannenberg makes of Barth's approach to the Trinity.

---

60   Pannenberg, *Systematic Theology*, Vol 1, 296. He cites *CD* I/1, 295ff & 311ff.

61.   *Ibid*, 303f.

62   *Ibid*, 299.

Christiaan Mostert

Pannenberg finds fault with Barth's understanding of the Trinity on the model of a single divine subject. This is actually a criticism of the development of trinitarian theology from Augustine's 'psychological' analogies for the Trinity. In the background lies the older idea of God as an absolute, simple and indivisible being. It is characteristic of the Western (Augustinian) approach that it seeks to derive the three Persons (*hypostaseis*) from the one God, a procedure which Pannenberg finds problematic. It is to 'subsume the threeness of the persons into the concept of a single personal God'.[63] He continues, 'for all the differentiation in the self-consciousness, the God of this understanding is a single subject. The moments in the self-consciousness have no subjectivity of their own'.[64] Pannenberg describes Barth's doctrine of the Trinity as 'an exposition of the subjectivity of God in his revelation'. In such an approach, he contends, 'there is no room for a plurality of persons in the one God but only for different modes of being in the one divine subjectivity'.[65] Pannenberg's own approach – which is critical of aspects of both Western and Eastern trinitarian theology, particularly in their exclusive concern with trinitarian relations as relations of origin—has as its starting point the subjectivity of each of the three Persons of the Trinity.[66] Only such an approach can do justice to the reciprocity of the intra-trinitarian relations.

---

63 *Ibid*, 294. He adds that Gilbert of Poitiers criticised this as Sabellian already in the 12th century.

64 *Ibid*, 295.

65 *Ibid*, 303f, 296. See also Pannenberg's essay, 'The Problem of the Absolute', in *idem, Metaphysics and the Idea of God* (Edinburgh: T&T Clark, 1988), Chapter 2, especially 40, where he criticises Hegel for essentially the same thing.

66 Pannenberg, *Systematic Theology*, Vol 1, 319: 'If the trinitarian relations among Father, Son, and Spirit have the form of mutual self-distinction, they must be understood not merely as different modes of being of the one divine subject but as living realisations of separate centres of action.'

Finally, it will not be surprising to find Pannenberg holding an Eastern position on the *Filioque*, in contrast with Barth's Western view. Barth can only see the Holy Spirit as in the closest relation to the Son, which, of course, is in itself unexceptionable. However, he goes further; '... it is one of the most self-evident themes that the Holy Spirit, and with the Holy Spirit all that makes the Church the Church, and Christians Christians, does not come from any place but only from Christ' (*CD* I/2, 250). This is seen as the essential justification of the addition of the *Filioque* to the text of the Nicene-Constantinopolitan Creed. This is exactly the kind of position that has reinforced Eastern suspicion of the christocentrism of the West. Pannenberg, on the other hand, stands with Eastern theology in its rejection of the *Filioque*. He regards it as both uncanonical and theologically inappropriate.[67] The basis for his view is that the Son not only sends the Spirit but, in the witness of the New Testament, also receives the Spirit. Against the Augustinian view of the Spirit as the bond of love between the Father and the Son, Pannenberg insists on the self-distinction of the Spirit from the Father and the Son, which constitutes the Spirit as a separate Person of the Trinity. It is as a distinct Person that the Spirit is related to the Son and the Father. The Spirit does not merely receive from the Father and the Son, but manifests the Son and thus completes the revelation of the Father by the Son. Pannenberg argues for a much stronger emphasis on the reciprocal nature of the intra-trinitarian relations, a point in which he is, formally speaking, closer to the Eastern view of the Trinity than the Western, though he is critical of both.

> The mistaken formulation of Augustine [of the Spirit
> as proceeding from the Father and the Son] points in
> fact to a defect which plagues the trinitarian
> theological language of both East and West, namely

---

67 *Ibid,* 318f. He does not, unlike Eastern theologians, regard it as heretical.

> that of seeing the relations among Father, Son, and
> Spirit exclusively as relations of origin. With this view
> one cannot do justice to the reciprocity in the
> relations.[68]

Pannenberg makes an important contribution to the doctrine of
the Trinity in his strong proposal that the relations of origin
have to be balanced by the eschatological relations. Only in this
way is justice done to the reciprocity of the intra-trinitarian
relations.

> In the handing over of lordship from the Father to the
> Son, and its handing back from the Son to the Father,
> we see a mutuality in their relationship that we do not
> see in the begetting. By handing over lordship to the
> Son the Father makes himself dependent on whether
> the Son glorifies him and fulfils his lordship by
> fulfilling his mission . . . The rule or kingdom of the
> Son is not so external to his deity that he might be
> God without his kingdom.[69]

Similar statements can be made about the Spirit, who raises
Jesus from the dead and, notably in the fourth Gospel, glorifies
the Son and the Son's relation to the Father. The Spirit is the
Spirit of truth, who brings the work of the Son to completion.
Despite claims to the contrary, Barth does not neglect the role of
the Spirit in God's great work of creation, reconciliation and
redemption.[70] But that is not the point. The difference between
Barth and Pannenberg on the Trinity—a difference reflected in
their different attitudes to the addition of the *filioque* to the text
of the Nicene-Constantinopolitan Creed—lies in their general
orientation to the Western and Eastern approaches to trinitarian

---

68. *Ibid*, 319. He considers that the (Eastern) concept of *perichoresis*, though containing the idea of reciprocity, is not sufficient by itself to express the reciprocity in the relations between the three Persons of the Trinity.
69. *Ibid*, 313.
70. For a strong defence of Barth on this point, see Johnson, *op cit*, 115f.

doctrine respectively and in their preference for thinking of God respectively in terms of a single subject of the divine action or in terms of three divine subjects. A doctrine of the Spirit that is at the same time thoroughly trinitarian will more likely follow the latter pattern. Pannenberg's emphases in contemporary trinitarian discussion, to which he has made a notable and distinctive contribution, are part of a broader shift of opinion among 'Western' theologians in recent decades.

Conclusion

There is every indication that the theology of Karl Barth continues to inspire and challenge theologians in many places, although his period of dominance of the theological landscape is now some decades behind us. The scope of his theological vision and the depth and richness of his theological insight are still found by many to be instructive, not least by those who have gone beyond Barth, sometimes in very different directions. Pannenberg is one such. Few theologians are referred to or taken account of in his work more than Barth, often with great approval. This paper has been mostly concerned with matters on which Pannenberg took a different view from Barth. These differences, though not to be exaggerated, are quite major. In the first place, there are fundamental differences in methodology. Basic to them all is Barth's determination as a theologian to say what he has to say, without recognising any obligation to satisfy the requirements of people who work at other things, notably philosophers and people in the natural and human sciences. Being an apologist was no part of Barth's view of a theologian. By contrast, in an age when serious theological claims are scarcely given a hearing, Pannenberg avails himself of support for the theological claims of the Christian faith wherever he finds it, more in the field of anthropology than in cosmology and the natural sciences. This does not mean that Pannenberg saw the theologian's task as one of making the Gospel palatable. Whereas for Barth no non-theological statement could exercise a veto over theological statements that were faithful to God's self-revelation, Pannenberg's view of theology includes both 'the exposition *and verification* of [the] truth [of Christian doctrine'.[71] For Barth the attempt to demonstrate the truth of the Word of God would be presumptuous in the extreme; for Pannenberg the truth of the Christian proclamation is something that has unavoidably to be argued, not presupposed.

Methodological differences aside, a sketch of the differences between Barth and Pannenberg on the doctrine of revelation revealed some significant points of convergence but more points of divergence. Each thinks of revelation in terms of God's self-revelation. Whether in the utterance of the Word or in the unfolding of the history of the cosmos, we have to do with an action of God in which the truth about God is (or is to be) disclosed on the initiative of God. Barth accentuates the mystery of God, the freedom of God, and the hiddenness of God even in the very act of self-disclosure; he never quite takes leave of Kierkegaard! Pannenberg, whose debt is rather to Hegel—though not Hegel alone, and by no means uncritically so—is always ready to take account of those who dispute or dismiss the very idea of God. On the question of the direct or indirect nature of God's revelation less difference was found than might have been expected. In addition, the eschatological shape of Pannenberg's entire theological project is well exemplified in his view of revelation. Only in the eschaton will the truth of God's being and purpose, which includes God's lordship over all created things, be established. This theme is clearly present in Barth, but Pannenberg works much more intensively and rigorously with the eschatological nature of the early Christian proclamation. It was also found that Pannenberg

---

71. Pannenberg, *Systematic Theology*, Vol 1, 23 (emphasis added). He rightly adds that verification is not merely a theoretical or intellectual matter, but also affective and practical.

was much more open to the idea of continuities between religion (that is, the actual religions in the world) and God's self-revelation, whereas for Barth the *cantus firmus* was about the discontinuity between them. Whilst Barth has legitimate questions to put to all world-views, religions and ideologies, events in the contemporary world have called for an exploration of the continuities between religion and revelation.

Finally, in a brief consideration of the trinitarian theology of Barth and Pannenberg, for both of whom it was of central importance, a number of differences were found. No departure from Barth's doctrine of the Trinity can lessen the importance of his contribution to the reinstatement of this doctrine to the centre of the theological agenda of this century. Standing on Barth's shoulders, as it were, a number of his former students, some of them closer to Barth's theological position than Pannenberg, have developed ideas about the Trinity that are more Eastern than Western in their orientation. This involves theological choices and commitments between which it is difficult to arbitrate, and for which biblical support is more or less equally strong. It is no discredit to Barth that intensive work on the doctrine of the Trinity in the last few decades has taken the discussion further and along some different lines. Pannenberg's work indisputably places him in the forefront of that discussion. If it is true that Barth continues to instruct, to question and to warn, Pannenberg's theological achievement is such as to provide both contemporaries and successors with rich theological fare, not perhaps as spicy as Barth's, but innovative, refined and highly nourishing.

Joy in the *Church Dogmatics?*
A Neglected Theme

John Mark Capper

Introduction

Numerous studies of Barth's theology have sought to find a key theme which would somehow unlock the gargantuan structure and reveal its secrets. This approach is both unfair to Barth and unlikely to be successful.[1] Joy is not posited as a controlling theme or a part of the formal structure which Barth adopted for the *Church Dogmatics*, rather it is shown to play a significant material role.

Joy functions as a major theme in Barth's doctrine of God, and carries a significant burden in his doctrine of election. It is reflected in Barth's doctrine of humanity, especially the crowning theme of his discussion of 'being in encounter'—the theme of gladness. This human dimension, grounded in his theology proper and rooted in his doctrine of the Word of God, flourishes in his exploration of Christian vocation, and underscores the praise of the people of God, their worship and witness and the vocation and destiny of the church.

Hardy and Ford suggest that

> while many (theologians) allow room for the discovery of the perfection of God in praise, most are so much preoccupied by formal and anthropological questions that they fail to go on to find the possibility

---

1.   George Hunsinger, *How to Read Karl Barth: An Outline of his Theology* (Oxford: Oxford University Press, 1991), 3.

of joy and freedom arising from the content of what is found.[2]

This essay shows that this is not the case for Barth. However, it is seen to be so for most of his major commentators. The result has been that the theme of joy which is evident in the *Church Dogmatics* is masked in most discussion of Barth's theology. A consideration of the limited extent to which previous commentators have noted the theme of joy in the *Church Dogmatics*, and how this correlates with their approach will help to indicate what kinds of approaches may best help in revealing the theme. The 'motifs' of Hunsinger's work, *How to Read Karl Barth*, will be used in this exercise, as selected works of T F Torrance, Hans Urs von Balthasar, G C Berkouwer, Robert P Jenson, Eberhard Jüngel and Alan Torrance are considered. Given the breadth of scope of the *Church Dogmatics*, this essay concerns itself primarily with a consideration of joy as part of Barth's Doctrine of God (CD II/1).

T F Torrance

Hunsinger argues convincingly for Torrance's weakness in underplaying the actualism[3] and particularism of the Word of God in Jesus Christ. The result is that '[t]he energy, dynamism, and sense of collision which enter Barth's theology by way of the actualistic and particularistic motifs never quite come through in Torrance's account'.[4] What is striking, given this apt description of the less than passionate portrayal of Barth's theology, is Torrance's enthusiastic evocation of Barth's character and personality. In outlining Barth's personal characteristics 'which have an intimate bearing upon all his life

---

2   Daniel W Hardy and David F Ford, *Jubilate: Theology in Praise* (London: Darton, Longman and Todd, 1984), 208.

3   The precise definitions of these terms as used are found in Hunsinger, *op cit*, 4-6.

4   *Ibid*, 11.

and work', he mentions Barth's 'joy and humour'.[5] Torrance notes that Barth (in Volume 3 of the *Church Dogmatics*) 'cannot repress his chuckles at the frightful seriousness with which too many theologians set forth their picture of *homo sapiens*—"What a pity that none of these apologists considers it worthy of mention that man is apparently the only being accustomed to laugh and to smoke"'.[6] Torrance attributes this not only to Barth's full and rich *Menschlichkeit*, but also to his awareness of the 'over-flowing self-communicating joy' of God.[7] That is a joy which awakens human response, and in which theology partakes, and in which Barth is 'constantly tuned to Mozart', and aware of the Augustinian conception of *fruitio Deo*, the enjoyment of God.[8]

Whilst this discussion of joy is linked to Torrance's biographical note on Barth, he does also note the theme of joy elsewhere.[9] For instance, he refers to the theonomous activity of thinking the truth, and notes that for Barth this entails an 'act of deep humility and courage, of reverence and joy'.[10] Torrance does not, however, explore the theme in the context of Barth's

---

5.   T F Torrance, *Karl Barth: An Introduction to His Early Theology, 1920-1931* (London: SCM, 1962), 19, 20, 23. In this latter respect he compares Barth with Heinrich Vogel who 'characteristically contributed to the 1956 *Festschrift* an essay entitled "Der Lachende Barth", (*Antwort: Karl Barth, zum siebstigsten Geburstag am 10. Mai 1956*, Zürich, 1956)'.

6.   T F Torrance, *Karl Barth*, 24, quoting *CD* III/2, 83. Torrance also enjoys pointing out other subtle humorous asides—the bad smell of demons, inclusion of Mozart among the Church fathers, and the humour of his (also angry) *Nein!* to Emil Brunner—the latter which, Torrance notes, 'Anglo-Saxons seem almost invariably to read with a Teutonic lack of humour'.

7.   *Ibid*, 24f, noting *CD* II/1, 653ff.

8.   *Ibid*, 25.

9.   In fact, Torrance is the only Barth commentator of whom I am aware who includes (as Barth does) *joy* in his index.

10. T F Torrance, *op cit*, 131.

theology of God. His concern with the objective dimensions of Barth's theology of the Word of God leads him to occlude the richness of the actuality and particularity of the Christ event. Yet there is more exuberance in Torrance's exploration of Barth's theology than Hunsinger suggests. Whilst he may not soar to doxological heights, Torrance can move from the knowability of God to a reminder of the way in which creation is called to rejoice in God.[11]

Hans Urs von Balthasar
Hunsinger considers that 'the strengths of von Balthasar's reading seem to be largely independent of his attempt to account for the unity of the *Church Dogmatics* as a whole'.[12] Von Balthasar offers an engagement with Barth which is rich and zealous, yet despite his appreciative comments regarding Barth's engagement of themes with which many Protestant theologians are either unfamiliar or uncomfortable, he does not note Barth's development of the theme of the joy of God.[13]

Hunsinger is right to recognize the commonality of Barth and von Balthasar in terms of actualism. However, by grounding his examination too firmly in the issue of the *analogia entis*, he fails to notice von Balthasar's rich analysis of Barth's

---

11. Torrance, *op cit*, 212.
12. Hunsinger, *op cit*, 20, referring to H U von Balthasar, *The Theology of Karl Barth: Exposition and Interpretation* (San Francisco: Ignatius Press, 1992).
13. H U von Balthasar, *The Glory of the Lord: A Theological Aesthetics*, *Vol 1: Seeing the Form* (Edinburgh: T&T Clark, 1982), 124-7, notes his debt to Barth's discussion of the perfections of God (*CD* II/1) in his development of the theme of the *beauty* of God. For von Balthasar, glory is a close associate of beauty, and he tends to follow the scholastics with their understanding of beauty as an aspect of being. Von Balthasar begins with the *analogia entis*, Barth with the *analogia relationis*. Perhaps von Balthasar's preconception blinds him to the theme of joy which pervades the *Church Dogmatics*.

doctrine of predestination. The result of this is that whilst von Balthasar moves closer to appreciating Barth's centring of actualism *in election*, Hunsinger, in over-emphasizing the act of God *in revelation*, has missed this important point. Whilst he does recognize this centring of actualism in election, von Balthasar's agenda, driven by his linkage of the concepts of glory and beauty in the fashion of philosophical æsthetics, fails to attend to Barth's greater emphasis on divine joy. The problem is not actualism, or any of Hunsinger's 'repertoire of "thought forms"',[14] but von Balthasar's own conception about the nature of divine glory, which is more dependent on the concept of beauty than on joy.

G C Berkouwer

Berkouwer considers that Barth's dogmatic stress is on grace, the *triumph* of grace. He often stresses the triumph more than the grace.[15] There could be many less adequate apertures through which to force the theology of Barth. In exploring the central issue of the work of Christ, Berkouwer states:

> It is in connection with the content of the gospel regarded from *this* point of view that Barth's theology bears a pronounced *triumphant* character and, in its

---

14. Hunsinger, *op cit*, 6.
15. At least partly the explanation for this is in how Berkouwer (in G C Berkouwer, *The Triumph of Grace in the Theology of Karl Barth* [Grand Rapids: Eerdmans, 1956], 49) sees and understands Barth's historical situation: ' . . . Barth wants to stimulate the preaching of the gospel in the sombreness of a catastrophic and depressing period of human history and to infuse new life into the witness to Jesus Christ as Victor. He wishes to do this in sharp antithesis to every kind of triumph that can be found in man or in the world. The 'sola gratia' and the 'soli Deo gloria' flow together for Barth from the one mighty glad tidings (sic) of the gospel as the only hope for our time.'

<blockquote>
service to the Church and her proclamation, shares in
the joy and gladness of the gospel.[16]
</blockquote>

That Berkouwer notes the missiological and joyful implications
of the objectivist understanding of the revelation of Christ as
the reconciling Word of God is significant (and is rather more
than Hunsinger achieves, with his focus on formal motifs).
Berkouwer is concerned to explore the credentials of Barth's
theology of election, and to that end explores this theme in
depth. Whilst he is right that the place of election is 'decisive',[17]
the focus on this doctrinal expression in terms of Berkouwer's
own expectations (shaped almost entirely by Calvin) of how the
doctrine should function means that Berkouwer is unable to
place the doctrine in its widest context, the nature of God, as
Barth locates it.

In discussing grace, Berkouwer does give joy a fuller place
than do any of the other commentators discussed by Hunsinger.
For instance,

<blockquote>
This grace does not confer a moderate, relatively
valuable gift, a temporal, limited, and uncertain joy. It
confers salvation, life which is life indeed . . . the
water which is drawn with joy from the wells of
salvation, . . . comfort, eternal comfort, light, joy, and
victory in all distress.[18]
</blockquote>

Berkouwer cannot, however, maintain the focus on this joy or
even this grace, but is led by his own concern with the *triumph*
of grace, to continue: 'And all this is preached to us with
authority which towers triumphantly above all uncertainty and
doubt and thereby lays the foundation for an inviolable
certainty.'[19] The triumph is linked to the preaching of the
Gospel, and above all to the need for authority and certainty.
Here Berkouwer and Barth part company as to their central

---

16. *Ibid*, 18.
17. *Ibid*, 52.
18. *Ibid*, 351.
19. *Ibid*, 351.

formal theological concerns.[20] This is the basis for Hunsinger's charge that Berkouwer has misread Barth.[21] Berkouwer has overlooked the richness of the theme of the joy of God due to his prior concern to show the centre of Barth's theology located in his preformed notion of the 'triumph of grace'. Hunsinger notes that 'by bypassing the complexity of Barth's thought forms, Berkouwer ends up by distorting the content and missing the unity of Barth's theology as well'.[22] Certainly Berkouwer has found an important theme, but he has elevated it to the role of interpretive key—a status which Barth withholds from it.

Robert P Jenson
In his analysis of Jenson, Hunsinger's motifs are at their most effective, delineating Barth from non-Barth in Jenson's analysis. A lack of attention to the motif of personalism is part explanation for Jenson's failure to detect the positive theme of joy in Barth. It must also be noted that the separation of eternity (Jenson's key focus) from glory (its partner in Barth's development of the divine perfections[23]) draws attention away from the theological context in which Barth's treatment of joy finds its richest and most original expression.

Eberhard Jüngel[24]
At a fundamental level, Jüngel is concerned with the means of expressing truth about God. He is concerned to explore the role and function of analogy, metaphor and anthropomorphism.[25]

---

20 In this regard, see Barth's response to Berkouwer, *CD* IV/3, 174.
21 Hunsinger, *op cit*, 15.
22 *Ibid*, 21.
23 *CD* II/1.
24 Hunsinger does not consider Jüngel or Alan Torrance in his work. Their importance in regard to the theme of joy is such that they will be outlined briefly, in the light of Hunsinger's motifs.
25 Noted by John B Webster, 'Eberhard Jüngel', in D Ford (ed), *The*

'I believe, therefore I speak.'[26] This is Jüngel's appropriation of Barth's understanding of Anselm's *Fides Quaerens Intellectum*, developed as faith *finding* understanding and expression. For Jüngel as much if not more so than Barth, the imperative of 'the Word' is speech *about* the Word, a truth which must be expressed and which liberates.[27] Thus Jüngel can say: 'I believe, therefore I speak, . . . I listen, . . . I am astonished, . . . I think, . . . I differentiate, . . . I hope, . . . I act, . . . I am (a new creature, called to represent the being of Christ in the communion of saints), . . . and I suffer'.[28] Theology which is 'never delivered from astonishment' grows in astonishment as it seeks to grow in understanding.[29] This understanding is constrained not by the contemporary philosophical traditions, but by its object. Thus, 'theology acquires its method by repeating in thought the movement of God's coming to the world'.[30] It is belief which asserts the new identity of the Christian self which enables both suffering and, amid suffering, the longing for rejoicing. Jüngel describes joy, in this context, as something *withheld* from believers and thus as a further cause of suffering. It is inextricably linked to the testing of the theologian, and the necessity for Christian theology to be a theology of the cross.[31]

Jüngel's appreciation of joy as a theme goes deep. It is linked with faith in the resurrection of Jesus Christ, but his basic theological analysis of it rings true with Jewish traditions of

---

Modern Theologians: An Introduction to Christian Theology in the Twentieth Century, Vol 1 (Oxford: Blackwell, 1989), 93.

26. E Jüngel, 'My Theology'—A Short Summary', *Theological Essays II*, J Webster (ed), (Edinburgh: T&T Clark, 1995), 4.

27. *Ibid*, 5. 'For faith must not seek. It finds. Faith lives from a discovered love whose liberating truth it then naturally seeks to understand and continually to understand better . . . I believe, therefore I speak.'

28. *Ibid*, 4-19.

29. *Ibid*, 8-9.

30. *Ibid*, 11

31. *Ibid*, 18-19.

rejoicing in God and of joy in God. It goes to the root of his conception of the self and of faith: ' . . . The self-definition for which man is determined in faith can thus be only the immediacy of divine joy'.[32]

Two things stand out in an analysis of Jüngel's treatment of Barth's theology. Firstly, he is seen to have woven together the motifs which Hunsinger outlines in a rich and productive theological appropriation of the theology of Karl Barth. His 'interpretation' is beyond simple restatement. His 'other words' are themselves evocative in ways parallel to Barth's theological enterprise. This is what has most been missing from the commentators with whom Hunsinger engaged. The reason for its presence in Jüngel is complex, but has at least some grounding in his desire to do theology in engagement with Barth, rather than to find particular keys to Barth's theology. Secondly, Jüngel has noticed the theme of joy in God which is present in the *Church Dogmatics,* and has (in his later work, especially) linked this to the joy possible in humanity, a possibility developed in consideration of the 'christological concentration' he finds in Barth's theology and exemplified in his own.[33] This awareness of the motif of joy in God is enhanced by Jüngel's preparedness to recognize joyful relationality as a constituent dimension of the intra-trinitarian life.

A J Torrance

Alan J Torrance's work focuses on CD I/1.[34] It is intended as a study on the nature of the Trinity as a theological theme, using

---

32 E Jüngel, *God as the Mystery of the World: On the Foundation of the Theology of the Crucified One in the Dispute between Theism and Atheism* (Edinburgh: T&T Clark, 1983), 192.

33 'Karl Barth's . . . entire life and thought as a whole announced that 'God' is a cheerful word.' E Jüngel, *Karl Barth: A Theological Legacy* (Philadelphia: Westminster Press, 1986), 21.

34 A J Torrance, *Persons in Communion: An Essay on Trinitarian*

Barth as a 'foil'.[35] A J Torrance aims to develop a richer understanding of the Trinity as a communion of persons, eschewing the limitations of Barth's term, *Seinsweise*, and to construct a methodology which has its semantic conceptions built from a concept of *analogia communionis*. The final goal is a 'form of semantic participation which stems from, and takes the form of, 'doxological participation''.[36]

It is in this context that A J Torrance, in exploring Barth's use of the term *Seinsweisen*, suggests that he has been significantly influenced by philosophical idealism.[37] This, in turn, has had a constricting effect on Barth's understanding 'of God's subjectivity, sovereignty, selfhood and personality'[38] and resulted in Barth's 'under-characterization of the doctrine of the Spirit'.[39] Whilst Torrance seeks to ameliorate the accusation of idealism,[40] he does note that despite Barth's 'continual reminders of the need to interpret the *Seinsweisen* in relational

---

Description and Human Participation with special reference to Volume One of Karl Barth's Church Dogmatics (Edinburgh: T&T Clark, 1996).

35. *Ibid*, 5.

36. *Ibid*, 3-5.

37. *Ibid*, 242, where he engages with T F Torrance, *Karl Barth: Biblical and Evangelical Theologian* (Edinburgh: T&T Clark 1990), 10, and Jürgen Moltmann, *The Trinity and the Kingdom of God: The Doctrine of God* (London: SCM, 1977), 241 n241, amongst others.

38. Torrance, *op cit*, 243, noting the comments of Moltmann, *op cit*, 139-44.

39. Torrance, *op cit*, 244, noting Moltmann, *op cit*, 142 and also Thomas A Smail, *The Giving Gift: The Holy Spirit in Person* (London: Darton, Longman and Todd, 1988), 43. On this issue, see also Smail's 'The Doctrine of the Holy Spirit', in J Thompson (ed), *Theology beyond Christendom: Essays on the Centenary of the Birth of Karl Barth* (Allison Park, PA: Princeton Theological Monograph Series, 6, 1986), 87-110.

40. Torrance, *op cit*, 245-51.

terms',[41] he falls short of a concept of intra-trinitarian *koinonia*.[42] The result of this is that Barth, constrained by his "'revelational model" . . . inadequately expresses the dynamic relations of mutual love within the Triunity on the one hand and . . . fails to integrate with an adequate conception of semantic participation (as this is constitutive of human thought and understanding) on the other'.[43]

A J Torrance has explored the dynamics of CD I/1, but has not referred to the many references there to the joy of God. Torrance's reworking of the central dynamics of Barth's theology allows him to posit the potential of doxological participation. On that basis he makes moves towards a very different interpretation of the divine-human relationality from that which is explicit in the *Church Dogmatics*. The outcome, in Torrance, is the opening up of a rich description of the intra-triune community.[44] Without explicit reference to the *joy* of that communality, however, Torrance's reading and reinterpretation of Barth prove less rewarding than they might in exploring issues of doxology and community, and offers a less rich understanding of the joy of relationality than Barth himself gives. The reason for this lies in Torrance's almost total concern with the formal dimensions of Barth's trinitarian communality. The result of this concern and its clear but selective focus on the cognitive descriptions of the intra-triune relationality means

---

41. *Ibid*, 259.

42. *Ibid*, 261.

43. *Ibid*.

44. In this context, the comments regarding 'Worship as the Place of Primary Verification (of Theology)' of D Ritschl, *The Logic of Theology: A Brief Account of the Relationship between basic Concepts in Theology* (London: SCM, 1986), 98ff, are a reminder of the whole purpose of the theological task, a context implicit in A J Torrance, but begging, in my view, to be made explicit. Cf Hardy and Ford, *Jubilate*, where the potential for theology to 'talk to God as well as about him', (Ritschl, *op cit*, 98), is allowed.

that Torrance has missed the affective dimensions and their connections to the material descriptions of the joy of God.

This brief engagement with important Barth commentators shows not only that joy is a neglected theme, but that it will not be found by concern with formal principles alone. Rather a beginning with material considerations will yield more evidence of the theme. Together with Barth's trinitarian framework, this helps to explain Barth's understanding of theology as a 'joyful science'. To this framework we must now turn.

Trinity and Joy

The structure of the *Church Dogmatics* rests on a trinitarian framework. For Barth the basic given in dogmatics is the reality of God as Father, Son and Holy Spirit. The role of dogmatics as a joyful exercise is set in the broader context of God and God's revelation. Dogmatics is a human response to God in revelation, and is set in the context of the responses of obedience, love, witness and worship which are incumbent upon those who are recipients of God's self-revelation. This overview of the theological task in the *Church Dogmatics* is grounded in Barth's own prolegomena, his Doctrine of the Word of God, the main theme of Volume One of the *Church Dogmatics*.

However, close attention to *Church Dogmatics* II suggests that, at least where a theology of joy is concerned, the centre is more usefully located here. This does not deny the importance of *Church Dogmatics* I, but rather suggests that undue attention to *Church Dogmatics* I risks blinding Barth scholars to other riches.

> For it is an honour and a joy, an inner necessity and a gracious privilege to serve and therefore to teach the Word of God. Indeed, it is the whole meaning of the Church's existence (*CD* I/2, 852-3).

109

We should note Barth's consistent call to keep theology focused on and by its central 'object'—God, Father, Son and Holy Spirit, who is revealed as triune.[45] It is the trinitarian dynamic, the recognition of God as Father, Son and Holy Spirit, which provides grounding for Barth's whole theological undertaking and a basis for the theme of particularity and universality which recurs throughout his theology.

Of great importance for the continuing appropriation of Barth is the recognition that theology is a joyful and worshipful task. In the ideal case, pure doctrine would be 'joyful and pleasant sounds . . . in [teachers'] mouths' (*CD* I/2, 803). In the worst, it is the false joy of a kind of police detection (*CD* I/2, 809). Then it becomes self-absorbed and of little or no value in the service of its purpose, and fails to display its 'characteristic beauty', which is the hallmark of the truth of God (*CD* I/2, 808).

Despite his iconoclastic warnings, Barth prizes the beauty of the theological task, and its concomitant joyfulness. As his reflection on Anselm's reference to the beauty of theology reminds us, '[t]he theologian who has no joy in his work is not a theologian at all' (*CD* II/1, 656). The abundant and gracious self-revelation of God, and the fact that this revelation is of a loving, free and joyful God of relationality, is the ground for a theological task which is joyful in the midst of a church called to a life of rejoicing service. The joyfulness of the task and the joyfulness of God do not preclude agony and suffering, but do exclude boredom and futility which are more likely to be destroyers of joy. The call to the church and the world to return to the Lord is a call to return to the joy of the Lord as well.

---

45   'The one God reveals Himself according to Scripture as the redeemer, ie, as the Lord who sets us free. As such He is the Holy Spirit, by receiving whom we become the children of God, because, as the Spirit of love of God the Father and the Son, He is so antecedently in Himself' (*CD* I/1, 448).

Joy and the Divine 'Perfections'

Barth's treatment of the perfections of God, especially the link which he makes with glory and eternity, undergirds the far-reaching sweep which joy is allowed. The constraints which he places on his discussion of the beauty of God and the greater freedom he allows joy point to limitations in Barth's own method, grounded in his own reformed tradition. These bias his understanding of divine glory. Nonetheless, the fact that he allows joy such a far-reaching sweep must be underlined.

With the basis of his theology of revelation outlined in *CD* I, Barth moves, in *CD* II, to explicate the nature of the God who reveals and is revealed. He asks: 'If we do not speak rightly on this Subject (the doctrine of God), how can we speak rightly of His predicates?' (*CD* II/1, 3). The problem of knowledge is both raised and answered in Jesus Christ.[46] It is Jesus Christ as truly God and truly human who provides the possibility of an answer or answers, and these will be found in the relationship offered by the call to 'Enter thou into the joy of the Lord' (*CD* II/1,11). Thus 'the real knowledge of God is concerned with God in His relationship to man, but also in His distinction from him' (*CD* II/1,10). In the light of Christ, the revelation of God is to be received with thanksgiving, joy and awe, because revelation reminds its recipient of the distance between God and humanity, as well as the closeness of the connection, made by grace (*CD* II/1, 223). Knowledge of God is participation in this 'veracity of revelation' with its centre in the act of God in Jesus Christ (*CD* II/1, 223).

In his groundwork for the discussion of the perfections of God, Barth stresses the call to enter into the joy of the Lord, and has grounded this in the act of God in Jesus Christ, the visible expression of the divine glory (*die Herrlichkeit des Herrn*). The God who reveals is the God who loves in freedom and is the

---

46 This is the main issue of CD II/1, 3-254, Chapter V, 'The Knowledge of God'.

God who is glorious as Father, Son and Holy Spirit. By holding love and freedom together Barth is affirming his aim to be true to God who is in fellowship and creates fellowship with humanity. It is in this context that we must place Barth's development of the perfections of God, and particularly his development of the 'perfection' of joy.

Using the imagery of light, Barth notes that the illumination by God's glory produces a reaction in that which is illuminated. 'It is a presence which opens [blind eyes]' (*CD* II/1, 647). It is in this context that Barth first links joy to glory. The doxological expressions in this context are significant, as Barth clearly considers that the appropriate response to God's self revelation of His glory is praise. His language becomes the language of worship: 'The creature has no voice of its own. It does not point to its own picture. It echoes and reflects the glory of God' (*CD* II/1, 648).[47] The rootedness of this movement of glorification from humanity towards God in praise and joy is for Barth located in the very nature of God. An extended quotation will serve to show the strength of the linkage which Barth makes between joy and the perfection which is God's glory:

> God's glory is the indwelling joy of His divine being which as such shines out from Him, which overflows in its richness, which in its super-abundance is not satisfied with itself but communicates itself. All God's works must be understood also and decisively from this point of view. All together and without exception they take part in the movement of God's self-glorification and the communication of His joy. God wills them and loves them because, far from having their existence of themselves and their meaning in themselves, they have their being and existence in the movement of the divine self-glorification, in the

---

47. Or further, 'the glorifying of God consists simply in the life-obedience of the creature which knows God. It has no alternative but to thank and praise God' (*CD* II/1, 674).

transition to them of His immanent joyfulness. It is
their destiny to offer a true if inadequate response in
the temporal sphere to the jubilation with which the
Godhead is filled from eternity to eternity (*CD* II/1,
647-8).

Whilst we will leave the aspects of the divine glory and joy
which pertain to humanity until another time, it is important to
note some key dynamics of Barth's understanding of joy and
glory in God which are focused in this passage, (though they
are also exemplified in numerous other places). The movement
of God's glory and God's joyful self-communication are
synonymous for Barth. The abundance of God's glory is seen in
God's joy. God's joy is perceived as the outpouring of God's
glory. The intratrinitarian joy evokes human responses of joy.
For the moment, however, let us ponder the remarkable
location of joy as tantamount to a perfection of God in Barth's
exposition, noting the close parallel drawn with glory. There
has been a development in the section quoted. In it, joy has been
elevated. Joy is no mere description of an aspect of divine glory.
Joy has been developed as being both the inward and the
outward aspect of divine glory. It is the basis of God's self-
communication, and the dynamic of that communication. Intra-
triune joy calls to humanity, and the invocation is to jubilation.
Joy is at least functioning as a perfection. It describes God and is
used to explore other perfections. Divine glory, the joy of God's
being God, becomes the central motif in explaining
jubilation—not just as human response to the divine, but the
jubilation 'with which the Godhead is filled from eternity to
eternity' (*CD* II/1, 648). Glory, the theme with which Barth
began his exploration of the perfections of God, returns as a
theme which refines and expands the whole conspectus of the
perfections.

Through participation in Christ's saving act, humanity
enters into the glory of God, and thus eschatologically leaves
the hindrances to joy: the groaning of creation and the burden

of sin.[48] This is the renewed human destiny. For Barth it is expressed in terms of glory and eternity. Thus in eternity and in temporal existence, Christians are called to 'live in the determination to be the reflection and echo of God and therefore the witnesses to the divine glory that reaches over to him, rejoicing with the God who Himself has eternal joy and Himself is eternal joy' (*CD* II/1, 648-9).[49]

That God has and is eternal joy is a remarkable statement, sure to surprise those who have only a passing or second-hand knowledge of the *Church Dogmatics*, yet it is essential to a full and rich understanding of Barth's treatment of the Doctrine of God. Barth has not yet finished his treatment of the joy of God. Already it has begun to assume the status of a perfection. But to understand his exposition, we must follow Barth into a discussion of a related theme, the possibility of speaking of the *beauty* of God.

Joy and the Beauty of God

In making the bold statement that 'God is beautiful' (*CD* II/1, 651), Barth opens a volume of historical theology normally left firmly closed by his fellow reformed theologians. Jürgen Moltmann has said, 'Karl Barth was the only theologian in the continental Protestant tradition who has dared to call God

---

48. The destiny of responding to God with joy in eternity is that which 'man received and lost, only to receive it again, inconceivably and infinitely increased by the personal participation of God in man's being accomplished in Jesus Christ' (*CD* II/1, 648).

49. Barth describes joy in Philippians as a defiant '"Nevertheless!"' which Paul sets like a full stop against the Philippians' anxiety . . . It is in fact a keynote that this joy is meant, beyond the joy one "has", feels, can show. *En kyrio* (in the Lord) is its location; at all times it can and must take place' (K Barth, *The Epistle to the Philippians* [London: SCM, 1962], 120f).

"beautiful"'.[50] Barth was well aware of the dangers of being misunderstood both in his use of the theme, and in his noting sources of the theme in the piety of the church.[51] Nevertheless, the fact is that 'God loves us as the One who is worthy of love as God. This is what we mean when we say that God is beautiful' (*CD* II/1, 651). This is a basis for worship and joy in the life of the recipients of the revealed joy, beauty and glory of God. It is also a necessary part of a fully biblical exploration of the divine perfections. Imploring caution with the concept of God's beauty and mindful of the propensity to idolatry within humanity, Barth defends the concept on two bases; firstly because to omit it leaves a gap in our knowledge, and secondly because it is biblically true.[52]

---

50. Jürgen Moltmann, *Theology and Joy*, Reinhard Ulrich (trans), with an extended introduction by David E Jenkins (London: SCM, 1973), 58.

51. 'When we say ['God is beautiful'] we reach back to the pre-Reformation tradition of the Church' (*CD* II/1, 651-2).

52. Or, perhaps more precisely, because it is not biblically prohibited for consideration (see *CD* II/1, 651-2). Interestingly, however, Barth marshals no biblical evidence at this point to support his assertion of the veracity of the concept of God's beauty, but rather, after having limited the use of the concept, he cites Ps 104:1f, 'where magnificence and sublimity and especially light are mentioned as God's garment and apparel. Ps 45:2 could also be mentioned, where the Messiah-king is addressed as "fairer than the children of men; grace is poured into thy lips: therefore God hath blessed thee for ever". In addition it is worth asking whether an important contribution could not and would not be made by a new and more penetrating exposition of the Song of Songs . . . Even then, the fact still remains that the idea of beauty does not have any independent significance in the Bible. Yet this does not mean that it is unimportant for the Bible or alien to it' (*CD* II/1, 653).

Barth's limitations on the use of the theme of beauty must be noted. He is unwilling for it to become a key theme, a 'leading concept' or a 'primary motif':

> Attention should be given to the fact that we cannot include the concept of beauty with the main concepts of the doctrine of God, with the divine perfections which are the divine essence itself. In view of what the biblical testimony says about God it would be an unjustified risk to try to bring the knowledge of God under the denominator of the idea of the beautiful even in the same way as we have done in our consideration of these leading concepts. It is not a leading concept. Not even in passing can we make it a primary motif in our understanding of the whole being of God as we necessarily did in the case of these other concepts. (*CD* II/1, 652)

A partial explanation of Barth's reluctance to allow beauty to be used as a means of explicating the other perfections is his concern to maintain sufficient theological distance between creation and its creator. 'Certainly we have every reason to be cautious here' (*CD* II/1, 651), he says, but notes that we should not 'hesitate indefinitely'(*CD* II/1, 651), nor can we avoid this step. Here is a tension for Barth: unable to ignore the concept of beauty, he is unwilling to use it further.[53]

For Barth, the concept of beauty is too closely linked to the attributes of Being to be employed without considerable circumspection, and he will not risk the association with the

---

53 'If we say now that God is beautiful, and make this statement the final explanation of the assertion that God is glorious, do we not jeopardize or even deny the majesty and holiness and righteousness of God's love? Do we not bring God . . . into the sphere of man's oversight and control, into proximity to the ideal of all human striving? Do we not bring the contemplation of God into suspicious proximity to that contemplation of the world which in the last resort is the self-contemplation of an urge for life which does not recognize its limits?' (*CD* II/1, 651).

analogia entis. As von Balthasar notes: 'Contemporary Protestant theology nowhere deals with the beautiful as a theological category'.[54] Yet having said this, von Balthasar goes on to note his debt to Barth.[55] Whilst Barth did not consider beauty as a category, he acknowledged it as a characteristic of the nature of God's glory, and as requiring adequate theological exploration (*CD* II/1, 666). By contrast, von Balthasar comes close to equating glory and beauty.[56] The key point of commonality for both theologians is the centrality of Jesus Christ, whom von Balthasar describes as 'our supreme object: the form of divine revelation in salvation-history, leading to Christ and deriving from him'.[57] For Barth, Jesus Christ is the centre of God's revelation, and whilst beautiful, is not a manifestation primarily of beauty, but of glory.

Yet despite Barth's reluctance to explore the theme itself, he notes that it has an important diagnostic function in discerning and expanding the understanding of the glory of God (*CD* II/1, 653). 'But we cannot overlook the fact that God is glorious in such a way that He radiates joy, so that He is all He is with and not without beauty'(*CD* II/1, 655).[58] The close link of beauty and joy in God and their use in understanding the glory of God must be noted as we explore Barth's longest discussion under the heading of beauty—the beauty which is a measure of the theological task (*CD* II/1, 657-66).

---

54 Von Balthasar, *op cit*, 56.

55 *Ibid*, 124-7.

56 Whilst acknowledging the limitations which are incumbent with Barth's treatment of beauty, von Balthasar commends his bravery: ' . . . neither the fact that more recent Catholic theology again takes the concept of beauty seriously, nor the fact that the liberal Protestant tradition misuses it, keep Barth from re-introducing it in *his* theology, albeit with evident care and precautions' (*Ibid*, 54).

57 *Ibid*, 29.

58 This, whilst praised by von Balthasar as an acknowledgment of the place of beauty in the divine attributes, is a severely limited and marginalised descriptive concept in Barth's theology.

Barth's three examples of beauty in theology are not given by way of proof. He mentions firstly 'God's being as it unfolds itself in all His attributes, but [which] is one in itself in them all' (*CD* II/1, 657). 'There can be no question,' argues Barth, 'of distinguishing between the content (*Inhalt*) and the form (*Form*) of the divine being and therefore of seeking the beauty of God abstractly in the form of His being for us and in Himself' (*CD* II/1, 658). Yet 'only the form of the divine being has divine beauty. But as the form of the divine being it has and is itself divine beauty' (*CD* II/1, 659). But for Barth this is not the end of the argument but a step in strengthening his case for divine joy. As he concludes:

> Inevitably when the perfect divine being declares itself, it also radiates joy in the dignity and power of its divinity, and thus releases the pleasure, desire and enjoyment of which we have spoken, and in this way, by means of this form, persuasive (*überführend*) and convincing (*überzeugend*). And this persuasive (*überführende*) and convincing (*bewegende*) form must necessarily be called the beauty of God(*CD* II/1, 659).

This develops into Barth's second example, the triunity of God. Here he emphasizes his recurrent theme—that the form with which we are dealing is not form *per se*, but 'the concrete form of the triune being of God, the being which is God the Father, the Son and the Holy Spirit' (*CD* II/1, 659). It is in this glory of the being and life of 'God Himself' (*CD* II/1, 661) that God's power and dignity are 'enlightening, persuasive and convincing' (*CD*, 661). 'It is radiant, and what it radiates is joy' (*CD* II/1, 661). Again we see the role of these discussions of beauty in developing the theme of joy within Barth's umbrella concept of the glory of God. As he says of God's joy: 'It attracts and therefore it conquers. It is therefore beautiful' (*CD* II/1, 661). Concluding with a return to the necessity of a concept of the beauty of God as a consequence of God's triunity, Barth denies again the possibility of beauty as a separate concept by noting it as derived from the doctrine of the trinity. He persists in linking it inextricably to the joy of God: 'the triunity of God is the secret of His beauty. If we deny this, we at once have a God without radiance and without joy (and without humour!); a God without beauty' (CD II/1, 659-61).

Barth's third example of beauty in theology is the incarnation. It is in the work of the Son that the beauty of God is revealed 'in a special way and in some sense to a supreme degree' (CD II/1, 661). The supreme degree is the sense that the beauty of God arouses joy. The beauty of Christ is to be found supremely for humanity in the fact that it is to arouse a response to the saving work of Christ. Here is God's glory in humility. This allows Barth to undergird his observation that (in Christ and His death) 'God's beauty embraces death as well as life, fear as well as joy, what we might call the ugly as well as what we might call the beautiful' (CD II/1, 665). This is because 'the beauty of Jesus . . . is the beauty of God' (CD II/1, 665). Whilst here the conclusion is not directed back to the encompassing theme of joy, joy has been evident as a continuous thread throughout the discussion and it soon returns to prominence in the further consideration of glory.

The link which Barth makes between divine joy and beauty and their constitutive part in the glory of God have been largely overlooked. Von Balthasar has noted the connection with beauty but not joy, and Protestants have tended to miss both. Yet joy is a strong material thread through Barth's doctrine of God. It recurs as part of Barth's doctrine of humanity. For the moment we must be content to conclude that joy is a theme in Barth's doctrine of God—and that it has been a neglected theme. Further effort can fruitfully be spent on exploring how this theme affected Barth's further theological developments. All this has its grounding in Barth's assertion that

> we cannot overlook the fact that God is glorious in
> such a way that He radiates joy, so that He is all He is
> with and not without beauty. Otherwise His glory
> might well be joyless (CD II/1, 655).

John Mark Capper

Conclusion

The perceptive reader will note that this writer has nowhere sought to define the concept 'joy'. There are two reasons for this. The first is that Barth does not, yet it does not stop him from using the term. The second is, I confess, because I cannot. The limitation here is both that inherent in the biblical record and the sheer difficulty of the term. It is clear what joy is not. (It is hard, however, to convincingly posit a simple antonym for joy. Suffering will not do, neither will pain, since the scriptures hold these together with joy). It is clear what some characteristics of joy are, and what it is associated with, yet a synonym is also hard to provide—happiness and pleasure carry too many human connotations, as do bliss and ecstasy. Barth's bold move is to explore this association with regard to perhaps the highest of his perfections of God—glory.

Let this limitation be described as making the concept of joy merely abstract, let me allow Karl Barth a final statement. Barth notes that if God's glory is not recognised as joyful, then:

> Even with the best will in the world, and even with the greatest seriousness and zeal, the proclamation of His glory will always have in a slight or dangerous degree something joyless, without sparkle or humour, not to say tedious and there[fore] finally neither persuasive nor convincing . . . Where it is neglected, and the legitimate answer to the question is not perceived or understood, the element in God's glory which radiates joy is not appreciated and His glory itself is not really perceived. But where this element is not appreciated—and this is why the question of form is so important—what becomes of the evangelical element of the evangel? (*CD* II/1, 655).

This is not an abstruse matter, then. It bears detailed examination because it has implications for the gospel. The God who reaches out to humanity in Christ does so in joy and for joy—for God's own joy and for the joy of the creature. This is a theme which Barth develops further in subsequent volumes of the *Church Dogmatics* and which bears fuller investigation, but that must wait for another occasion. However, to point to the fuller implications of the joy of God, we can note that just as the joy of God undergrids Barth's sense that revelation and the theological task are joyful, so it provides a basis for his understanding that the fullness of humanity is found in gladness and gratitude and that eschatology points from the joy of the Easter event to the joy of eternal life in the presence of God. Thus we can conclude that God calls from joy to joy, for the joy of redeemed people. In that joy we are called to live and witness to the God of joy in the joy of God.

Dialectics of Communion: Dialectical Method and Barth's Defence of Israel

Mark Lindsay

I

It has long been the received wisdom of Barth scholarship that Barth's theological methodology began dialectically before switching to an analogical approach. In the immediate aftermath of Barth's break with Neo-Protestant liberalism, he had viewed the dialectical *Denkform* as a necessary outcome of the confrontation with 'the superior, new element which limits and determines any human self-understanding . . . [It] describes a way of thinking arising from man's conversation with the sovereign God who encounters him'.[1]

According to Michael Beintker, the dialectics of this post-liberal period took two forms.[2] The first was illustrated in Barth's Elgersburg lecture of 1922, in which he set out the principle that for every theological statement there must be a counter-statement, with the two theses remaining in unresolved tension. Dialectic, he says, 'is the way of Paul and the Reformers', and it sets as the basic theological task the interpretation of 'the Yes and the No and the No by the Yes without delaying more than a moment in either a fixed Yes *or* a fixed No'. It is only by such an approach that we can recognise the living truths that truly God became truly man, and that

---

1.   K Barth to Kroner Verlag, 7 March 1954, cited in E Busch, *Karl Barth: His Life from Letters and Autobiographical Texts* (Grand Rapids: Eerdmans, 1994), 144.
2   M Beintker, *Die Dialektik in der 'dialektischen Theologie' Karl Barths* (Munich: Christian Kaiser Verlag, 1987).

precisely as an *impius*, humanity is a *justus*. 'My friend', insists Barth, 'if you ask about *God* and if I am really to tell about *him*, dialectic is all that can be expected of *me* . . .[3] The other predominant form of Barthian dialectic was that which provided the essential flavour of the second edition of his *Romans*. Fundamentally ontic in character (as opposed to the noetic nature of the first type), it was designed to highlight the Kierkegaardian 'infinite qualitative difference' between God and humanity, time and eternity.[4]

In the chronology of Barth's work, the zenith of dialectical theology ostensibly occurred during his Safenwil and Göttingen years, and the representative text was *Romans* II. Between 1927 and 1931, however, this dialectical approach to theology was rejected in favour of analogy. According to Hans Urs von Balthasar's classic 1951 analysis,[5] this 'turn to analogy' was slow but irrevocable. Both Barth's *Christliche Dogmatik* and the *Anselm* book[6] were regarded by von Balthasar as undeniable

---

3. K Barth, 'The Word of God and the Task of the Ministry', in *idem*, *The Word of God and the Word of Man* (Gloucester, Mass: Peter Smith, 1978), 206-209. [The lecture was originally delivered on October 3rd 1922.] Beintker has labelled this form of dialectic 'complementary dialectic', and it is characterised by a ceaseless to-ing and fro-ing of the two poles, with neither resolution nor progress being made.

4. See for example B L McCormack, *Karl Barth's Critically Realistic Dialectical Theology: Its genesis and development 1909-1936* (Clarendon Press, 1997), 11f. Note, of course, that it is precisely this ontic difference which establishes the need for the previously discussed noetic dialectic.

5. H U von Balthasar, *The Theology of Karl Barth* (San Francisco: Ignatius Press, 1992).

6. K Barth, *Die christliche Dogmatik im Entwurf. Erster Band: Die Lehre vom Worte Gottes: Prolegomena zur christlichen Dogmatik* (Christian Kaiser Verlag, 1928; repr Zurich: TVZ, 1982); *Fides quaerens intellectum: Anselms Beweis der Existenz Gottes im Zusammenhang seines theologischen Programms* (Christian Kaiser Verlag, 1931; repr

examples of a change in Barth's theological style, away finally from the dialectical approach, although with the qualification that even analogy did not become fully integrated into his 'system' until *CD* II/1.[7]

That, at least, has been the long-standing assumption which has driven Barth scholarship. In recent times, however, the whole notion of a 'turn to analogy' has come under intense scrutiny. Ingrid Spieckermann, Michael Beintker and, more recently, Bruce McCormack have all criticised the rigidity of the former paradigm.[8] Spieckermann's breakthrough was in discovering a form of analogy in the period traditionally thought of as Barth's dialectical phase. Such a discovery clearly undermines the assumption that Barth progressed from the one to the other. McCormack, on the other hand and building on Beintker's work, has tackled the problem from the other direction. Instead of focusing on the presence of analogy in Barth's dialectical period (a presence he does not deny), he has argued strongly that dialectic remains present in Barth's theology *even after* the 'turn to analogy' allegedly took place.

The consequence of this new research is that any strict periodisation of Barth's theological development is inherently problematic, as both analogy and dialectic now appear to have operated side-by-side in Barth's work, from the Safenwil pastorate right through into the *Church Dogmatics*. From the perspective of methodological paradigms, this is profoundly significant. The interest of this article, however, lies in exploring what effect the ongoing presence of dialectic has on the interpretation of the *material* of Barth's mature theology, specifically in relation to his doctrine of election.

Zurich: TVZ, 1981).

7.   Balthasar, *op cit.* 72, 93f.

8.   I Spieckermann, *Gotteserkenntnis: Ein Beitrag zur Grundfrage der neuen Theologie Karl Barths* (Munich: Christian Kaiser Verlag, 1985); Beintker, *op cit*; McCormack, *op cit.*

Before considering Barth's formulation of this doctrine and the role of dialectic within it, it is necessary to locate this aspect of his work in its rightful historical context. The material content of *CD* II/2, where Barth's most thorough analysis of election appears, was delivered in lecture form between the winter semester of 1939-40 through to the winter semester of 1941-42.[9] Thus, the final lectures that comprise this volume of the *Church Dogmatics* were given at roughly the same time as the Wannsee Conference of 20 January 1942, at which the systematic execution of the Nazis' *Endlösung* was planned. This does not in itself indict either Barth or his theology with Antisemitism, as the historical order makes it highly unlikely that Barth knew any details of genocidal activity during the period in which he was teaching the material of *CD* II/2.[10]

Contextually, however, Barth *was* formulating his particular doctrine of election at the very time when a general doctrine of election was being violently manipulated to suit the exterminationist nationalism of Nazi ideology. On the one hand, the propaganda machine of Nazi Germany was deifying the German *Volk*, idealising (and idolising) it as God's new chosen race. On the other hand, with the status of 'elect' thus removed from Israel, Nazi racial politics condemned the Jews to the penalty that accrues to the rejected. In being vilified as 'life unworthy of living', the Jews were elected to death[11]—a death that was executed in the hells of Auschwitz, Belzec, Chelmno

---

9. E Busch, *Unter dem Bogen des einen Bundes: Karl Barth und die Juden 1933-1945* (Neukirchen-Vluyn: Neukirchener Verlag, 1996), n401
    3.

10. This is so for the following two reasons: the decisive turn to genocide did not begin until mid-1941; and it was not, therefore, until Barth was nearing the completion of *CD* II/2 that there was any such information to be known. In other words, the material on the doctrine of election was developed *before* the start of the Holocaust proper.

11. G M Kren & L Rappoport, *The Holocaust and the Crisis of Human Behaviour* (New York: Holmes & Meier, 1980), 73f.

125

and Sobibor. Consequently, whatever is to be said of Barth's understanding of election—and the Jews' place within it—as proposed in *CD* II/2, must be said in light of this context.

II

In order to appreciate the significance of dialectic within Barth's doctrine of election, the outlines of the doctrine itself must be understood. The first point to stress is that Barth's treatment of this doctrine is, strictly speaking, neither analogical nor dialectical. It is, rather, a *dogmatic* treatment that is strongly Christocentric. In the first part of his 'Doctrine of God', Barth insists that the dynamic of election is the freedom of God to be with those who are not God; His turning towards us is purely a function of His grace. It is a turning towards, not in equality, but in condescension (*CD* II/1, 311f).

With the graciousness of God's turning thus established as foundational, the correlative question then becomes, who is the object of election? Barth does not argue that generic humanity is the elect of God.[12] He refutes the notion that God's covenant partner is an abstract conception of 'humanity'. Nor is it 'a large or small total of individual men [*sic*]' (*CD* II/2, 8). Rather, the particular partner 'over against God which cannot be thought away . . . , which is so adjoined now to the reality of God that we cannot and should not say the word 'God' without at once thinking of it', is the man Jesus of Nazareth '*and the people represented in Him*' (*CD* II/2, 8).[13] That Israel and the Church are

---

12   This is despite what he says in *CD* III/3. In this volume, Barth suggests that the purpose of creation is the history of the gracious covenant between God and humanity. The divine decision for a covenantal relationship precedes creation as its presupposition and so, therefore, creation as such means election and not rejection (see *CD* III/1, 330-334).

13   My emphasis. Barth's position was based almost entirely on Pierre

the people represented in the primary election of Jesus is an idea to which we shall return later, and in which we shall see clearly a theological defence of both Israel and present-day Jews. We cannot proceed to that point, however, until we have delved into the essentially prior (and primal) election of Jesus, on which all the rest hangs.

Barth first submits that the idea of election denotes 'God in His movement towards [humanity] . . . ' (*CD* II/2, 7, 9). This movement is personalised in its identity with Jesus Christ, the Jewish man of Nazareth. It is here that Barth diverges from earlier theological paradigms, for the God-man exists as *both* the subjective and objective grounds of our election. In other words, Jesus is at once the electing God and the elected man. With this, we are referred back to the Chalcedonian formula of true God and true man, but the anhypostatic pole of Barth's Christology compels him to prioritise the *vere Deus*.

> Jesus Christ is the electing God. We must begin with this assertion because by its content it has the character and dignity of a basic principle, and because the other assertion, that Jesus Christ is elected man, can be understood only in the light of it (*CD* II/2, 103). [14]

On the basis of his exegesis of John 1:1-2, Barth claims that there can be no separation between the electing God and the Word

---

Maury's paper 'Election and Faith', which was presented at the 1936 'Congrès internationale de théologie calviniste' in Geneva, and at which Barth had been a delegate. See P Maury, *Erwählung und Glaube* (Theologische Studien 8: Zurich: EVZ, 1940). Maury's thesis, that outside of Jesus Christ we can know nothing of either the electing God or of His elect, and the subsequent corollary of a cross-centred understanding of election and reprobation, to which we shall come shortly, all find their clear echoes in Barth's doctrine. See McCormack, *op cit*, 455-458.

14. See also *CD* II/2, 107: 'the Son, too, is an active Subject of the *aeterna Dei praedestinatio* as Son of man, that he is Himself the electing God, and that only in this way . . . is He the Elect [man]'.

who is with Him in the beginning, and who is identifiable as Jesus Christ. How, Barth asks, 'are we to distinguish God's electing from His Word . . . ? Are we not forced to say that the electing consists in this Word and decree in the beginning; and conversely, that this Word' whose name is Jesus Christ . . . 'in the beginning [is] God's electing . . . ?' (*CD* II/2, 95-100). Barth's logic is simple. He contends that the question of election enjoys a precedence over all other tenets of faith that relate to the work of God, because 'in the act of love which determines His whole being God elects' It is the work which is intrinsic to the divine being. Or, as Barth puts it, God's electing of Himself for humankind and humankind for Himself 'is not one moment with others in the prophetic and apostolic testimony'. Rather, because it is enclosed 'within the testimony of God to Himself, it is the moment which is the substance and basis of all other moments in that testimony' (*CD* II/2, 76, 91).[15] This being the case, God is, in pre-temporal eternity, an electing God. But because the Word of God is with God in this pre-temporal beginning (John 1:1), and because the doctrine of *perichoresis* insists that the three persons of the Godhead are all mutual subjects in all the works of God, then the Word, who is Jesus Christ, is as such the electing God.

From here, Barth proceeds to add that Christ is also, and on the basis of the above, the elected man. While the eternal decree of God has the salvation of all humanity in its scope, it only moves to this universality from a prior particularity in the man from Nazareth. He stands as not merely one of the elect, but as *the* elect of God, with all others being subsequently elected only 'in him' (*CD* II/2, 116).[16] If, therefore, we are to understand our

---

15. See also C Gunton, 'Karl Barth's Doctrine of Election as part of his Doctrine of God', *Journal of Theological Studies* 25 (1974): 383f.

16. See also *CD* II/2, 51: 'In itself . . . the particular leads us to the general, which it includes within itself. For finally, of course, the election has to do with the whole of humanity . . . although materially it has to do first and exclusively with the one man, and

election, we must look solely to Jesus Christ, who is 'the particularity and concretion of the true God and true man' and who, for that reason, is *the* elect man (*CD* II/2, 51, 58f).

III

From this vantage point, Barth discusses the community of those who are elected in Christ, which is identified as 'the reality both of Israel and of the Church' (*CD* II/2, 196). It exists in the twofold form of Israel-Church, and it offers a twofold function of witness. Crucially, however, even in this duality of form and service, the *comm*unity of Israel and the Church is above all a *unity*.

> [T]he community as the primary object of the election
> which has taken place and takes place in Jesus Christ
> is one. Everything that is to be said of it in the light of
> the divine predestination will necessarily result in an
> emphasising of this unity (*CD* II/2, 197).

The existence of this unity is a function of the fact that 'the bow of the one covenant'—of grace—arches over both Israel and the Church.[17] As the presupposition of this claim, however, and to that extent the most fundamental basis of unity, stands Jesus

---

then with the specific members of the people which belong to
Him . . . [Thus] the doctrine of election is rightly grounded when
in respect of elected men as well as the electing God it does not
deal with a generality or abstraction in God or man, but with the
particularity and concretion of the true God and true man. It is
rightly grounded when only from that starting-point it goes on to
perceive . . . whatever there is of consequence about God or man
in general; from that starting-point, and not *vice versa*'.

17. As Barth notes in reference to Calvin, God's covenant with Israel
is '*substantia et re ipsa* not different from God's covenant with us
but identical with it' (*CD* I/2, 75). The difference between the two
testaments is merely 'a difference of *administratio* not of *substantia*'
(*CD* I/2, 76). See Calvin, *Institutes*, II x.2 & II xi.1.

Christ who, as the personification of the gracious covenant under which both exist, is

> the promised son of Abraham and David, the Messiah of Israel. And He is simultaneously the Head and Lord of the Church . . . In both these characters He is indissolubly one. And as the One He is ineffaceably both. As the Lord of the Church He is the Messiah of Israel, and as the Messiah of Israel He is Lord of the Church (*CD* II/2, 197f, 200).[18]

Consequently, Barth insists that we 'cannot, therefore, call the Jews the "rejected" and the Church the "elected" community. The object of election is neither Israel for itself nor the Church for itself, but both together in their unity' (*CD* II/2, 199).[19]

Barth seems clearly to be suggesting that he wants to present to us, not a dichotomous either-or, but a dialectical both-and, the poles of which must be held in tension. It is here that we can see the employment of Beintker's complementary dialectic, that species of dialectic which characterises the Elgersburg lecture

---

18 Note that Barth frequently recalls the Church to a recognition of solidarity with the Jews on this account, and says that where the Church sunders this unity it is no longer the Church (See, for example, *CD* II/2, 201, 234, 240). Moreover, as Busch says, 'In fact, the Christian Church can be the Church only in its inseparability from Israel . . .' Busch, *Unter dem Bogen*, 457).

19 Katherine Sonderegger also acknowledges Israel's election but insists that, according to Barth's doctrine, Israel has been 'elected for rejection', thus implying that God's No has the final word. K Sonderegger, *That Jesus Christ Was Born a Jew: Karl Barth's 'Doctrine of Israel'* (Pennsylvania: The Pennsylvania State University Press, 1992), 123, 129. David Demson ('Israel as the Paradigm of Divine Judgment: An Examination of a Theme in the Theology of Karl Barth', *Journal of Ecumenical Studies* 26 (1989): 613) does more justice to Barth's intention when he writes that 'Israel [the Jews] is not an anachronism. Barth referred to Israel as the passing form of the community, yet not as an anachronism, for Israel lives, and by God's will its members live as members of the one community of God'.

and which posits two opposing poles which engage in a perpetual to-ing and fro-ing, with neither progress nor resolution being made. In this case, neither Church nor Israel can be equated with each other but, just as surely, neither can be regarded in isolation from the other. They are, in effect, each other's flip-side and as shall be seen, what accrues to one accrues to the other, whether that be judgement or mercy. If the Church is Israel's future, Israel is nevertheless the origin from which the Church derives and without which it can and could never exist. As Barth puts it, '[o]nly unbelief with regard to Jesus Christ can try to separate here what God has joined together'(*CD* II/2, 201).[20]

> Whoever has Jesus Christ in faith cannot wish not to have the Jews. He must have them along with Jesus Christ as His ancestors and kinsmen. Otherwise he cannot have even the Jew Jesus. Otherwise with the Jews he rejects Jesus Himself. This is what is at stake, and therefore, in fact, the very basis of the Church, when it has to be demanded of Gentile Christians that they should not approach any Israelite without the greatest attention and sympathy (*CD* II/2, 289).

Indeed, the existence of Israel is the 'presupposition without which there would be no Church and no Gentile Christians' (*CD* II/2, 285). Evidently, because of the fact that the Elector-Elected Jesus of Nazareth, in all his necessary Jewishness, is himself the unity of the Church and Israel, there is a reconciliatory attitude of Christians towards Jews that Barth here enjoins.

A brief consideration of the so-called 'Judas passage' of §35 reveals the same commitment. Much of the objectionable

---

20 Busch notes that in dealing with the question of the Church-Israel relationship, Barth insists that the answer cannot be supplied by 'free floating positive or negative impressions, ideas, interpretations and wishes . . . ' (Busch, *Unter dem Bogem*, 402). Rather, it must be decided theologically, in conformity to the witness and sovereignty of Holy Scripture.

character of this excursus arises from Barth's focus upon Judas as the archetypal figure of rejection who, in turn, represents Israel as such. Significantly, however, Barth consistently refuses to regard Judas and/or Judas-Israel in isolation as the sole ciphers of sin and rejection. On the contrary, Judas himself stands in the closest proximity to the Church. He is 'undoubtedly a disciple and apostle'. Indeed, Barth suggests that of all the twelve, Judas is the one most appropriately called an apostle because 'he alone . . . belongs like Jesus to the tribe of Judah, the seed of David' (*CD* II/2, 459). Judas was in no sense a 'docetic' apostle, having only the appearance of apostleship. He was, rather, 'genuinely elect', albeit at the same time rejected (*CD* II/2, 459). But Barth goes even further. Far from identifying Judas exclusively with Israel, he insists that 'Jesus was handed over . . . *from within the Church*'. At this most decisive juncture 'the Church stands and acts in identity with the Israel which rejected its Messiah, together with the heathen world which allied itself with this Israel, and made itself a partner in its guilt' (*CD* II/2, 460). At this point, 'the apostles'—plural!—'have to share the guilt of Israel and the Gentile world . . . ' (*CD* II/2, 461). Not only was the work of Judas an act done within the Church, but it was something which *any* of the apostles *could* have done. 'To be sure, they have not actually done it or co-operated with him. But the point is that they obviously could have done it'. To this extent, the Church shares a point of contact with Israel. So, while 'the basic flaw was revealed in Judas . . . , it was that of the apostolate as a whole' (*CD* II/2, 471f, 475). Barth refuses to ascribe guilt for Jesus' death exclusively to either Judas or Israel. Sonderegger's argument that Barth sees the betrayal and death of Christ as a Jewish act is, therefore, too one-sided.[21] Barth does not suggest that Jews were totally innocent of the death of Jesus but, by arraigning the Church on the same charge, substantially reduces the potency

---

21. Sonderegger, *op cit*, 116.

with which the accusation can be used as a justification for Antisemitism.

Without gainsaying this indissoluble unity, it is nonetheless true that the Jewish form of the community has a very different function to the Church form. Whereas the service of the Church is to witness to God's mercy and proclaim the new life for which humankind has been elected in Christ, the distinctive witness of Israel is to the judgement of God and, therefore, to the frailty and death of the 'passing man [*sic*]'. When read in the ethical twilight after Auschwitz, this paradigm sounds disturbingly hostile.[22] The overall tenor of the section, however, argues against this being Barth's intention and, in fact, strongly suggests that his meaning lies in the very opposite direction.

The disobedience, or infidelity, of Israel to its election[23] does not negate Israel's service, even if this service is now executed unwillingly. While Barth's portrayal of unbelieving Israel's history and involuntary service is undeniably gloomy, this is not the final word. The key is to remember that Barth locates the doctrine of election within the doctrine of *God*. Because the electing God (Jesus Christ), who is eternally faithful to His election, is the basis of Barth's treatment of Israel, Barth is able to affirm a great 'Nevertheless', according to which faith, hope

---

22 Busch makes the comment that this is the very reason why some recent scholars (*e.g.* B Klappert, F-W Marquardt, W Krötke) have decided that they either cannot follow Barth at all in this part of his theology, or must severely recast his thinking in a post-Auschwitz world. Klappert, particularly, questions the legitimacy of speaking of Israel as a witness to the divine judgement after the Holocaust. See Busch's discussion of Klappert and his response in Busch, *Unter dem Bogem*, 438-440.

23 It is 'the people of the Jews which resists its divine election' in that it 'deliver[ed] up its Messiah, Jesus, to the gentiles for crucifixion . . .' (*CD* II/2, 198). Insofar as it is this disobedient community, it is represented in Barth's schema by the unbelieving Synagogue that exists over against the Church.

133

and life are posited as Israel's future, in contrast to its present misery and suffering.

Throughout §34, Barth repeatedly returns to the inviolability of God's faithfulness and election in the face of Israel's resistance. 'By their resistance to their election they cannot create any fact that finally turns the scale against their own election, separating them from the love of God in Jesus Christ, cancelling the eternal decree of God' (*CD* II/2, 209). Not by any action of its own—or, for that matter, by the actions of any other nation, such as Nazi Germany—can Israel 'annul the covenant of mercy . . . [or] alter the fact that the promise is given and applies to itself, that in and with the election of Jesus Christ *it and no other* is God's elected people . . . ' (*CD* II/2, 237).[24] There can be a dishonouring of one's election, a futile attempt to live in contradiction to it, but no such attempt can change the reality of the Jews' divine election which is, as such, an election to grace and life (*CD* II/2, 243, 249).[25]

IV

Perhaps the most instructive of Barth's statements that confirm the Jews' ongoing election occur in his exegesis of Romans 9-11 with which he punctuates this section. It is here that we once again begin to see his employment of dialectics.[26] Referring to

---

24. My emphasis. Similarly, '. . . the grace of God cannot weaken, the covenant of peace cannot fail' (*CD* II/2, 399).
25. Or, as he was to say in 1945, 'Yahweh is always the Lover, the Bridegroom and Husband. And His lost people is always His Beloved, His Bride and His Wife . . . We have to reckon with the unfaithfulness of the Wife, but never with the unfaithfulness of the Husband. We have to reckon with her rejection and abandonment, but not with a bill of divorce' (*CD* III/1, 316).
26. Significantly, Busch notes that although these Pauline chapters are the *locus classicus* for a biblical exposition of the relationship between Israel and the Church, this theme did not occupy Barth

Paul's analogy of the potter (Romans 9:20-21), Barth identifies Israel as the 'vessel of dishonour' and the Church as the 'vessel of honour', with Israel's distinctive service being to 'witness to the divine judgment' (CD II/2, 223f)[27] Initially, it seems that Barth is positing two qualitatively different futures for the two communities (or better, the two parts of the *one* community). He insists, however, that this is not the case. We completely misunderstand the thrust of Paul's argument if we assume that the analogy implies 'a juxtaposition of two different purposes of God'.

> The twofold action of the potter does not by any means take place along parallel lines, in symmetry and equilibrium, so that proceeding from a centre of indifference . . . God will now accept and now reject . . . [Rather] His operation εἰς τιμήν is one thing and His operation εἰς ἀτιμίαν is another, and they stand in an irreversible sequence and order (CD II/2, 224).

---

in either of his two earlier commentaries on the epistle in 1919 and 1922. Rather, Busch feels that it was due to the 'confrontation with the anti-Semitic struggles of the [Nazi] time' that Barth's eyes were opened to the necessity of this theme. Once he had come to this realisation, however, Barth did not ignore it. As he said at the World Conference of Churches in Amsterdam in 1948, the 'Jewish question' is the 'central theological question' for Christianity, to which Christianity cannot approach without recourse in the first instance to these three chapters. For this discussion see Busch, *Unter dem Bogen*, 404 and cf K Barth, 'Amsterdamer Fragen und Antworten', *Theologische Existenz heute*, (1949): 14.

27. Demson says that Barth did not intend to speak disparagingly of the Jews. Moreover, he believes that Barth's exegesis of Romans 9-11 is 'extensive, profound, and coherent . . . '. It does not stray far from Paul's presentation and, therefore, cannot lightly be dismissed. Demson does, however, argue that Barth's treatment can, in the light of the Holocaust, be recast in such a way as to make Gentile Christians, rather than Jews, paradigmatic of divine judgement. See Demson, *op cit*, 611f, 619-627.

135

There is a Yes and a No spoken, but they are related in an unequal dialectic whereby the No exists only for the sake of, *and on the way towards*, the Yes. If, as has been argued above, the unity of Church-Israel complies with the characteristics of complementary dialectic, this rather more asymmetrical image of the two services offered by the Church and Israel conforms to a 'supplementary dialectic'. This type of dialectic, which Michael Beintker finds in the 1919 *Romans* commentary, insists that the two opposing poles do not remain in unresolved tension, nor are they resolved into the synthesis of a higher third. Rather, one overpowers and subsumes the other.[28] In other words, the 'harsh appearance that can descend . . . as if God's mercy and hardening, the existence of 'vessels of honour' and of 'dishonour' were the two goals of two different ways of God—is now finally dispelled' (*CD* II/2, 224f, 227). To Barth's mind, the end of the ways of God is the resolution of the dialectic in favour of the Yes, that is, of His mercy. And this, it is to be stressed, is as applicable to Israel as to the Church. Indeed, '[i]f God's mercy is so rich and powerful even upon Gentiles who were standing wholly under His curse and sentence of rejection, how much more so upon [Israel] to whom He has already promised it!' (*CD* II/2, 231).[29]

This fidelity of God to His people and His promise, and the inability of humankind in any sense to condition or delimit the efficacy of God's work, is the reason why Barth is compelled to affirm a vital and hopeful future for Israel. The Jews remain the original elect community, whose election is neither abrogated nor suspended by their present resistance to the gospel. Despite this resistance, 'the fundamental blessing, the election, is still

---

28 Beintker, *op cit*, 38f; McCormack, *op cit*, 163.
29 Barth's reference is to the fact that, prior to the incarnation, the Gentiles were outside the covenant community and only *post Christum natum* have been included in the promises of election which were previously Israel's alone. See Ephesians 2:11-13.

confirmed . . . [The] final word is one of testimony to the divine Yes to Israel . . . ' (CD II/2, 15).[30] According to him,

> Beloved! . . . is the last word which in every present and in respect of every member of this people has to be taken into account in relation to Israel's history from its beginnings into every conceivable or inconceivable future. Not the first, but definitely the last word! . . . But this is also the last word even in relation to the present of unbelieving Jews (CD II/2, 303).

The Jews of all ages, in faith or in unbelief, are the beloved of God. With this as the ultimate divine attitude towards Israel, Barth was unable—especially in the midst of the Nazi atrocities—to demand anything less from the Church with which Israel was and is bound in indissoluble unity.

---

[30] Has God cast off His chosen Israel?, Barth asks in relation to Romans 11:1. Μη γενοιτο, he answers, along with Paul. This question faced by the apostle is 'the question asked by Christian anti-semitism, whether the crucifixion of Jesus Christ does not settle the fact that the Jews are now to be regarded and treated only as the people accursed by God'. But this question is an 'anti-semitic question . . . of unbelief, and those who put this question can only be called to repentance with the utmost urgency' (CD II/2, 269, 273). Because this question has this character, Barth not only rejects its validity, but also insists that it can only be answered negatively. In no sense, therefore, does Barth sanction traditional Christian supercessionism. Sonderegger (*op cit*, 6) is mistaken in her opinion that Barth's language and logic inevitably entail this commitment. He does not, as she wants to argue, represent 'the broadest tradition of Christian anti-Judaism, preserving, sharpening, and elaborating the controversial doctrine [of supercessionism] that has been standard . . . since Justin Martyr'.

V

To return finally to Barth's Christological formulation of this doctrine, it can be demonstrated that the impact this dogmatic base has on his understanding of the individual's election is incompatible with any notion of a general and final reprobation of the Jews. Barth renegotiates the Calvinistic idea of double predestination (to life and to death) by centring it upon the incarnation. There is a double predestination, to both election and rejection, but its object is not humankind in part or in full, but is once again located in the person of Jesus Christ. Not only, therefore, is he the electing God and the elected man, he is also the elected and *rejected* man. We must recognise both Abel *and* Cain, Isaac *and* Ishmael, as types of Christ (*CD* II/2, 366). As well as both the subjective and objective poles of election finding their focus in Christ, so too do the subjectively experienced realities of election and rejection.[31]

This entails far-reaching consequences for our view of both humankind and God. According to Barth, the humanity which is elected by God is a fallen humanity, in resolute enmity towards God. Necessarily, therefore, God's condescension into the state of this humanity—in the incarnation—means that 'He declared Himself guilty of the contradiction against Himself in which man was involved . . . 'By electing to rescue humankind from its fate through the assumption of full humanity by the Word of God, God 'made Himself the object of the wrath and judgment to which man [sic] had brought himself . . . He took upon Himself the rejection [damnation and death] which man had deserved' (*CD* II/2, 164).[32] What God has done is to have

---

31. Barth has adopted this directly from Maury's *Erwählung und Glaube*.

32. See also *CD* II/2, 315: 'Predestined man is simply forgiven man [who] . . . is not met by honour and approval, but by justification by grace alone, by forgiveness; who is not the object of divine election in virtue of a life which is acceptable and welcome to

elected Himself to suffer vicariously the punishment deservedly placed on humankind, in order that humanity may be elected to life. Thus,

> [F]or man it means infinite gain . . . But for God it means inevitably a certain compromising of Himself that He should determine to enter into this covenant. Where man stands only to gain, God stands only to lose. And because the eternal predestination is identical with the election of Jesus Christ, its twofold content is that God wills to lose in order that man may gain (*CD* II/2, 162).[33]

Consequently, we are forbidden by Barth's programme to think of God's election as 'bifurcating into a rightward and a leftward election' in respect of humanity. 'There is a leftward election. But God willed that the object of this election should be Himself and not man' (*CD* II/2, 172).

Barth's recurring theme, therefore, is that humankind—not the *Jews* specifically, but *humankind as such*—is fully deserving of rejection, but that this rejection has been borne by God Himself (*CD* II/2, 306, 322-324, 348). There is no one who stands apart from this promise. Indeed, the chief service of the community of God is to proclaim to everyone that they are elect. If the witness of the Church is to be 'solely Gospel, this cannot be an exclusive Gospel, to be withheld from this or that one, and having a serious reference and application only to this or that other one' (*CD* II/2, 325). This implies, moreover, a

---

> God, but because God covers, transforms and renews his unworthy and rebellious life; whom the sovereign God . . . encounters, not with a natural Therefore, but with a miraculous Nevertheless'.

33. Regarding Jesus Christ as elected to suffer, see *CD* II/2, 177-118. To a certain degree, Jesus' passion is the goal of his election. See also J Daane, *The Anatomy of Anti-Semitism and Other Essays on Religion and Race* (Grand Rapids: Eerdmans, 1965), 58; E Allen, *The Sovereignty of God and the Word of God: A Guide to the Thought of Karl Barth* (London: Hodder & Stoughton, 1950), 36-37.

fundamental ignoring of the question of faith or unbelief. As far as Barth is concerned, the proclamation of the Church must continually call the divided together by proclaiming to believers their merited rejection and to unbelievers their unmerited election, and to both the One in whom they are elect and not rejected (*CD* II/2, 326).

Consequently, there can be belief only *for* unbelievers, not *against* them. On what possible grounds can the unbeliever be regarded as rejected? Rejection is not, for Barth, an equally open and valid course (*CD* II/2, 326f, 349f, 416). With this in mind, it should be clear that Barth's explication of election, and of our rejection which is borne by Christ, permits no privileging of Christians over against Jews on the spurious, anti-Judaic assumption of Christian theological tradition, that the latter are rejected and the former elected by God. On the contrary, Christ's vicarious bearing, and therefore the rejection, of our rejection entails a level playing field on which the question of faith or unbelief is radically subordinated to the power and universality of the divine work.

It is, of course, true that not everyone lives according to their election. As has been seen in respect of Israel, however, Barth insists that this does not negate God's decision. According to his paradigm, all exist within the sphere of the divine election of grace, some obediently, others disobediently, but nevertheless all. For those who exist there in disobedience, their attempt to deny their election is futile. Because God has elected Jesus to be *the* rejected, it is 'objectively impossible' for anyone else to ultimately triumph against their own election (*CD* II/2, 346).[34]

---

34. It is important to see that Barth explicitly rules out the validity of the teaching of *apokatastasis*—universal salvation (*CD* II/2, 416-417)—although many commentators have queried the logical coherency with which he does so. Such commentators include C Brown, *Karl Barth and the Christian Message* (London: Tyndale Press, 1967), 130-133, 151; G C Berkouwer, *The Triumph of Grace in*

There is, in other words, a 'triumph of grace' in Barth's theology of election that renders the No of God against humanity ultimately impotent in the face of the divine Yes. In other words, if we return to the central argument of the paper, we can say that while the dogmatic basis of this doctrine is assuredly Christological, the methodological framework makes creative use of dialectic. In the 1919 edition of *Romans*, the relationships he posited between 'real history' and 'so-called history', and between real and unreal humanity (the one in Christ, the other in Adam respectively) exemplified supplementary dialectic. In 1942, it was the Yes of God triumphing over the No, the election over the rejection. In both examples, from *Romans* and *CD* II/2, the two opposing poles do not continue in perpetual contradiction, but find resolution in an ultimate prioritising of one over against the other. Therefore, as far as the triumph of election is concerned, the doctrine

> is not a mixed message of joy and terror, salvation
> and damnation . . .It does not proclaim in the same
> breath good and evil, both help and destruction, both
> life and death. It does, of course, throw a shadow . . .
> The Yes cannot be heard unless the No is also heard.
> But the No is said for the sake of the Yes and not for
> its own sake (*CD* II/2, 13, 27-29).

The end result is that all people, irrespective of their attitude of faith and of their race, are enclosed within the sphere of election and, therefore, of grace and life. If there exists the threat of

---

the Theology of Karl Barth (Grand Rapids: Eerdmans, 1956), *passim*; perhaps also A E McGrath, *Christian Theology: An Introduction* (Blackwell Publishers, 1994; repr 1995), 364f, 400-402. What can and must be said, however, is that, if Barth does admit the possibility of the actual rejection of some, the primacy of election means that it cannot be argued that according to his formulation of the doctrine, Jews *per se* are rejected or even specifically prone to it. The question is, for Barth, totally irrespective of race.

rejection, there exists as the greater reality in which it is enclosed, the promise of election (*CD* II/2, 324).[35]

VI

We began our consideration of Barth's doctrine of election by noting that it was formulated during the Holocaust. In spite of this context, and the fact that many of his fellow theologians were using the Holocaust to vindicate their belief in Israel's rejection, the above study shows that Barth's doctrine offers an affirmation of Israel and present-day Jews. He does so by utilising both a Christological dogmatic base and (just as importantly) a dialectical methodology. His employment of complementary dialectic forbids us from separating the Church and Israel—what can be said of one, must be said of the other, and there can be no resolution *against* one in favour of the other. But Barth also uses a supplementary dialectic to privilege election over rejection. Certainly, some of Barth's language remains offensive when read in the aftermath of the *Shoah*, and must be reworded if his work on election is to be used within the context of Jewish-Christian dialogue. But, when both the Christological *and dialectical* aspects of his critical apparatus are recognised, we can legitimately claim that Barth's more unfortunate phraseology is not representative of his doctrine itself, but that indeed the intention of his approach, when purged of these linguistic short-comings, is to conclusively affirm the elect status of the Jews.

---

35. To put it the other way around, Busch (*Unter dem Bogen*, 405) argues that Barth was determined to prove that if one lets the text of Romans 9-11 speak for itself, it speaks of 'God's irrevocable covenant with Israel and of the indissoluble connection between the Church and Israel'. But, to speak of this means that one must also utter statements that, in isolation, appear to be harsh and deprecatory.

To conclude, Barth did not cease his employment of dialectical theology in 1931. Just as analogy was present in his *Romans* days, dialectic was present within the *Church Dogmatics*. Moreover, it is vitally important that this is the case, because it was precisely this usage of dialectic which gave affirmatory strength to his doctrine of election, at the very time when the 'Final Solution' threatened to rob it of all integrity.

Part Three

Studying Barth after Modernity:
Emerging Challenges

Barth's Theology of Work and Vocation for a Postmodern World[1]

Gordon Preece

I

Karl Barth's theological correction to the modern over-estimatio[n] work and the identification of vocation with paid employment [?] has much to offer a post or hyper-modern world torn betw[een] overwork and underwork and where life-long 'vocation' relatively rare. The modern master narratives of vocation and Protestant Work Ethic have, when read with a hermeneutic suspicion, been seen to be often ideological justifications for s[o] becoming masters and others slaves. Miroslav Volf's *Work in Spirit* has questioned the adequacy of these models fo[r] postmodern theology of work and thus provides a useful foil to the contemporary adequacy of Barth's view of work and rework of the vocation tradition.[2]

While space constraints forbid a full discussion of the Protes[tant] vocation tradition, suffice it to say that it begins with Luth[er's] application of 1 Corinthians 7:20 'stay in the calling in which [you] were called' to not only Christian conversion (the general N[ew] Testament sense), nor to monastic calling (the post-Constantin[ian]

---

1. Adapted from G Preece, *The Viability of the Vocation Tradition in Trinitarian, Credal and Reformed Perspective* (Lewiston NY: Edwin Mellen Press, 1998), Chapter 5. Used by permission. Chapter 4 of the same work provides substantial background on Barth's primarily christocentric theology.
2. M Volf, *Work in the Spirit: Toward a Theology of Work* (New York: Oxford University Press, 1991). My primary focus, though, is not to set Barth and Volf in opposition.

sense), but to one's calling to ordinary work, familial and citizenship roles.[3]

Volf criticises the Lutheran protological vocation tradition as incapable of transforming postmodern work. Its identification of work and vocation is unbiblical (misreading 1 Corinthians 7:20 as calling to work not conversion), socially conservative (sanctifying rigidly hierarchical roles), susceptible to ideological misuse (to religiously justify dehumanising work as God's calling) and unable to consistently justify change of one's work because of the analogy between immutable spiritual and external vocation (if once called to salvation, always called, so also to one's secular vocation. You have one vocation and it is a life sentence, like it or not).[4]

To claim that Barth could meet Volf's tests, we must demonstrate that Barth's christologically revised Reformed vocation theology is more biblical, less susceptible to ideology, and more open to change and transformation of working situations than Lutheran and modern views of work and vocation.

I will argue that Barth anchors his theology and ethics of work and vocation to the divine and human freedom focussed on God's self-election in Christ and our election of God in Christ. In partnership with his threefold trinitarian, but primarily christocentric view of God's eternity as pre-, supra- and post-temporal, Barth successfully revises the idea of the immutability of God's nature, election and vocation so central to Volf's critique and so problematic in a mobile postmodern working world.

Further, Barth sees vocation's christological centre in election (*CD* II/2) and the covenant of reconciliation (*CD* IV/3) as the inner dynamic of vocation in the ethics of creation (*CD* III/4). This largely overcomes the problems of overly static and protological views of vocation. However, this is perhaps achieved by pushing work too far to the margins under the banner of creation and divine providence.

---

3. See Preece, *op cit*, Chapters 1 and 3.
4. Volf, *op cit*, 107-10. See Preece, *op cit*, Chapter 3 for responses to Volf's critique.

I will next explore Barth's criteria of human work in the light of his christocentric and personalist anthropology, asking whether it provides a suitable basis for resisting work ideologies and transforming alienating work. Then, Barth's view of vocation will be examined for its biblical credentials and capacity to maintain the biblical dynamism of vocation or calling to God's kingdom in the light of his central doctrine and ethics of reconciliation and his treatment of vocation. Finally, Barth's theology of work and vocation will be evaluated in the light of the criticisms levelled against it.

A Christocentric Theology of Divine and Human Temporality

For Barth, Christ is the ground of all human activity and vocation - 'in him is the impulse to work, to struggle, and also the impulse towards fellowship, towards human solidarity'[5] and justice. This is a consistent thread from Barth's 'socialist' Safenwil period as pastor-theologian on to his mature academic (but not apolitical) theology.[6]

Barth's christological revision of notions of eternity, immutability and election (spiritual calling) breaks down the alleged analogy between immutability in spiritual vocation (election) and external vocation. It thus provides a possible basis for a revamped and more mobile view of vocation (external calling). Though Barth's Reformed theology is thoroughly trinitarian, that trinitarianism pivots around the Word incarnate through the key doctrines of election (*CD* II/2) and reconciliation (*CD* IV/1-4). Their twin affirmations of God and humanity in Christ function like an

---

5.   E Busch, *Karl Barth: His Life from Letters and autobiographical Texts* (London: SCM, 1976), 496.
6.   See Barth's 1911 lecture, 'Jesus Christ and the Social Movement', in G Hunsinger (ed), *Karl Barth and Radical Politics* (Philadelphia: Westminster, 1976), Chapter 1; Eberhard Jüngel, *Karl Barth, a Theological Legacy* (Philadelphia: Westminster Press, 1986).

hourglass[7] through which all concepts must pass, including divine and human temporality.

Barth's innovative perspective on God's 'pre-, supra-, and post-temporality', does not follow the traditional opposition of time and eternity but reconciles them in Christ, in correspondence to creation, reconciliation, and redemption. God's triune, christologically conditioned temporality allows no static theological or anthropological categories, but requires 'an attitude of continual openness and receptivity'.[8]

Barth's radical revision of the immutability of God's being, electing and calling is applied through his Christ-centered, relational and temporally oriented anthropology (*CD* III/2). It sets humanity in the time of Christ and views providence as a divine accompanying of humanity on its temporal journey (*CD* III/3). This anthropology then undergirds both his ethics of creation (*CD* III/4) and his dynamic views on work and vocation which help overcome the immutability Volf criticises in the classical vocation tradition.

Structural Priority of Election, Covenant & Reconciliation over Creation

Barth further counters the tendency towards immutable vocation of Luther's relatively static first article theology, by focusing on Christ as the centre of election, and covenant and reconciliation as the inner dynamic of creation (*CD* III/1). 'The Command of God the Creator' (*CD* III/4) does not isolate protology but anticipates 'The Doctrine of Reconciliation'(*CD* IV/1-4).

This structurally relativises work by earthing it in Christ, 'the inner ground of creation and the centre and meaning of the whole cosmos and history' (*CD* III/4, 660). The creation orders are revealed, renamed and reframed through his christological

---

7.   H U von Balthasar, *The Theology of Karl Barth* (San Francisco: Ignatius Press, 1992), 197f.

8.   R E Willis, *The Ethics of Karl Barth* (Leiden: E J Brill, 1971), 121f.

anthropology as the four freedoms or 'definite spheres and relationships' constituting humanity (*CD* III/4, 29-31).[9] The table below highlights the parallels to Barth's incarnational anthropology in III/2 (noted in *CD* III/4, 43-5):

III/4	III/2
§53 'Freedom Before God' on the Holy day, in confession & prayer	§44 'Man as the Creature of God'—an elect being in a covenantal history
§54 'Freedom in Fellowship' as male and female in community, family and neighbourliness.	§45 'Man . . . as Covenant partner of God'—a being in I thou encounter as God's image
§55 'Freedom for Life' as God's loan and for the active life as our task	§46 'Man as Soul and Body' under God's Spirit
§56 'Freedom in Limitation"	§47 'Man in His Time'—a being with a God-given limited span.

Barth corrects the horizontal tendency of the created orders of his 1928 *Ethics*[10] by placing the vertical dimension of 'Freedom before God' (election, human freedom and responsibility to love God, remembered in sabbath, confession and prayer), before the horizontal relations of co-humanity, life and limitation. This effectively subordinates human work to God's work.[11]

---

9   The four horizontal relationships in the spheres of divine-human encounter "might very well be called orders [*Ordnungen*]" except for the risk of legalistic misunderstanding (III/4, 29). See further, Nigel Biggar, *The Hastening that Waits: Karl Barth's Ethics* (Oxford: Clarendon Press, 1993), 52.

10   K Barth, *Ethics* (New York: Seabury Press, 1981).

11.   Biggar, *op cit*, 57f, 62.

Gordon Preece

The Holy Day as First and Last Day Relativises Work

This vertical stress is exemplified in the structural priority of 'The Holy Day'. There is, for Barth, no positive scriptural command to work, whereas there is an emphatic call to rest. We rest before we work (*CD* III/4, 52, cf 482). This reminds increasingly totalitarian work societies that we live by God's work and creation, not by our own, nor even by our participation in God's complete and inimitable work (*CD* III/4, 60, 63).

Yet while Barth's vertical emphasis on the Holy Day subordinates human work, it also sustains it. As throughout the *Church Dogmatics*, the pretended autonomy of all created realities is subject to a dialectical No-Yes pattern. So, 'The Holy Day' relativises human work (*CD* III/4, 49, 50) before reaffirming it christologically. Barth thus asks: 'Is not the paradoxical 'activity' of the holy day the origin of all other activity?' (*CD* III/4, 51).

Therefore the week begins, not ends, with a holy day, a reminder of 'true' or resurrection time in which all things are realised. Calling upon God for salvation precedes our secular calling (*CD* III/2, 458), for we are not justified by our jobs, but by God's sabbatical yes to creation in Christ. Humanity is therefore more than Marx's or managerialism's *homo faber*. Nonetheless, in a less Promethean sense, we are still workers (*CD* III/4, 54) sent forth 'into the other days of the week' (*CD* IV/3, 53). Humanity is no mere *homo religiosus* either

Work as Part, not the Whole of the Active Life

Under the heading 'Freedom in Fellowship' Barth further subordinates work by first applying his personalist and Christ-centered anthropology to male-female, parent-child and neighbourly relationships. This accent on the relational and sexual interpretation of God's image is designed to avoid the problematic links between, on the one hand, the Reformed tradition's tendency to interpret God's image in terms of dominion over creation[12], and on the other hand, the development of capitalism, technology, the work ethic and western culture.[13]

In the paragraph 'Freedom for Life', life is firstly a gift and a loan, and only then a task within the broader category of 'The Active Life' (*CD* III/4, 470-564). Barth downplays the modern western employment ethos by locating work at the circumference of human activity in analogy to divine providence at 'the circumference of God's activity' (*CD* III/4, 517). Vocation will then mainly be related to God's coming kingdom community as the paradigm of divine action. Thus, for Barth, the distinctively *human* action is neither Marxism's social labour[14] nor capitalism's individualistic labour, but our vocation or calling to God's kingdom (*CD* III/4, 475, 493). Put christologically rather than eschatologically, the center of human action and vocation is witnessing to reconciliation in Christ at the center of God's triune action, and invoking social transformation through God's coming kingdom (*CD* IV/3, 481-680 and *CL*, 85-109).[15]

Ordinary work, the creation mandate and culture are thus put in their place. Instead of cultural enterprise, economic necessity is the basic biblical reason for work.[16] Hence Protestant fascination with

---

12 The Reformed interpretation of God's image as dominion is backed by D Clines, 'The Image of God in Man', *Tyndale Bulletin* 19 (1968): 53-103 and John Paul II's *Laborem Exercens* 4.1.

13 For Barth, 'the myth of modern Western civilisation with its ethos of work' is not due to God's command but to 'the pressure of recent developments in European economy and economics'. 'We search . . . the New Testament in vain for the passion with which the 'subdue the earth' of Genesis 1:28 has been interpreted and applied since the 16th century' (*CD* III/4, 472f).

14 P West, 'Karl Barth's Theology of Work: A Neglected Resource for the Late 1980s', *Modern Churchman* 30.3 (1988): 14-17.

15 See Preece, *op cit*, 176-83 and G Badcock, *The Way of Life: A Theology of Christian Vocation* (Grand Rapids: Eerdmans, 1998), who, however, ignores creational vocation in *CD* III/4.

16 Quoting Psalm 90:10, 104:23 and Proverbs 6:6-11, Genesis 3:17 and

'the importance of work to human personality and as a cultural enterprise, is very much in the background'. Christ called his disciples away from their ordinary work rather than to it. Paul has no positive view of work in general, nor of his tentmaking, which is marginal to his apostolic calling. He merely corrects by example and exhortation abuses of apostolic privilege, escapology (escapist eschatology) and the perception of Christians as disorderly (*CD* III/4, 472).[17]

By picturing work as only part of 'The Active Life', Barth salvages the best of the contemplative tradition[18] while retaining the Reformation critique of its Greek and monastic elitism and indolence. But he rejects the Reformers' identification of the active life with secular work only and their divinising of work as worship (*CD* III/4, 474), the danger of which was hidden by a less openly exploitative economic order than prevailed in the nineteenth century (*CD* III/4, 536-37).

Rather than any spiritualising direct analogy between divine and human work[19] advocated by modern co-creationist work theologies,[20] Barth prefers the more modest concept of creaturely 'correspondence' to God's work,(*CL* 175)[21] or 'service' to the kingdom community (*CD* III/4, 471-75). Humanity is neither 'co-creator, co-saviour or co-regent in God's activity', not a 'co-God' nor 'a second Jesus Christ' (*CD* III/4, 482).

Barth establishes an analogy between divine and human action as both having a centre and circumference. The centre corresponds

---

Ecclesiastes.

17. Citing Acts 18:3, 2 Thessalonians 3:8, 10f.
18. See *CD* IV/2, 551 on Protestantism's 'fear of the bogey of monasticism' and its ignoring of Jesus' proclamation of freedom from family and other orders (cf *CD* III/4, 472).
19. Barth can even say there is an 'absolute unlikeness' between God and humanity (*CD* III/4, 104).
20. On the modesty of Barth's ethics generally see John Webster, *Barth's Ethics of Reconciliation* (Cambridge: Cambridge University Press, 1995), 97.
21. See further, *Ibid*, 197-99.

to the internal covenant of election in Christ while the circumference corresponds to its external setting in creation. The basis of analogy and criterion for truly human action in accord with God's primary covenantal/kingdom action and secondary creative action is 'the active life of Jesus Christ Himself'. We mimic Christ's gracious activity in word and deed for the world within our own creaturely circles by doing the primary 'work of discipleship'. Service corresponds 'centrally' to the coming of Christ's kingdom community (*CD* III/4, 483, cf III/1 and III/3, 3), not 'cultural activity', and 'around this centre' to God's providential rule (*CD* III/4, 485-87, 474f, cf III/3, § 48, 49) over creation and work. The unique and urgent work of proclaiming Christ pushes secular work to the 'circumference' under the banner of God's providence (*CD* III/4, 487).

Yet in Barth's schema the creation circumference of God's covenantal action is still significant. Here human work corresponds to God's providence in affirming creaturely existence. Because God's providence previews 'the coming of His one kingdom on earth' there is no duality of divine or human action into separate spheres or laws as in the Lutheran 'double kingdom' (*CD* III/4, 517f).

However, there is a hierarchy. Work keeps body and soul together, but reflects the intimate but hierarchical relation between the two in Barth's anthropology (*CD* III/2, §46). Ordinary work is a '*parergon* of that *ergon*' or proper work of obedient faith (*CD* III/4, 523f, cf 487). It is 'man's active affirmation of his existence as a human creature'. We work to survive as creatures in order that we might serve and thrive as Christians (*CD* III/4, 518-19, cf 525-26).[22]

---

22   I. Siker ('An Unlikely Dialogue: Barth and Business Ethicists on Human Work', D M Yeager (ed), *The Annual of the Society of Christian Ethics* [Washington: Georgetown University Press, 1989] 134) notes: 'Whereas for Barth self-preservation functions positively as a springboard for serving God and neighbour, in the field of business ethics it functions negatively as a justifiable limit to other-oriented action . . . moral obligation ends where

Gordon Preece

Yet, work distinguishes humans from other non-working creatures and from God (*CD* III/4, 521-23). Barth thus partly accepts Marx's Hegelian view of work as humanity's distinctiveness.[23] However, work is not only an act of autonomous 'self-affirmation' as in Hegel and Marx but for Barth also an act of creaturely 'self-moderation', 'marking a line of demarcation' from the Creator.[24]

Christo-Anthropology and the Criteria of Human Work

As noted earlier, the motifs of Barth's christological anthropology predominate in his general treatment of work and vocation in *CD* III/4. This is particularly so in his criteria for work at the (still significant) circumference of human activity which actively affirms human existence as illustrated below.[25]

III/4 §.47 Work Criteria	III/4 Four Freedoms	III/2 Christo-Anthropology
Objectivity—purposeful work with heart & soul	§.53 'Freedom Before God' on the Holy Day, in confession & prayer	§.44 'Man as the Creature — an elect being in a covenantal history
Worth—not trivial, dishonest, harmful, dehumanizing		
Co-humanity—community not competition or isolation	§ 54 'Freedom in Fellowship' as male & female in community, family & neighbourliness.	§.45 Man as God's Covenant partner — in I-thou encounter as God's image.

livelihood is threatened'.

23. Cf K Marx, *Capital*, Vol 1, (Moscow: 1954); 173f and K Marx, *Grundrisse* (Hammondsworth: Penguin, 1973) 611 cited in T J Gorringe, *Capital and the Kingdom* (London/Maryknoll: SPCK/Orbis, 1994), 74 and 182 n66. Gorringe, however, fails to qualify Barth's following of Marx in his enthusiasm for parallels (cf 59, 75).
24. Willis, *op cit*, 322.
25. Cf Siker, *op cit*, 140.

156

| Reflectivity—rational & soul work | §.55 'Freedom for life' as God's loan & for the active life as our task | §.46 'Man as Soul & Body under God's Spirit |
| Limitation—allowing for leisure & Sabbath rest | §.56 'Freedom in Limitation' | §.47 'Man in His Time' —with a God-given limited span |

The first criterion of objectivity[26] or purposeful work involves the distinctively human immersion in doing justice to a task's object or end (*CD* III/4, 527-29). Though work is not an end in itself, it as a relative end demanding our best efforts.

The second criterion asks whether the purposes of work towards which humans give their best are worthwhile. Is work honest and useful, promoting 'advancements, ameliorations, illumination and perhaps even adornments of human existence?' This could exclude 'whole industries' including much amusement, consumerism, bureaucracy, even academia, which, despite their diligence and objectivity, is often mere 'busy idleness'. At least work should not be 'injurious or ruinous' *e.g.* the armaments industry or financial speculation. Such work should be condemned as it was by the Early Church (*CD* III/4, 530-31).

Thirdly, Barth's personalist anthropology anchors 'our co-existence and co-operation' in praying for and earning '*our* daily bread'. Work should be social work, not isolated, competitive and inhuman—violating our co-humanity (*CD* III/4, 536-38). His democratic socialism criticises both Communist managerially manipulative forms of co-operation and 'free' labour contracts dictated by western capitalists. Both approaches reduce workers to inhuman means to their economic ends (*CD* III/4, 542f).

Fourthly, the criterion of reflectivity is based in Barth's anthropology of the human being as soul and subject. Therefore the internal or spiritual work of reflection and planning precedes external work. This is Barth's more optimistic equivalent of Marx's

---

26   In German '*Sachlichkeit*' has some different connotations to English 'objectivity' *i.e.* 'matter-of-factness' or 'getting down to business'. See Siker, *op cit*, 143, n6.

famous contrast of the architect and bee, humanity and animals.[27] Reflective work is possible even in situations of unemployment, mind-numbing mechanical work, sickness or domestic drudgery (*CD* III/4, 546-49).

Finally, for work to further our freedom it must be restricted against all totalitarianisms of work, whether capitalist or communist. Human work is secondary to God's completed work in creation and redemption, as the sabbath regularly reminds us. This is the antidote for the tension and compulsion of work (*CD* III/4, 550-53).

In sum, Barth's criteria for work are similar to Marx's and Volf's criteria for ensuring that work and workers are not alienated as mere means but rather treated as ends in themselves.[28] He is concerned that workers are not alienated from their task (objectivity and worthwhileness), their humanity (reflectivity) nor their fellows (co-humanity). Barth affirms social and ecclesiastical ways of countering such alienation, but they are only partial solutions compared to our real end found in the coming of God's kingdom and anticipated in the weekly sabbath. Barth's criteria provide a basis for a postmodern work ethic, especially for those most effected by the current corrupted version, the unemployed (including the sick and disabled), the bored worker and the workaholic.

---

27. 'What distinguishes the worst architect from the best of bees is this, that the architect raises its structure in imagination before he erects it in reality. At the end of every labour process, we get a result that already existed in the imagination of the labourer at its commencement' (Marx, *Capital*, 174).
28. Though Volf (*op cit*, 170-72) is more explicit in his use of these Kantian and Marxist themes.

Vocation as Freedom in Created Limitation

In response to Volf's critique of the vocation tradition, I stressed earlier the importance of Barth's view of divine and human temporality in Christ for reformulating the immutability of spiritual and external calling. I will now examine its vocational outworking as 'Freedom in Limitation' (§.56). In creaturely limitation rather than false exaltation we find the definition that is true freedom, freedom to act out our true nature in Christ (*CD* IV/3, 575f).

As Christians first we only know true creatureliness and humanity as centred and elected in Christ (*CD* III/4, 578) in a specific time, place and opportunity. Like Christ we should revel in the 'long and mighty opportunity' (*CD* III/4, 580) provided by our temporality and finitude (*CD* III/4, 569f)[29] as a 'moment' of His time.[30] In relation to Barth's threefold view of temporality there is a threefold opportunity: to find one's true time in Christ (supra-temporality); preserved for a future 'pregnant with promise' of God's kingdom (*CD* III/3, 85) (post-temporality); and covenantally elected as creation's centre (pre-temporality). Here, as earlier, Barth's dynamic concept of divine and human temporality provides an alternative basis to the traditional immutable vocation concept which Volf questions, especially its equation with a life station.

In the context of this 'unique opportunity' Barth defines calling as 'this particularity, limitation and restriction in which . . . God . . . calls and rules' and humanity obeys (*CD* III/4, 597). Yet he distinguishes, without divorcing, divine calling from vocation: the former is a 'special and constantly renewed intention', or 'summons' stretching our humanity towards its kingdom destiny (*CD* III/4, 595f, cf 565) and ultimate, ontological vocation as a 'witness to Jesus Christ'[31]; the latter is our providential '"place of

---

29. Cf *CD* III/2, 63f on the finitude of Jesus Christ, III/3, 61f and 229ff on 'The Divine Preserving'.
30. Willis, *op cit*, 313.
31. *Ibid*, 312, 320.

responsibility" (D Bonhoeffer)' in creaturely limitation (*CD* III/4, 595-98).

Barth further distinguishes the 'comprehensive sense' of vocation from its 'narrower technical sense' of an occupation. Vocation is not exhausted in a profession, but is lived out in 'widely different spheres'. It is the 'totality of particularity' of individual existence claimed by God's call and command. Comprehensive vocation is a divine summons 'proper to all' including the unemployed, housewives, children, the sick and elderly. Barth thus guards against a dangerous identification of vocation with one's job and answers one of Volf's key criticisms of the vocation tradition. A job can be 'part' but not the *heart* of their Christian vocation or humanity (*CD* III/4, 599f, 630).[32]

In an historical dialogue with the vocation tradition Barth first disagrees with its medieval monastic limitation. Luther rightly reopened vocation to God's whole people, but his separation of law and created order from gospel, led to acceptance of a fixed order and a secular commandeering of vocation, whether by feudal or later capitalist society (*CD* III/4, 600-2).

Like Volf, Barth criticises Luther's identification of vocation and station in 1 Corinthians 7. 'The divine calling comes from above into all . . . human spheres, cutting diagonally across them. Thus the New Testament *klesis* has nothing to do with the divine confirmation of these spheres as such, nor with the direction to enter such a sphere' eg of work (*CD* III/4, 600). Calling comes from heaven, not the social hierarchy, nor the heart, nor tradition. It is a 'revolutionary' and 'new thing'. This sounds like the No of Barth's *Romans*.

But there is a christological Yes. Since '*klesis* is the calling of God issued in Jesus Christ', this cannot hang above humanity docetically, for Jesus became truly human, entering all spheres of life. God's call is then not *equated* with these spheres, but is closely *related* to them in Christ. God is free in Christ to call people within

---

32   Cf O Guinness, *The Call: Finding and Fulfilling the Central Purpose of Your Life* (Waco: Word, 1998), 29-31.

them without being bound by them. Barth affirms the difference, as well as the likeness, of divine calling and human vocation, through the flexibility of his christological analogy, thus answering Volf's critique of the analogy equating spiritual and external calling.

This transcendent divine calling also enables change of vocation or gifts. God's Word and Spirit is free to call us beyond our old humanity and its states of life and aptitudes, yet maintains continuity with it. God's command finds us at the 'sum of those points' at which God calls each one in their uniqueness (*CD* III/4, 604f). It relativises the vocational criteria of age, history, personal aptitude and place in life (*CD* III/4, 600) but without renouncing them as God's creation. These various limitations in Christ become forms of liberation.

Barth also builds on the Reformers' inclusion of gifts in vocation and so can include Volf's charismatic approach (or perhaps *vice versa*). God's 'one *klesis* is differentiated and variously issued' within the *ekklesia* to each uniquely gifted and called individual (*CD* III/4, 603).[33] Similarly to Volf, Barth also allows for a changeability of charisma and aptitude, according to the demands of the situation and the command of God—'one ability now comes to the fore and another steps back' (*CD* III/4, 624-26).

Change is thus possible in vocations, contrary to Luther's reading of 'abiding' in one's calling (1 Corinthians 7:20). For Barth, like Calvin, 'What abides is the calling, the Word, the command of God, not the sphere of operation' to which it leads and rules. God's call requires a constantly fresh faithfulness and openness to change in one's vocational sphere.

By maintaining the supremacy of gospel over law, and the distinction and irreversible relation between divine calling and human vocation, Barth provides grounds for transformation and

---

33 Citing Matthew 25:14f, 1 Corinthians 12, Romans 12:3f, and 1 Peter 4:10f. He also notes the equation in 1 Corinthians 7 of gift (v 7) and calling (v 17) with singleness or marriage, and describes vocation in terms of the Spirit's distribution of gifts 'as he wills' (See *CD* III/4, 604-6).

change of the latter (*CD* III/4, 646f). The biblical dynamic of 'divine calling' (*CD* III/4, 606f) is maintained, as God's change-agent in the world, as transcendent to specific spheres/vocations, and as relevant to occupationally mobile postmodern societies. It also stands against the ideological distortion of particular stations identified with God's order. This too is a liberating word for those who do not fit the employment ethic; divine calling is different to human vocation, and vocation different to a job, though it may include it.

Evaluation and Critique

Having examined Barth's view of work and vocation the time has come to evaluate its adequacy and relevance for a postmodern work situation, primarily using Volf's critique of the vocation tradition as a framework, but also drawing on others. Firstly, Barth has a more eschatologically oriented, though even more christological perspective than Luther's protological perspective criticised by Volf. For Barth 'the kingdom of God is the most profound need of the world around' (*CD* III/4, 502)[34]—even more than the need for work. Barth agrees with Volf on 'the single, underlying universal need, the need for the *new creation, which is the kingdom of freedom*'.[35]

Volf expounds this as the fulfilment of 'four fundamental needs' or ways of limiting the postmodern economy's 'permanent expansion of human needs'. They are the need: '*for God, . . . for solidarity with nature, . . . for fellow human beings, . . . for personal development*.[36] All except the second (due to fear of natural theology, his christo-anthropocentricity, and a lack of ecological vision) are covered by Barth also.

---

34. P West, 'Towards a Christian Theology of Work: A Critical Appropriation of the Thought of Jürgen Habermas', (PhD dissertation, University of Cambridge, 1986), 248.
35. Volf, *op cit*, 154.
36. *Ibid*, 150-54.

However, Volf sees Barth's view of work, like that of many theologians, including Aquinas, as operating under the assumption of the eschatological annihilation of the world, thus neglecting the continuity between creation and new creation. For many, work is eschatologically insignificant apart from its influence on human souls and the proper work of faith, sanctification and service. Volf is correct in general, but misreads Barth here. Barth, though holding to a relative dualism (*e.g.* regarding soul and body), held to the Blumhardts' earthy eschatological hope.[37] This enabled him to provide a basis for provisional action for the transformation of worldly work now, although he gives work a lesser place than Volf.

A second criticism, by Willis, concerns the way Barth's single-minded christological vision of culture effectively demythologises work and culture,[38] but is insensitive to their empirical complexity.[39] Russell Palmer and Graeme Smith, however, argue that having affirmed the 'need of the Gospel' to explain why work is finally necessary (*CD* III/4, 523), Barth is least christological and most practical in his criteria of human work.[40]

However, I have shown that Barth's Christ-centred anthropology undergirds his criteria for humane work and vocation. Admittedly, Barth's christo-analogical method is stronger on the personal dimension of, for example, work alienation, but weaker on the structural. Nonetheless, I agree with Nigel Biggar and social scientist Stuart McLean that Barth's occasional abstraction and lack of empirical specificity is not a fundamental defect.[41] With McLean I believe Barth's insights have great undeveloped potential for

---

37. See Preece, *op cit.* 50, 124, 185.

38. Willis, *op cit*, 322.

39. Barth, *Ethics*, 383, cf 381-91, 418-20, 428-33.

40. 'Karl Barth and the Orders of Creation: A Study in Theological Ethics', (PhD dissertation University of Iowa, 1966), abstract. 'It is by no means clear Barth's ethical guidelines derive from his Christology any more than Brunner's derive from the orders of creation'.

41. Biggar, *op cit*, 158-160.

empirical analysis given that 'Barth's anthropology, which frames his theology of work/vocation is the most profound in western thought'.[42]

Barth's analogical method is very different to the favored 'application method' of modern secular and Christian business ethicists where general principles eg utility, justice etc are applied to cases. He resists casuistry, lest it squeeze out the particularity of the encounter between God and humanity in Christ, and between individuals and the great variety of social reality (cf CD III/4, 533f). Barth's more postmodern focus on particularity, rather than a more modern application of universal rational principles, provides a way forward in our highly particularistic context.

Thirdly, Volf argues that the classical vocation tradition does not encourage transformation of work. However, we have shown how Barth maintains the New Testament dynamism of the divine calling to Christ and the kingdom without divorcing it from human vocation, thus providing ever-fresh stimulus for the transformation of human vocations. 'The *Dogmatics*' Christology latently retains the Safenwil insight that Jesus Christ is God's movement for social justice' and can be developed to 'meet the very inside of humanity's and nature's travail'.[43]

Fourthly, Volf argues against the ideological susceptibility of the vocation tradition.[44] A theology of work must be liberative and

---

42 S McLean, *Humanity in the Thought of Karl Barth* (Edinburgh: T&T Clark, 1981), 40 Cf Webster on 'the accounts of 'The Unique Opportunity' and of 'Vocation' as imbued with a sense of the *density* of particular human history' (*op cit*, 75) and Joan O'Donovan ['Man in the Image of God: The Disagreement Between Barth and Brunner Reconsidered', *Scottish Journal of Theology* 39 (1986): 435] who regards Barth's 'transcendent-relational, Christological-Trinitarian' anthropology as the best safeguard against today's assault on human uniqueness.

43 E A Barnes, *Affront to the Gospel? The Radical Barth and the Southern Baptist Convention* (Atlanta: Scholars Press, 1982), 37f.

44 An ideology uses language as 'a medium of domination and social power' legitimating 'relations of organised force' and

transformative and ideologically self-critical.[45] Willis agrees, but argues perceptively that Barth's christological opposition to the ideologies of natural and cultural Christianity drives him reactively toward an ideological minimisation of creation and work.[46]

Philip West and David Attwood, however, see Barth's theology of work and vocation as the most powerful antidote against the politically pervasive (Left and Right—Marxist and managerial) 'ideology of work' which has affected the liberationist *homo faber* theology of Moltmann, Sölle and others, the co-creationist theology of John Paul II and Michael Novak, and the evangelical 'work as worship' theology of Stott.[47]

If our 'litmus paper' to test for the presence of ideology is the work ethic's victims, the 'under and over-employed', then Barth provides us with criteria for constructive, though incomplete change towards more human work in the light of God's kingdom.[48]

---

disguising injustice (J Habermas, 'A Review of Gadamer's *Truth and Method*', in F R Dallmayr and T A McCarthy (eds), *Understanding and Social Inquiry* [Notre Dame: University of Notre Dame Press, 1977], 360).

45. Volf, *op cit*, 83f. 108. Cf West, *op cit*, 213-15.

46. Willis, *op cit*, 420, though he admits that the immediacy of God's command keeps human action '(relatively) free of ideological constraint and confusion, and provides for a total openness to each situation' (426).

47. J Moltmann, 'The Right to Meaningful Work', in *idem, On Human Dignity: Political Theology and Ethics* (Philadelphia: Fortress Press, 1984), 37-58; D Sölle with S A Cloyes. *To Work and to Love: A Theology of Creation* (Philadelphia: Fortress Press 1984); John Paul II, *Laborem Exercens*, M Novak, *Business as a Calling: Work and the Examined Life* (New York: Free Press, 1996); J Stott, *Issues Facing Christians Today* (Basingstoke, UK: Marshall, Morgan & Scott, 1984), Chapter 9.

48. D Attwood, 'Exaggerated Christian Doctrines of Work: Co-Creation, Redemption and Worship', Tyndale Ethics Lecture, (Cambridge: 1987), 1-4, 6. Cf P D Anthony, *The Ideology of Work* (London: Tavistock, 1977).

This practical test is as pertinent as Volf's valid concerns about work mobility and alienation, for the great problem today is the unequal distribution of work.[49] Barth's relativisation of social labour by making it *part* but not the *heart* of vocation, his stress on the sabbath's priority and that justification is not by a job, and his critique of work as co-creation, all have radical implications for re-evaluating paid work and unemployment.[50]

Fifthly, do Barth's criteria of human work (and vocation), which correctly stress the purposeful, ethical, communal, reflective and limited nature of work, provide a practical alternative to alienation as Volf is rightly concerned to do? Certainly Barth's emphasis on work expressing and contributing to human relationships has immense implications for a new work ethic that guards against the ideological distortions of the vocation tradition.[51] But it raises questions as to who or what will initiate such work—the individual, society, the Church, or God's coming kingdom? Barth gives a qualified answer. He puts an onus now on employers and exhorts workers to engage in collective and individual action within a communal ethos (*CD* III/4, 532f). Yet he sees that only God's future kingdom will bring complete liberation.

Even Jacques Ellul criticises the abstraction and lack of practicality of Barth, his theological mentor. Barth's advocacy of employers offering dignified work not preying on 'human folly, vanity, lack of taste, errors or vices' is theologically correct but economically impractical. It does no justice to human nature nor the nature of capitalism or socialism. It would send employers bankrupt and put employees on the dole. Physically, morally, and ecologically harmful work would be obliterated, but also much merely trivial work.

Ellul also challenges Barth's anachronistic nineteenth century liberal individualism of vocational 'choice' based on an idyllic Swiss

---

49. Volf (*op cit*, 156) does, however, have a helpful excursus on 'Spirit, Work and Unemployment'.
50. Cf West, *op cit*, 13-15.
51. Attwood, *op cit*, 6.

situation of full employment. For most people vocational selection is an illusion. Barth's 'academic hypotheses' ignore such constraining factors as premature educational choices, qualifications, multinational labour planning and quotas, environment, bureaucratic control, market and advertising pressures and propaganda, diverse discriminations, and a permanent pool of unemployed. Barth discounts these concrete sociological and environmental determinations of modern work for fear of metaphysical fatalism.[52]

Ellul, like his sociological mentor Marx, differs with Barth over how far economic and technological 'things' shape thought and how far freedom can escape the necessity of work (determined by the Aristotelian dialectic of freedom and necessity). Nevertheless, Ellul's criticism is somewhat extreme. Barth recognised many of these collective and technological pressures, answering some of Ellul's criticisms in advance.[53] Barth also better maintains the realism of grace grounded in the cross and divine freedom against any determinism or non-christological dialectic. This provides the ultimate basis for action against work alienation as a denial of divinely endowed human freedom.

Sixthly, and most seriously to my mind, are criticisms of the insufficient trinitarian basis of Barth's theology of work and vocation. Jonathon Gibbs argues that Barth and others (*e.g.* West and Moltmann) following his sabbatical relativising of work, underplay the greater relativisation and yet relevance of the triune God's continuing creative, sustaining and redeeming action to work.[54] Christ can still be the paradigm of human response to God,

---

52 J Ellul, *The Ethics of Freedom* (Grand Rapids: Eerdmans, 1976), 457-60. Cf G R Preece *Changing Work Values: A Christian Response* (Melbourne: Acorn), Chapter 4.

53 As G Bromiley notes in his preface to Barth's *Ethics* (vi). See Barth on the '*chthonic forces*' in *CL* 228-49 where he finally treats the theme of dominion, and indicates his awareness of the restrictions upon choice of vocation in *CD* III/4, 618-23.

54 J Gibbs, 'The Challenge of Transformation: Towards a Theology of

but so that creative activity and 'social labour is acknowledged as an integral and not as a peripheral aspect of human life before God'.[55] This is a re-affirmation of the 'Great Tradition' of Augustine, Luther, Calvin and Edwards.[56] The priority Barth gives to Christology, reconciliation and sabbath, and the relative marginalisation of creation, providence, Spirit and work, indicate areas where Barth, for all his creativity, does some injustice to this 'Great Tradition'.

The overt trinitarianism of Barth's ethics is spelt out in the three dimensional ethical outlines in paragraphs 36, 52, and 74. This linking of each ethical section is based on the indivisibility of God's external operations in creation, reconciliation and redemption. Barth insists that the first article 'anticipate' the second and third (*CD* III/4, 515f) for there can be no order of creation or redemption separate from the order of reconciliation without splitting the divine economy. Yet God's oneness thus brackets and 'encloses the first article' (*CD* III/4, 38) overshadowing the trinitarian appropriations (Father as primary Creator, Son as primary Reconciler etc), the biblical and credal order, and pushing creation to the periphery. Soteriology then effectively precedes ontology. The teleological overpowers the original.[57] Thus the command of God the Son—the Reconciler has 'material primacy' over the others:

Work in the Light of the Thought of H Richard Niebuhr' (PhD dissertation, University of Cambridge, 1989), 7, cf 22, 67, 185.

55.   *Ibid*, 191, 193.

56.   *Ibid*, 78 citing H R Niebuhr's term.

57.   'The grace of God in Jesus Christ also includes within itself creation, and therefore the command of the Creator'. Again true creatureliness is discovered in the light of Christ who is the ontic and noetic and internal basis of creation by virtue of God's eternal decree of election (*CD* III/4, 33, 35, 37, 39). Cf Webster (*op cit*, 63-4): creation for Barth is not 'the necessary' and 'complete' 'ground' for God's other works, but the 'necessary *implication* of God's primary work of grace in Jesus Christ'. In *CD* III/1, 44, 231, 31f: 'Creation sets the stage for the story of grace'. It is simply 'equipment for grace'. Knowing Christ's humanity is our way of

> That God is Lord of the covenant of grace is
> materially the first thing by which his being and
> work, and therefore his speaking and commanding,
> as Creator and Redeemer are also determined and
> stamped . . . The core of every statement in the first
> and third chapters of special ethics will thus consist of
> statements taken from the second, from specific
> Christological and soteriological statements (CL, 9f).

For all the strengths of Barth's christological primacy in countering the conservatism of Luther's protological approach and implied immutability of vocation it trespasses too far onto the trinitarian 'territory' of the Father and the Spirit. I agree with O'Donovan that:

> It was a mistake to think that everything that needed
> to be said about human society could be included
> under the doctrine of reconciliation. Each area has to
> be given, as it were, a salvation-history of its own . . .
> Work is a gift of creation; it is ennobled into mutual
> service in the fellowship of Christ; it gives place to the
> final sabbath rest. And so on.[58]

Finally, despite the danger of Barth's downplaying of creation almost lifting callings 'beyond any historical context' Barth's 'discussion of calling is the greatest that exists in modern theology'.[59] For Barth's trinitarian and christological revision of God's eternity, his notion of enacted being and his taking time seriously for vocation and work provides an important corrective to the classical Reformation tradition's Platonic and static tendencies. By abandoning the immutability of God, election and calling he revised the vocation tradition in a more biblical and relevant way that answers the key elements of Volf's critique of that tradition: its

---

'assuring ourselves of the reality of creation'. For Barth, the covenant of grace is more concrete and real than consciousness of self, creation or God (CD III/1, 365).

58　O O'Donovan, *Resurrection and Moral Order: An Outline for Evangelical Ethics* (Leicester: InterVarsity Press, 1986), xvii.

59.　P Marshall, *A Kind of Life Imposed on Man: Vocation and Social Order from Tyndale to Locke* (Toronto: University of Toronto Press, 1996), 125 n7.

analogous immutability of spiritual and external calling, its equation of vocation and station, and its irrelevance to postmodern occupationally mobile societies. He also provides a basis in the freedom of divine calling over human vocation and in his Christo-anthropology for social transformation and criticism of alienating and dehumanising work. Within a more thoroughly trinitarian theology that does more justice to the role of creation and the Holy Spirit, Barth's development of a more dynamic notion of work and vocation provides an essential stimulus to a postmodern theology of work and vocation.

The Counterpart of Others: Some Questions for Barth's Doctrine of Reconciliation

Nancy M Victorin-Vangerud

I

So when you are offering your gift at the altar, if you remember that your brother or sister has something against you, leave your gift there before the altar and go; first be reconciled to your brother or sister, and then come and offer your gift (Mathew 5:23-24).

A Passion for Reconciliation

In his 1983 *Journal of Religion* article on 'Karl Barth and Liberation Theology,' George Hunsinger claims that 'two very different controlling passions' separate the two.[1] Barth's passion, according to Hunsinger, is to give 'unqualified precedence to the sovereign Word of God' whereas liberation theology, in particular the theology of Gustavo Gutiérrez, presents its passion for 'the liberation of the oppressed'.[2] On Barth's side is the integrity of the biblical tradition and its unique Word; on Gutiérrez' side is the pragmatic criterion of liberation praxis. 'Of course,' as Hunsinger reminds us, 'it would be just as false to suggest that the liberation theologians give no precedence to God's Word as it would be to suppose that Barth cared nothing about the oppressed and their needs'.[3] Still, the controlling passion for each theologian orients his theology in specific ways.

---

1. G Hunsinger, 'Karl Barth and Liberation Theology', *The Journal of Religion* 63 (1983): 247-263.
2. *Ibid*, 254.
3. *Ibid*.

What is the controlling passion of my inquiry into Barth's theology of reconciliation and our postmodern future? Simply put, my passion is for re-imagining Christian theology's soteriological picture, for not only do human beings stand as sinners before God, they also stand as sufferers, sufferers who have suffered the sins of those who stand beside them before God. What does reconciliation with God mean in a day when we recognise the social contextuality of oppressors and oppressed, victims and perpetrators, the powerful and the powerless? Certainly, as Miroslav Volf reminds us, it is easy in a genocidal century to fall into a simplistic schema of *innocent* oppressed and *guilty* oppressors. From his own Croatian-Serbian war context, Volf claims that the oppression-liberation scheme is good for fighting but not for negotiating or living together afterwards side-by-side.[4] But if theologians do not recognise the complexity of soteriological need, we run the risk of mystifying, individualising, privatising and ahistoricising sin and evil, as liberation theologies so clearly warn against.[5] The passion of this inquiry is for re-imaging a Christian doctrine of reconciliation in light of the 'reconciliation of peoples'.[6]

The inquiry draws on two distinctive, yet related theological themes of the twentieth century. The first theme is the '*krisis* of human knowledge' regarding God and God's relation to the world that interrupts modernity's grand narrative of human rationality,

---

4. J Gundry-Volf and M Volf, *A Spacious Heart: Essays on Identity and Belonging* (Harrisburg: Trinity Press International, 1997), 33-60.

5. For example, see L Boff and C Boff, *Introducing Liberation Theology* (Maryknoll: Orbis, 1993); R Chopp, *The Praxis of Suffering: An Interpretation of Liberation and Political Theologies* (Maryknoll: Orbis, 1986); E Fernandez, *Toward a Theology of Struggle* (Maryknoll: Orbis, 1994); G Gutiérrez, *A Theology of Liberation: History, Politics and Salvation* (Maryknoll: Orbis, 1973); and M Taylor, *Remembering Esperanza: A Cultural-Political Theology for North American Praxis* (Maryknoll: Orbis, 1990).

6. G Baum and H Wells. (eds), *The Reconciliation of Peoples: Challenge to the Churches* (Maryknoll: Orbis, 1997).

self-certainty, piety and autonomy.[7] For Karl Barth, God's radical Otherness shatters modern theology's anthropocentric monologue through the counterpart of God's self-revealing Word. Barth explains in *The Epistle to the Romans* (second edition):

> In announcing the limitation of the known world by another that is unknown, the gospel does not enter into competition with the many attempts to disclose within the known world some more or less unknown and higher form of existence and to make it accessible to men. The gospel is not a truth among other truths. Rather it sets a question-mark against all truths.[8]

In Barth's theological vision, God's Word of judgement and grace, God's infinite No! and Yes! 'explodes' like a shell in the modern world.[9]

But the second theme brings a different theological crisis—the interruption of suffering, which deepens the *krisis* for modernity. The voices and presence of 'non-persons' from 'the underside of history' have ruptured modernity's grand narrative as well. Their cries comprise, echoing Barth's terminology, a *counterpart of others* who reflect to modernity a groaning world (Romans 8:22). Rebecca Chopp clarifies the character of this groaning: 'As the calamities of nature once rattled the tower of divine omnipotence, so the disasters of history now explode the freeways of progress'.[10] The explosion of non-persons who have 'retrieved their humanity' challenges liberal and neo-orthodox interpretations of theological doctrines and calls theology to accountability and transformation.[11] The second theme of the twentieth century may be characterised by a *turn to the other* (in contrast to modernity's *turn to the subject*), who is both stranger and counterpart.

---

7. K Barth, *The Epistle to the Romans* (London: Oxford University Press, 1933, 1968), 362-374.
8. *Ibid*, 35.
9. Barth, *The Epistle to the Romans*, 29.
10. Chopp, *op cit*, 1.
11. J Comblin, *The Retrieval of Humanity* (Maryknoll: Orbis, 1990).

The two themes find their correlation in representing what Steven Smith terms 'the argument to the Other'.[12] For Barth, the Other is the wholly Other God revealed in Jesus Christ. For liberation theologians, the Other is God encountered in the marginalised, suffering non-person of history. If we include Sallie McFague's analogy of nature as 'the new poor,' then the argument to the Other is expanded even more widely.[13] It is this awareness of the *many* others that has shifted modern consciousness toward a new postmodern consciousness. Zygmunt Bauman defines postmodernity as 'a state of mind . . . marked by a view of the human world as irreducibly and irrevocably pluralistic'.[14] But the focus on pluralism may fan the flames of ethnocentrism, racism and xenophobia leading to 'rampant tribalism' in 'the soft world of communities'.[15] According to Bauman, the postmodern accolade of difference may in the end create 'a series of soliloquies, with the speakers no more insisting on being heard, but refusing to listen into the bargain'.[16] Bauman's warning is serious, but if the otherness of others is not recognised in a theo-ethic of reconciliation, repressive violence and despairing silence will continue.

The goal of this preliminary examination is to question Barth's doctrine of reconciliation in light of the argument to the Other.[17]

---

12 S Smith, *The Argument to the Other: Reason Beyond Reason in the Thought of Karl Barth and Emmanuel Levinas* (Chico, California: Scholars Press, 1983). In this work, Smith compares and contrasts Barth with Levinas, not liberation theology, but as will become clear later in this chapter, I claim that a similar 'argument' can be made.

13 S McFague, *The Body of God: An Ecological Theology* (Minneapolis: Fortress, 1993), 165.

14 Z Bauman, *Intimations of Postmodernity* (London: Routledge, 1992), vii, 35.

15 Z Bauman, *Postmodernity and Its Discontents* (New York: New York University, 1997), 79-82.

16 Bauman, *Postmodernity*, 81.

17 A more expansive study of Barth, liberation and reconciliation is

174

The key texts will be from *CD* IV/1, *CD* I/2 and *CD* II/2 as informed by Hunsinger. While Barth will be a resource for theology in the twentieth-first century, his work must be pursued through a more focused and sustained dialogue with liberation theologies. Thus, the questions for this paper are what is the relation of reconciliation with God in Barth and the reconciliation of people in liberation theologies? What is the theological status of the neighbour as other? What does the argument to the Other imply for the meaning of justification?

The Reconciliation of God and Humanity in Jesus Christ

Our first step is to gain an understanding of Barth's concept of reconciliation. For Karl Barth, theology does not begin with any other foundation or subject, than God's own self-revelation. The amazing grace of Christian faith is that God addresses God's Word to and for humanity. But if theology is to speak of God, theology must also speak of humanity. Barth claimed that theology must be understood as *the-anthropology*, 'for an abstract doctrine of God has no place in the Christian realm, only a 'doctrine of God and of man,' a doctrine of the commerce and communion between God and man'.[18] But to view Barth's the-anthropology as merely about reorienting epistemology, is to miss Barth's bigger picture. In his book, *Barth's Ethics of Reconciliation*, John Webster clarifies that

---

beyond the scope of this chapter. But I am grateful to Dr J Michael Owen who suggests that additional pathways into Barth's theology of reconciliation can be found through Barth's own involvement in Swiss-German reconciliation. See K Barth, *Eine schweizer Stimme 1938-1945* (Zollikon, Zurich: Evangelischer Verlag AG, 1945).

18   K Barth, *The Humanity of God* (Atlanta: John Knox, 1978), 11. For Barth, the-anthropology is inclusive of women and men, but even though there is vital concern about his order of A (man) and B (woman), I am choosing to leave his language as it has been translated in the text.

Barth's dogmatics in fact represents a 'moral ontology'.[19] Thus, 'what Barth has to say about any topic in theology cannot be adequately grasped unless we bear in mind this larger scope of the argument of the *Church Dogmatics* as 'the-anthropology' and therefore as theological ethics'.[20] As Barth himself states, 'For without ceasing to be dogmatics, reflection upon the Word of God is itself ethics' (*CD* 1/2, 371). The grace of God in Jesus Christ, which reconciles human beings to God and restores covenant relations, further grounds human agentiality in true freedom for loving God and neighbour.

But we need to look closely at Barth's understanding of reconciliation. In *CD* IV/1 (22-66), Barth opens with the affirmation that humanity exists out of the gracious, eternal election of God in order to live in covenant with God. Humanity, though, has not been able to fulfil the covenant. Barth explains:

> This history of man from the very first—and the same is true of the history of every individual man—consisted, not in keeping but the breaking of the covenant, not in the receiving but the rejecting of the promise, not in the fulfilling but the transgressing of the command, not in the gratitude which corresponds to the grace of God but in a senseless and purposeless rebellion against it, a rebellion which at bottom is quite negative, but terribly real even in this negativity (*CD* IV/1, 67).

The human condition is enmeshed in sin, thus in light of the covenant, there is need for atonement. For Barth, reconciliation is not an afterthought or a best solution to a failed project in need of cleaning up. The election of humanity to the covenant is based on the eternal reality of God-with-us, Jesus Christ, the one who fulfils the broken covenant and restores peace for humanity with God (Romans 5:1).[21] The picture is even bigger—in Christ, God has

---

19. J Webster, *Barth's Ethics of Reconciliation* (Cambridge: Cambridge University, 1995), 4.
20. *Ibid*, 4.
21. *Ibid*, 74, 83.

reconciled the *world* unto Himself (2 Corinthians 5:19). God in Christ has reconciled 'all things' (*ta panta*) to Godself (Colossians. 1:19).[22] But in terms of human existence, the broken status of the covenant means a 'yawning abyss' lies between God and 'man, not merely the creature, but the sinner, the one who exists in the flesh and who in the flesh is in opposition to Him'.[23] This oppositional context means that humans have lost their right to covenant partnership and live under 'a verdict, which disowns and renounces'.[24] The crisis for human beings is that they have no means—morally, epistemologically and ontologically—by which they can cross the abyss themselves.

For Barth, reconciliation with God is God's own activity. In the verdict of God, the No! also includes the Yes! of God's continued faithfulness to the covenant. Atonement is accomplished by God in Jesus, the mediator, substitute and representative of humanity before God.[25] His history founds the meaning of all human history and in his death and resurrection, human subjectivity is freed and grounded in God's mercy for a life of faithfulness with others. Barth emphasises that the grace of God is for humanity as a whole, thus reconciliation mediates a new social reality lived as intersubjective freedom. Challenging modern individualism, he explains, 'But I am not Man, I am only a man, and I am a man only in relation to my fellow men. Only in encounter and in communion with them may I receive the gift of freedom. God is *pro me* because He is *pro nobis*.'.[26]

Barth sets forth justification, sanctification and promise (or calling) as three inter-dependent dimensions to God's reconciliation. Each dimension is differentiated from the other, with justification assuming precedence, but united into one whole event together. In justification, God establishes the righteousness that restores the covenant and converts the human status from sinner to

---

22 Barth, *The Humanity of God*, 61.
23 *Ibid*, 82.
24 *Ibid*, 93.
25 *Ibid*, 230.
26 *Ibid*, 77.

friend, child and partner. Barth explains God's justice in Jesus' atoning death:

> (M)an is no longer the transgressor, the sinner, the covenant-breaker that God has found him and he must confess himself to be, that as such he has died and perished from the earth, that he cannot be dealt with as such, that as such he has no future. Jesus Christ has taken his place as a malefactor. In his place Jesus Christ has suffered the death of a malefactor. The sentence on him as a sinner has been carried out. It cannot be reversed. It does not need to be repeated. It has fallen instead on Jesus Christ (*CD* IV/1, 94).

Jesus' mediatorial role establishes the bridge across the yawning abyss between God and humanity. Freed from the sentence and reoriented to God's sovereign direction rather than his or her own illusory autonomy, the sinner receives a new reality, a new subjectivity. No longer is the human person the self-caused actor in his or her own drama. Christ's representative atonement justifies human beings within God's drama and God's own providence. It is important to see that reconciliation for Barth is not the fulfilment of human history as if all has been said and done. Reconciliation does not render history and existence superfluous. In fact, it reveals the very opposite. Reconciliation is the radical, fundamental orientation of the relation of God and humanity that enables human beings to live in freedom. Barth uses the language of living in the 'kingdom' of peace:

> Jesus Christ is God's mighty command to open our eyes and to realise that this place is all around us, that we are already in this kingdom, that we have no alternative but to adjust ourselves to it, that we have our being and continuance here and nowhere else. In Him we are already there, we already belong to it. To enter at His command is to realise that in Him we are already inside *CD* IV/1, 99f).

We can hear Barth stressing in his words that justification is not a *de jure* reality now needing a *de facto* instantiation. Webster explains, 'The telos of grace is the evocation in its human recipients of a new

178

life-act . . . (Barth) refuses to see the move from *de jure* to *de facto* as one in which the "objective" becomes "subjectively real"'.[27] Justification is a new creation, or given Barth's emphasis on the eternal love and election of humanity in Christ, justification is creation.

The second dimension in Barth's order of salvation is sanctification, or living within the direction of God. Barth makes clear that sanctification is not our initiative or contribution to reconciliation. Sanctification cannot be separated from justification; it is 'a form of the atonement, of the conversion of man to God' (*CD* IV/1, 101). Thus, sanctification is our summons 'to use the freedom in which man has already been put in Jesus Christ' (*CD* IV/1, 101). As God so loves the world to fulfil the covenant, so now in sanctification do human beings respond with love in 'a kind of silhouette' of the 'elective, free and total activity of God' (*CD* IV/1, 104). This sanctifying love comprises two directions—a vertical direction of love to God and a horizontal direction of love to the neighbour and brother (and sister). Barth writes: 'The love of God in Jesus Christ brings together Himself with all men and all men with Himself. But at the same time it is obviously the coming together of all men one with another' (*CD* IV/1, 105). Again, love to God and love to others is a differentiated, yet united love, with love to God taking precedence.

Barth relates love to God and love to others through the parable of the sheep and goats (Mathew 25). He claims that the criterion of faithfulness for our love to God will be judged in and through our love for 'the least of these'. But he is careful not to identify the two. Others are witnesses to the 'poverty' Jesus Christ accepted to establish the fellowship of God and humanity and they must not be ignored or overlooked (*CD* IV/1, 106). But the neighbour or brother is not separate from loving God. Barth writes that 'God can not be had without them, nor can reconciliation with Him nor conversion to Him' (*CD* IV/1, 106). What can be said of love to God must also be said of love to others. Thus while the vertical and the horizontal

---

27.   Webster, *op cit*, 96

dimensions of Christian love are only possible through the preceding love of God for the world, love to neighbour does serve as (emphasis added) 'a perfect *counterpart* to the vertical coming together of God and man . . . (I)t cannot be exhausted by mere feelings, or a mere outlook, let alone mere words. It is an active being' (*CD* IV/1, 107). In sanctification, the *counterpart of others* is necessary for the fulfilment of Barth's complex moral vision. The direction of God's freeing love is not for human passivity or God's monarchical domination, but human agentiality of love to God and others. As Webster succinctly states, 'The ethics of reconciliation is an exploration of the shape of existence in analogy to Jesus'.[28]

More insight into Barth's connection of love to God and love to others is found in his discussion on 'the greatest commandment' (Mark 12:29-31) in *CD* I/2 (381-454).[29] The themes of God's original love for the world, Jesus Christ's representative death, and the responsive obedience of human love are heard here as well. Love to God and loving our neighbours as ourselves are not two absolute commands, nor are they identical loves. Love to God is the absolute commandment, but loving our neighbour as ourselves is derivative and relative, but not arbitrary or with a lesser degree of divine seriousness. Barth explains (*CD* I/2, 410):

> If we try to love God as the neighbour, it will not be
> the God whom we are commanded to love. And if we
> try to love the neighbour as God, it will not be the
> neighbour whom we are commanded to love. If we
> are not to deviate from the divine revelation, if we
> really want to obey the one command of God, we can
> only love God and our neighbour.

But since the Christian life involves the integrity of love to both God and neighbour, the relationship of the two needs clarification. Barth challenges anthropocentric understandings that view loving the neighbour as a humanitarian good or extension of human love. Human love to neighbour does not consist in extending our own

---

28 *Ibid*, 98.
29 In addition, see Smith's discussion, *op cit*, 161-164.

high esteem or self-regard to those like ourselves and thus, to God as well. The afflicted neighbour is loved unfaithfully if we relate to the neighbour in ways that inflate or call attention to our own human virtue. The neighbour brings into focus God's amelioration of our common human condition. Again Barth explains:

> This work of reconciliation, in the consummation to which Jesus Christ pointed and which He is to fulfil, is the divine removing of the things under which we now see both ourselves and others suffer. We are not told that we have to cooperate in this removing as such . . . What we are told is that we should love our neighbour by proclaiming to him—not only in word of course, but in deed—the true amelioration and therefore Jesus Christ (CD I/2, 428).

In contrast to religio-social teaching, Barth claims that the neighbour does not present a task for us, but the opportunity to acknowledge the true ameliorating humanity of Christ. A fellow-human becomes a neighbour as her or his shame, guilt, torment and misery mirrors our own sinful state and also mirrors what Jesus Christ was willing to take on in order to reconcile humanity to God. Thus, in loving the neighbour as ourselves, we recognise ourselves as sinners and we receive the Christ who served the sentence for our sin. This neighbour is not the accommodating neighbour of charity, but the disconcerting neighbour of grace:

> The neighbour shows me that I myself am a sinner. How can it be otherwise, seeing he stands in Christ's stead, seeing he must always remind me of Him as the Crucified? How can he help but show me, as the reflection of myself, what Christ has taken upon Himself for my sake? (CD I/2, 431).

In loving our neighbour as we love ourselves, we stand together before God in a 'common bankruptcy,' a 'fellowship of sin and misery' (CD I/2, 436). We stand in *solidarity* with our neighbour as *co-sinners*, whose guilt has incurred the same condemnation. Yet we are co-recipients of grace; we live by forgiveness and receive Christ's reprieve from death. In free response to God's love for us (I John 4:10) we give praise to God, which breaks out in love to God

181

and love to neighbour. We live this love to our neighbour thro
witness to Jesus Christ (our words), assistance as a sign of Gc
true assistance (our deeds), and an evangelical attitude (*CD*
443-447). For Barth, justification and sanctification form one g
work of love—God's work. Human beings stand together be
God and the broken covenant in the solidarity of sin. It is onl'
light of God's love in spite of humanity's status of guilt
unworthiness that theology can speak of love. As Barth states, 'F
Scripture speaks of man always and exclusively from
standpoint of his sin and reconciliation' (*CD* I/2, 404).

Barth's majestic hymn of love resounds as wave after wave u
the shore, but his vision of reconciliation raises questions in w
José Miguez Bonino terms 'an *oikoumene* of domination'[30] Is Bar
the-anthropology of the solidarity of sinners before God enou
either in terms of a biblical witness to reconciliation or in terms
socio-political context? This is not to say that Barth was
seriously concerned with politics (to the contrary!), nor
contradiction to the opening claim that Barth's dogmatics
theological ethics.[31] But what if biblical exploration and so
political analysis provide a challenge to what Barth has definec
the Word of reconciliation? What if there is an even *bigger pic*
than the solidarity of sin? What if the afflicted neighbour reveals
just the 'yawning abyss' between God and myself, but the at
between myself and my neighbour? What if the afflicted neighb
reveals not only my rebellion against God, my intractable break
of obedience to God, but my abuse, violence, prejud
indifference, hatred and fear of my neighbour? Why should
suffering of the counterpart of others point away to what Christ
done for us, rather than upon what I have done to them?

---

30 In T Wieser (ed), *Whither Ecumenism? A Dialogue in the Transit
Lounge of the Ecumenical Movement* (Geneva: WCC, 1986) 29-30,
quoted by K Raiser, *Ecumenism in Transition: A Paradigm Shift in
the Ecumenical Movement?* (Geneva: WCC, 1991), 63-64.

31 See G Hunsinger, *Karl Barth and Radical Politics* (Philadelphia:
Westminster, 1976).

Barth's doctrinal norm of the solidarity of sinners marginalises the soteriological complication of standing before God as those afflicted with unjust suffering. Human beings need atonement for guilt, but also inclusion, healing, dignity and righting of the wrong against them. Even Miroslav Volf, who maintains the universality of sin as the biblical norm, qualifies this by saying that from a biblical perspective, all sins are not equal and some are more guilty than others.[32] He writes, '"Solidarity in sin" is disturbing because it seems to erase distinctions and unite precisely where the differences and disjunctions matter the most—where dignity is denied, justice trampled underfoot, and blood is spilled'.[33] Thus we can join with Barth in affirming that no one is innocent. Yet, we cannot stay with Barth in confining the theological significance of the violated, the oppressed and the marginalised to providing a reflection of the abyss between their violators and God. Reconciliation of humanity with God must also incorporate reconciliation within humanity as well.

The Counterpart of Others from the Perspective of Liberation

In the latter half of this century, theologies of liberation have brought the presence of *others* to the centre. The standpoint of reflection no longer remains with 'universal man' or even the 'universal Christ', but with the particular subjects of cultural, sexual, economic or political marginalisation. From a diversity of contexts, theologies of liberation have interrupted Cartesian certainty, Kantian morality and Hegelian history with the counterpart of others who reveal the discontinuities (the abyss) separating nations, peoples, communities and individuals.

In the terms of Smith's 'argument to the Other', theologies of liberation articulate 'a reason beyond reason' in which the other as an 'event' breaches our experience and knowledge (the No!) with

---

32   M Volf, *Exclusion and Embrace: A Theological Exploration of Identity, Otherness and Reconciliation* (Nashville: Abingdon, 1996), 82.

33   *Ibid.*

what is absolutely new.[34] The other addresses us with authority
and height and calls us to accountability and justice. But how can
we stand justified before the other? Our representations and actions
have served as totalities for mastering the relation. Thus, we must
defer to the other, serve the other and recognise in the face of the
other both a veiling and unveiling. As Graham Ward claims in his
work on Barth (and Levinas), the epiphany of the vulnerable other
not only negatively accuses, but positively calls persons to
responsibility as living for the other—the stranger, the widow and
the orphan.[35] In both the address of the Word (Barth) and the gift
of the Saying (Levinas), the other effects an 'ethics of kenosis'.[36]

Could it be that in the interruptive Saying of liberation
theologies the Word is heard anew, maybe a different Word than
the one of neo-orthodoxy? In *The Amnesty of Grace*, Mexican
theologian Elsa Tamez claims that liberation theology provides the
opportunity to recover anew Paul's understanding of reconciliation
and justification.[37] The key is the contrast in Paul between the logic
of death-dealing sin and the logic of life in the Spirit. The former
characterises social, political and economic realities based upon
merit, profit, privilege and power which do not affect individuals
equally, but judge some as worthy and righteous, while the
majority are condemned literally to death without basic necessities
and significance. Thus, while all people participate in systemic sin,
Tamez calls attention to the dynamics of exclusion that force non-
persons to 'bargain away' their humanity.[38] The justice of these
necrophilic systems renders only injustice for those enslaved, poor
and marginalised. In Tamez' liberation hermeneutic, the

34.   Smith, *op cit*, 8.
35.   G Ward, 'The Revelation of the Holy Other as the Wholly Other:
      Between Barth's Theology of the Word and Levinas' Philosophy
      of Saying', *Modern Theology* 9 (1993): 159-180.
36.   *Ibid*, 159-180.
37.   E Tamez, *The Amnesty of Grace: Justification by Faith from a Latin
      American Perspective* (Maryknoll: Orbis, 1993).
38.   *Ibid*, 37-43.

representative figure of justification shifts from Cain, the blood-spiller, to Abel, whose blood is spilled.[39] This shift expresses the soteriological complexity of structural sin. Tamez explains:

> Justification by faith must be oriented toward the affirmation of life—real life for real persons. When what is at stake is the life of the poor, the theme of justification must necessarily be read according to a logic different from the usual one that affirms that God justifies the sinner. This different reading is necessary because the poor introduce a concrete life and a history in which they are the primary victims of sin.[40]

For non-persons in the sphere of sin, the logic of Spirit involves God's act of solidarity which restores dignity, affirms the *imago Dei*, and incorporates the previously condemned slaves as heirs (daughters and sons) of God's abundant life. This new realm of freedom is made possible through the life, death and resurrection of Jesus Christ, 'the excluded person par excellence'.[41] Jesus' inclusive praxis restored personhood to non-persons, challenged the structures of sin that condemned people to death and broke down the walls dividing the privileged from others. He died under the unjust law of structural sin, abandoned and excluded as the preferential option meted out for those who live against the dominant logic. But in *God's* preferential option, God subverted the determinative power of structural sin and asserted God's justice through Jesus' resurrection. The excluded are now included as partners in God's just economy of 'life for all'.[42] A new humanity is raised that is not subject to the bondage of sin, for death no longer holds its tortuous sting. Dignity, life and community become God's inalienable gifts for those justified by the Spirit of the crucified. Tamez writes:

---

39. *Ibid,* 197.
40. *Ibid,* 42.
41. *Ibid,* 133.
42. *Ibid,* 42f, 140.

With the eruption of the logic of life in Jesus Christ
and verified in justification by faith and not by works
of any law, the excluded recover their ability to
distinguish God's truth about themselves and about
others. Together with this discovery they also become
aware of their freedom as historical subjects,
participants in the divine lineage, by being children of
God and brothers or sisters of Jesus Christ.[43]

For Tamez, justification means the affirmation of life for
excluded and the re-making of people who are truly free to
justly for the sake of all. The justified recognise that they are
'above' the privileged, for they acknowledge the potentiality
humans enmeshed in sin to live from the blood of others. Inst(
they call the privileged into God's great work of amnesty.

By re-viewing Paul's doctrine of justification within the bibl
tradition of justice, Tamez challenges 'one-dimensio
interpretations of reconciliation.[44] The problem is when the v(
dikaioo, 'to justify' is reduced only to 'the "vertical" relationshi(
humankind to God—neglecting implications on the "horizon
plane concerning relationships between human beings'.[45] Tl
justification and reconciliation are ahistoricised and solidarit'
suffering is relegated to a secondary position. Tamez cites Bar
attempt to hold together justification and reconciliation, but
links more closely the relation of God's justice with interhur
justice.[46] 'The justice of God and justification cannot be reduce(
"being at peace with God," for peace with God is seen when p(
is realised'.[47] Thus, for Tamez, reconciliation of God and huma:
incorporates the historical struggle of justice-making within hur
life.

In summary, theologies of liberation call attention to
complexity of soteriological need. Human beings not only st

---

43   *Ibid*, 143.
44   *Ibid*, 24.
45   *Ibid*.
46   *Ibid*, 24, 172.
47   *Ibid*, 24.

before God as covenant breakers with blood on their hands; they stand as persons whose blood has been shed in the dehumanising and deadly structures of sin. Sin is not abstract, but historical and concrete, thus for liberation theologies the Word of reconciliation incorporates historical and concrete dimensions. In this century, the counterpart of others interrupts modernity's arrogant and forgetful self-reflection. In analogy to Jesus Christ, the violated and excluded, the oppressed and suffering become included as heirs, restored to dignity in the image of God and freed for God's reconciling ministry of justice-making.

Conclusion: Turning to the Other

Is there a connection between the otherness of God and the otherness of neighbours? This paper represents some preliminary work in examining two major emphases of twentieth century theology toward a postmodern Christian theology of reconciliation. Theologies of liberation provide an opportunity to 'begin anew at the beginning'—faith in the triune God's reconciling love for the world.[48] But they challenge liberal and evangelical theologies with 'the strange new world of the Bible' as Barth once said of his own encounter with Romans in Safenwil.[49] The soteriological complication in theologies of liberation does not simply project or absorb a Christology, but empowers the deconstruction of evangelical and liberal Christologies. Deconstruction need not imply the death of God, but affirms 'a way of uncovering the gospel of the living God'.[50] Through the interruptive Saying of insignificant others, modernity and postmodernity may be

---

48 K Barth, *Evangelical Theology: An Introduction* (Grand Rapids: Eerdmans Publishing Company, 1963), 165.

49 Recounted by S Grenz and R Olson, *Twentieth Century Theology: God & the World in a Transitional Age* (Downers Grove: InterVarsity, 1992), 66.

50 K Hart, 'Nietzsche, Derrida and Deconstructing the True Gospel', *Zadok Perspectives* No 60 (Autumn, 1998): 11.

addressed by the Word of the living God. The key is viewing the solidarity of sinners as part of the more encompassing horizon of the solidarity of suffering.

Now Hunsinger suggests that Barth's theology of grace is right in principle and liberation theologies are right in practice.[51] For Hunsinger, liberation theology ends up with a sectarian vision because it loses sight of the great and decisive dialectic between God's grace and human sin. The Bible is 'so comprehensive and all-encompassing, that it also embraces within it the lesser dialectic of liberation and oppression—not excluding or trivialising the latter, but certainly emphatically relativising it'[52] Hunsinger affirms Barth's concern for a differentiated unity between theology and politics and asserts that according to Barth, the concrete political tendency of the biblical message is for the rights of the oppressed. Hunsinger cites Barth's own words (CD II/1, 387): 'God stands at every time unconditionally and passionately on this and only on this side: always against the exalted and for the lowly, always against those who already have rights and for those from whom they are robbed and taken away'. But Barth grounds these political reflections in the larger theological truth that God's mercy is for all in distress. Hunsinger summarises Barth's 'logic to the Other':

> It is precisely because God has acted once for all apart from us, against us, and for us in Jesus Christ—doing for us that which we most needed but were in no position whatsoever to do for ourselves—that we are in faith made responsible for all those who are poor and oppressed, that we are summoned to espouse the cause of those who suffer wrong. *For in them it is manifested to us what we ourselves are in the sight of God.*[53]

When we go to Barth's text quoted by Hunsinger, we read that before God all people are like the widow, the orphan, the alien, the wretched and the poor who cannot procure right for themselves.

51. Hunsinger, *op cit*, 260.
52. *Ibid*, 258f.
53. Hunsinger, *Ibid*, 259. Emphasis added.

Thus, because of God's right for all humanity, human beings cannot avoid the question of human rights and must affirm a state based on justice. The important connection for Barth is that people of faith cannot divorce their principle of grace from their praxis of advocacy and support of human rights.

Liberation theology, though, presses Barth to take things further, not just because it is a praxis, but because it also bears a Word. By generalising the human condition of inability to plead humanity's case before God from the figures of the widow and orphan, Barth neglects the great abyss between the wretched and persons whose mastery or participation in the sinful system gives rise to the cry in the first place. The insignificant, hungry and violated not only reflect something about the individual need of the significant ones, but the 'historical consequences' of the power disparities between the significant and insignificant.[54] This legacy of violence means that the significant are accountable for not only advocating the cause of the violated but seeking reconciliation with them. In Barth's and Hunsinger's view, privileged human beings become *responsible* for the neighbour, but not *respondable* to the neighbour who challenges their heroic, paternalistic status *vis à vis* him—or herself. The new Word to be received is the risen One, the excluded Christ. This Word, with the dignified yet wounded hands, reaches out to touch those without dignity, re-humanising them in God's image and freeing them for God's just covenant in which even the inhumane are hopefully restored.

Barth's theology of reconciliation is not abstract, but in light of the counterpart of others, a doctrine of reconciliation must go further. The neighbour is not just a reflection of my own need for God's justification, but a counterpart with whom I am accountable for making justice. A postmodern doctrine of reconciliation needs to cross the abyss between both God and neighbour. The excluded

---

54. J Sobrino, *Christology at the Crossroads: A Latin American Approach* (Maryknoll: Orbis, 1978), 201-216. Sobrino presents the cross and death of Jesus as the 'historical consequence' of his life in the service of God's Kingdom.

Christ continues to confront me in the voices of the counterpart of others with whom I am in wrong relation, broken relation, and abusive relation. Their dignity in Christ unmasks the idolatrous, stolen dignity I presume and invites me into the larger picture of the justification of all life. God's great amnesty holds out the hope of solidarity in suffering and restoration of dignity.

In closing, theologies of liberation provide an argument to others and to ultimately the Other. Neither a new foundation for dogmatics, nor an ideology dictating to theology, the counterpart of others provides the complication of soteriological need enabling theology to receive anew the gospel of the living God. Again, theology can begin at the beginning, in a way that reorients the whole and enables us to recognise that our doctrines of reconciliation need ongoing reformation.

'Our lines and concepts continually break apart': Language, Mystery and God in Barth

Geoff Thompson

> God is inapprehensible . . . .In other words, the lines which we can draw to describe formally and conceptually what we mean when we say 'God' cannot be extended so that what is meant is really described and defined; but they continually break apart so that it is not actually described and therefore not defined. In relation to God the means of definition at our disposal are not sufficient to reassure us, when we have applied them to Him, that we have thought what must be thought and said here. The being apprehended by us in thoughts and words is always either not yet or else no longer the being of God (*CD* II/1, 187).

It is remarks such as these, highlighting Barth's acknowledgment of some measure of instability in theological language, that provide much of the impetus to the various links made between Barth's theology and the postmodern preoccupation with language and the questions that are raised about its ability to refer to anything beyond itself.

My purpose in this paper is not primarily to enlist Barth for some or another self-consciously postmodern theology of the Word (although I will be arguing *against* one attempt to enlist Barth for such a theology). I am, instead, more interested in a network of explicitly doctrinal (rather than linguistic) considerations that cluster around Barth's specific ideas of mystery, language and God. In short, my primary question is not 'What is it about language that brings this instability to our thoughts and words about God?' but 'What is it about God that

191

means that our thoughts and words lack stability when put to this purpose?' As the answer to this question emerges, the discussion will be moved away from the problems of linguistic instability and towards the possibilities associated with its constructive correlate: the dynamism of theological discourse.

Nevertheless, the particular contours of this approach will be sharpened by setting them against the background provided by some of the recent attempts to bring Barth into dialogue with the deconstructionism of Jacques Derrida.

Barth and Derrida: Parallels and Proposals

The theological interest in Derrida stems from what appear as overlaps between the apophatic element of the Christian tradition and the endless deferral of reference which Derrida's concept of *différance* seeks to describe. Indeed, Derrida himself has drawn attention to the parallels between negative theology and deconstructionism: 'This thought seems strangely familiar to the experience of what is called deconstruction. Far from being a methodological technique, a possible or necessary procedure, . . . deconstruction has often been defined as the very experience of the (impossible) possibility of the impossible, of the most impossible, a condition that deconstruction shares with the gift, the 'yes' the 'come' decision, testimony, the secret etc'.[1] His thought provides a kind of heuristic tool, and even a philosophical foundation, for those theologies which have been sensitised by postmodernists to the allegedly infinite interpretability of language, and which are also nervous about the propensity of theological discourse for exceeding its own limits. According to Robyn Horner, '[t]he question which Derrida brings to theology has to do with the possibility of thinking the One who cannot be reduced to the dimensions of

---

1.   J Derrida, 'Sauf le nom', in T Dutoit (ed), *On the Name* (Standford: Standford University Press, 1995), 43.

thought'.[2] Similarly, although perhaps less pessimistic about the possibility of bringing God to thought, Graham Ward writes:

> *Différance* draws attention to the fact that theology cannot make dogmatic claims about God, not without also accepting that it speaks with and through metaphors. This ineradicable metaphorical character of language *does not* negate the meaning of theological statements but it puts them into question. It demands that they recognize that they are not, nor ever can be, unequivocal statements of truth.[3]

The specific link between Derrida and Barth has been pursued along a variety of lines. For my purposes, however, the major

---

2 R Horner, 'Derrida and God: Opening a Conversation', *Pacifica* 12 (1999): 16.

3 G Ward, 'Why is Derrida Important for Theology?', *Theology* 95 (1992): 265. Of course such an assessment of theological language is hardly dependent on Derrida's concept of *différance*, a fact which Ward readily acknowledges through his reference to 'theologians of the stature of Augustine, Aquinas and Barth' (265). Indeed, that theological appropriation of Derrida's deconstructionism wants to offer a more radically negative theology than traditional qualifications of positive theological statements is made clear in Kevin Hart's *The Trespass of the Sign: Deconstruction, Theology and Philosophy* (Cambridge: Cambridge University Press, 1989). Hart's case rest on a distinction between *restricted* and *general* negative theologies. The former includes most of what has passed for negative theology in the past but which in fact serve only to caution and supplement and are themselves eventually overcome by positive theological claims. The latter—more akin to deconstructionism—would not serve a merely cautionary function *vis à vis* positive theologies but would condition them such that they would 'seek[ ] to abstract our attention from concepts of God to the true God who cannot be conceptualised' (177).

193

focus will be restricted to the work of Graham Ward[4] and, to a lesser extent, that of William Stacy Johnson[5].

Ward not only sees parallels between Barth and Derrida, but employs Derrida to solve what he believes is a fundamental flaw in Barth's account of revelation and language. The parallels consist in what Ward observes as commitments by Barth to the kind of deferral of reference implied in my opening quotation from Barth. Ward claims that for Barth 'the truth of theology lies in [the] necessity yet impossibility of rendering an account'.[6] Consequently 'the revelation of the Word does not occur and cannot occur in Barth's theology, and so its meaning is maintained in mystery'.[7] Indeed, in relation to mystery in Barth, Ward offers this summary: 'The very lack of explanation and clarity constitutes the mystery'.[8] With such alleged commitments Barth is said to share a core concern with Derrida: for both thinkers 'the central problematic is the ineradicable otherness which haunts discourse and yet the impossibility of transcending metaphoricity and positing a real presence'.[9]

Nevertheless, Ward believes that he has exposed a fundamental flaw in Barth's account of how the Word comes to expression in human words. He claims that Barth employs two antithetical models of language: the 'communication model' and the 'semiotic model'. According to Ward, Barth employs the constructivist 'semiotic model' to explain the reality of human language in general. In such a model there is no guarantee of any correspondence between objects and the

---

4.   G Ward, *Barth, Derrida and the Language of Theology* (Cambridge: Cambridge University Press, 1995).

5.   W S Johnson, *The Mystery of God: Karl Barth and the Postmodern Foundations of Theology* (Louisville: Westminster John Knox Press, 1997)

6.   Ward, *op cit*, 244.

7.   *Ibid*, 250.

8.   *Ibid*, 244.

9.   *Ibid*, 247.

human perception of them. In reference to God, though, this problem is overcome in the event of revelation when, according to the 'communication model', certain words are 'conscripted by revelation'.[10] Summarising Barth on this point, Ward states: God 'perfects that correspondence, restores the appropriateness or the adequate proportion between views, concepts and words'.[11]

To the extent that Barth himself at all considers that he is working with two models of language, he holds them together by an analogical appeal to the Incarnation: the Word is to Jesus of Nazareth as the Word is to the words of human beings. Ward, however, rejects this appeal to the Incarnation on the basis of his claim that in his considerations of language and revelation, Barth really is attempting a 'general theology of language'[12] and for that purpose something more general than the particularism of the Incarnation must be offered as an account of the Word in the words. In what is a key statement in the development of his argument, Ward writes: 'The incarnation of Christ is an historically particular event, . . . but the incarnation of the Word in the words is not a particular event – it is the condition of language when language is viewed from its proper and original perspective'.[13]

In the end that 'something more general' which solves the alleged aporia in Barth's work, turns out to be Derrida's economy of *différance* in which 'discourse is the presentation of otherness and human representations of it'.[14] It offers one model which coherently achieves what Barth, on Ward's reading, fails to achieve by an alleged recourse to two antithetical models. So, Derrida is said to provide Barth's

---

10   For Barth's use of this phrase see *CD* I/1, 324.

11   Ward, *op cit*, 27.

12   *Ibid*, 21.

13   *Ibid*, 31.

14   *Ibid*, 245.

theology of language with a 'philosophical supplement'.[15] Ward thus offers a theory of discourse itself as the confirmation and legitimation of the movement, instability and open-endedness of theological language as proposed by Barth. God's hiddeness, says Ward, is 'constitutive of discourse itself'. He continues: 'It is the process of discourse, the logic of its referring and deferring in which the hermeneutical project is both disrupted and returned to, which is the focal interest of both Barth and Derrida'. More specifically, 'Barth's theological discourse traces how the mystery of otherness evades domestication, how this evasion prevents foreclosure, and generates supplementary attempts to argue for or to this otherness'.[16]

Much of the force of Ward's claim to expose an aporia in Barth's argument lies in his claim that Barth is in fact seeking a general theology of language *per se*. Bruce McCormack is, I suggest, entirely correct when he argues in his vigorous rebuttal of Ward's thesis that Barth's appeal to the Incarnation and its particularism succeeds precisely because Barth's principal interest in language is in language as it is employed in the particular events of revelation in particular human words.[17] As McCormack explains it, Barth's appeal to the *assumptio carnis* and the associated communication of attributes means that for Barth 'the use made by the divine Logos of human language effects no divinisation of that language' and 'no permanent gain in meaning accrues to that language, no stabilization of the relation between God and language such that revelation is made to be a predicate of the language employed'.[18]

Nevertheless, there is an element of Barth's treatment of the relationship between the Word and words which is not

---

15.   *Ibid.*, 256.

16.   *Ibid*, 245.

17.   See B L McCormack, 'Graham Ward's *Barth, Derrida and the Language of Theology*', *Scottish Journal of Theology* 49 (1996): 101f.

18.   *Ibid*, 107. On this see *CD* II/1, 227-232.

accounted for by an appeal to the Incarnation. Its particularism does indeed do justice to the particularity of revelatory events which Barth champions over and against any claims for a general revelatory capacity of language. Yet its very particularity could be seen to be precisely what prevents an appeal to the Incarnation—with its associations of finality and completeness—from providing a theological ground for what Barth terms, 'further insights'—a notion which warrants brief explanation.

For all Barth's emphasis on the indirectness of revelation, he is clear that God's self-revelation has a specific *terminus ad quem*: 'Not the veiling, however, but the unveiling is the purpose of His revelation'. Whilst the veiling and unveiling must be held in tension, 'these two moments in His revelation and in faith are not equally balanced' (*CD* II/1, 215). If there is, as George Hunsinger observes, a reticence in Barth's concept of analogy, there is also a commitment to the 'perspicuity of God's self-revelation'.[19] On the other hand, this 'teleological ordering' (see *CD* II/1, 236) and 'perspicuity' do not overwhelm the 'reticence' (to use Hunsginer's terms). A certain provisionality remains. When elaborating on his statement that God's Word is both

---

19   'The reticence of analogy honoured the mystery, the predication of analogy the perspicuity, of God's self revelation as attested in scripture.' G Hunsinger, 'Beyond Literalism and Expressivism: Karl Barth's Hermeneutical Realism', *Modern Theology* (3): 1987, 218. For a recent and general discussion of the relationship between Barth's particular concept of analogy and the concerns of deconstructionism see S F Du Toit, 'Revelation or Reveilation? Barth and Posmodernism', *Heythrop Journal* 40 (1999): 1-18. More basically, the issue underlying these discussions is the precise nature of Barth's realism. On this, in addition to the above essay of Hunsinger, reference would also need to be made to such works as I Dalferth, 'Karl Barth's eschatological realism', in S W Sykes (ed), *Karl Barth. Centenary Essays* Cambridge: Cambridge University Press, 1989, 14-45, and B L McCormack, *Karl Barth's Critically Realistic Dialectical Theology* (Oxford: Clarendon, 1995).

'provisionally comprehensible and comprehensible in all its incomprehensibility', Barth says: 'to say "provisionally" is to indicate the possibility of further insights and that to say "in all its incomprehensibility" is to imply that we shall still be moving within fixed limits even in all these further insights'(*CD* I/1, 249). In other words, it is not a question of an endless deferral of reference which prevents revelation from occurring, as Ward would have us believe, but a question of actual reference within an ongoing history of revelation.

A simple appeal to the Incarnation cannot provide the grounds for this type of history of revelation. Nor, though, does Ward's offer of something 'more general' in the form of a 'process of discourse'. Even less so when Ward understands that for Barth it is theological discourse itself that, in his words already quoted, 'generates supplementary attempts to argue for or to this otherness'. To grasp a more comprehensive picture of the grounds of the provisional and occasional character of revelatory events, it will be necessary to move beyond Barth's specific comments on language and beyond general theories of discourse and explore something of the pattern of divine action in the world. This task will be taken up in the second section of this essay.

Before coming to that section, though, there is one more issue to emerge from the comparisons between Barth and Derrida. It is raised in William Stacy Johnson's *The Mystery of God: Karl Barth and the Postmodern Foundations of Theology*, and can be brought to the surface quite quickly. Johnson puts Derrida to a more modest heuristic use. He sees certain parallels between Derrida's critique of the logocentrism and dualism of the Western intellectual tradition, on the one hand, and Barth's own critique of the metaphysical concept of God and his attempts to offer a non-dualistic account of God's relationship to the world, on the other. Johnson sees Barth's own emphasis on the mystery of God as strongly shaped by these concerns and translated into Barth's commitment to the open-ended

198

character of the theological task.[20] His thorough doctrinal reading of Barth ultimately issues in a playing out of these concerns in ethics: theology that takes the mystery of God as axiomatic, he writes, 'stands poised between the explication (*explicatio*) and application (*applicatio*)'.[21] He does, however, make one brief comment of greater relevance to my concern. Suggesting that Barth's theology is more like a constitution than a statute, Johnson suggests that it does not impose 'narrow limits on the type of discourse to be permitted, but that it opens up possibilities for an expansion of discourse'.[22] If this is so, then there must be certain linguistic acts carried out by humans to facilitate such an expanded discourse. Although Johnson himself does not elaborate on this point, I will use the third section of this essay to explore whether Barth does allow for human linguistic acts which would make some such 'expansion of discourse' possible.

'The Possibility of Further Insights':
A History of Revelation

What follows is not an exhaustive account of Barth's understanding of the history of revelation. The specific issue to be highlighted here is the grounding of the possibility of 'further insights' in the being of God. This movement towards 'further insights' has the character it does and not some other character because, at least in part, God has the nature He has and not some other nature. Barth claims that any event of revelation is a 'provisional part or moment of the history of the covenant between God and us. It is a reference which always needs to be confirmed and completed by other references' (*CD*

---

20. W S Johnson, *op cit*, 21-30.
21. *Ibid*,190.
22. *Ibid*.

Geoff Thompson

II/1, 53). It is the pattern of 'confirmation and completion' proposed by Barth that will show itself to be deeply rooted, not in a general theory of language, but in a distinctively Christian doctrine of God.

'Everything depends', says Barth, 'on the fact that God does not cease to bear witness to Himself as the one eternal God in new manifestations of his presence, in new revelation of His former ways, leading His people continually from old to new faith' (*CD* II/1, 23f). Taken on its own, this line of thought would suggest that this promise of further insights is related to the provisionality—even fallibility—of the faith of the people of God. The dynamic that is at work here could be taken to be located in movement from old faith to new faith in response to new revelations of God's former ways.[23] Yet, Barth is predictably careful to identify the primary subject of this history of revelation: it is not the person to whom God is revealed, but Jesus Christ who is the 'basic reality and substance of the sacramental reality of [God's] revelation' (*CD* II/1, 53).[24] That the knowledge of God has a history derives not just from movement within human apprehension of revelation, but from the fact that 'the man Jesus is a beginning of which there are continuations; a sacramental continuity stretches backwards into the existence of the people of Israel, whose Messiah He is, and forwards into the existence of the apostolate and the Church founded on the apostolate' (*CD* II/1, 54).

The question of agency does not, however, exhaust the discussion. Barth is also keen to insist that the limitations which do condition human knowledge of God are not quantitative in character (see *CD* II/1, 52) To make this point, he turns to his

---

23 This is made even more explicit in *CD* II/1, 53.
24 This is of a piece with the fundamental trinitarian conviction of Barth's account of the knowledge of God: 'We have to understand God Himself as the real and primarily acting Subject of all real knowledge of God, so that the self-knowledge of God is the real and primary essence of all knowledge of God' (*CD* II/1, 10).

much used image of a circle and its centre. Revelation, he maintains,

> happens in the whole circumference of this centre, in the whole circumference of sacramental reality, in a succession of attestations and cognitions, which all expect and indicate each other, which all determine and are determined by each other. Not as if each one does not always exist in complete truth. But it does so in such a way that the whole truth is always truth for us temporally. It is truth which always needs to be repeated. It has to become truth afresh in a new attestation and cognition (CD II/1, 61f).

This way of perceiving events which 'expect and indicate' each other is further developed in the Doctrine of Reconciliation where Barth develops his idea of secular parables of the kingdom. Although of great interest in its own right, this text indicates in a more systematic manner the relationship between events of revelation. Whereas in the passage from the Doctrine of God, Jesus Christ is the centre, and the sacramental reality the circumference, here Barth has the one Word of God constituted by the centre and the periphery. You cannot have the centre without the periphery. Any event of revelation—here described as a true word—is such by virtue of being simultaneously related to the centre *and* the remainder of the periphery.

> They are true words, genuine witnesses and attestations of the one true Word, real parables of the kingdom of heaven, if and to the extent that . . . as true segments of the periphery of this circle they point to the whole of the periphery and therefore to the centre, or rather to the extent that the centre and therefore the whole of the periphery, i.e., Jesus Christ Himself, declares Himself in them. Hence they do not express partial truths, for the one truth of Jesus Christ is indivisible, yet they express the one and total truth from a particular angle, and to that extent only implicitly and not explicitly in its unity and totality (CD IV/3, 64).

201

Geoff Thompson

The way which Barth portrays segments, centre and periphery mutually 'pointing' to each other, and his resistance to 'partial' expressions of the truth indicate an appropriation of a certain perichoretic conceptuality. [25] The proximity of this aspect of the history of revelation to trinitarian doctrine, indeed to the triune being of God, is strikingly reinforced in a passage from earlier in the Doctrine of Reconciliation.

> The recognition of Christian faith can and should be varied. The reason for this is as follows. Although its object, the Jesus Christ attested in Scripture and proclaimed by the community, is single, unitary, consistent and free from contradiction, yet for all His singularity and unity His form is inexhaustibly rich, so that it is not merely legitimate but obligatory that believers should continually see and understand it in new lights and aspects. For He Himself does not present Himself to them in one form but in many—indeed, He is not in Himself uniform but multiform. How can it be otherwise when he is the true Son of the God who is eternally rich (CD IV/1, 763).

'He is not in Himself uniform but multiform'. The line of argument here is actually quite straightforward: God is triune and therefore internally multiform or differentiated; and because God is in his works what He is in Himself (see CD II/1, 260), then God's work *ad extra* is also multiform and differentiated.

This line of thought is no accident. It reflects moves made by Barth early in the development of the *Church Dogmatics*. Again in the Doctrine of God, Barth writes of the 'infinite individual variation of the divine action *ad extra*' (CD II/1, 316). The context is Barth's discussion of the Being of God in Freedom,

---

25. For further discussion on this application of perichoretic/Chalcedonian conceptuality of mutual indwelling, see G Hunsinger, *How To Read Karl Barth: The Shape of His Theology* (Oxford: Oxford University Press, 1991), especially 271-273.

202

and in particular, his claim that God's freely given immanence to the finite creature does not in any way restrict God's freedom, or limit the mode of God's work. There is, he writes 'no mode of action proceeding uniformly from Him' (*CD* II/1, 315). The divine action is not 'something generalised which as such certainly cannot be divine' (*CD* II/1, 316).

Here, then, lies the ground for the particular pattern of events of revelation which expect and indicate each other. The unity of God's triune being and His work means that the history of revelation reflects the same combination of differentiation and mutual indwelling that characterises God's triunity.

The Expansion of Theological Discourse:
Human Linguistic Events

Although Barth never denied, and roundly insisted upon, the human character of theology[26], his notion of the divine conscription of language has often been understood to render extremely problematic anything he may have said about the human task of theological discourse.[27] Indeed, we touch here on the vexed question of human agency in Barth's theology generally. In this section, I want to make two general points about Barth's account of the divinely-given room for human agency and then a more specific point about the human task of developing the church's discourse about God.

The first general point focuses on the coherence of Barth's account of human agency. This controversial aspect of Barth's work can be barely touched on here except to appropriate John

---

26. See the discussion of the church's 'active' response to the hearing of the account of the teaching role of the church in *CD* I/2, 844-861, and also comments in *CD* II/1, 227f.

27. See, for instance, J W Richards, 'Barth on the Divine Conscription of Language', *Heythrop Journal* 38 (1997): 247-266.

Webster's exposition of Barth's account of the 'correspondence' of human action to the prior divine action.[28] The key text in Webster's work is Barth's treatment of water baptism which Barth describes as a 'human action which corresponds to the divine action' (*CD* IV/4, 105). The concept of correspondence allows Barth to prevent any confusion of divine and human works, and thereby to ascribe a proper dignity to the latter. Webster demonstrates how this concept of correspondence is 'further refined' in *The Christian Life*. Barth writes there of the divine-human partnership: ' . . . it is very proper for [God] . . . to let his action be co-determined by his children who have been freed for obedience to him' (*CL*, 104). This ascription of a proper dignity to human agency, coupled to a willingness to consider a co-determination of God's action will be shown below to assume some significance for Barth's account of human linguistic events which can be seen to expand theological discourse.

The second general point stems directly from the issues raised in the previous section of this essay. The room which God makes for human activity and the theological contours of that activity are directly related to God's triune identity. The issue emerges with some particular clarity in the Doctrine of Providence when Barth describes God's rule as one which does not impose itself upon the creature by allowing a merely uniform and homogeneous human response. That it is the rule of the triune God means that there corresponds to it a variegated, heterogenous creaturely response. The events in God's rule are 'not so many "cases" in the one rule, but individual events which have their own importance and have to be considered in and for themselves' (*CD* III/3, 138). Once again there is an affirmation of the unity of the divine act linked to the rejection of its uniformity. God's 'unified plan has nothing whatever to do with a levelling down and flattening out of

---

28   J Webster, *Barth's Ethics of Reconciliation* (Cambridge: Cambridge University Press, 1995), especially 148-213.

individuals and individual groupings' (*CD* III/3, 168). Barth
again stresses that the claim that God's rule does not obliterate
diversity is not simply a divine accommodation to a creaturely
diversity that exists independently of God's rule, but is rooted
in God's own being. 'Like the divine essence, the divine activity
is single, united and therefore unitary, but it is also manifold
and therefore not uniform, monotonous and undifferentiated.'
(*CD* III/3, 137)

Because God is triune, the diversity of creaturely occurrence
is not alien to God: ' . . . the differentiated nature of the world
created by Him derives from himself even as the one'. Indeed,
Barth seeks to strengthen his argument by considering the
alternative, the 'notion of a god who in himself is uniform,
monotonous and undifferentiated' (*CD* III/3, 138). Such a god
could only deal with the manifoldness of the creature by
suppressing that diversity or accommodating itself to it (see *CD*
III/3, 138). But no such suppression or accommodation is
required of the 'eternally rich' triune God. Nor does this
richness compromise God's simplicity:

> [God's] simplicity has not to be explained as the
> simplicity of the absolute as compared with the
> relative . . . It is the simplicity of the God who is
> eternally rich in His threefold being . . . [I]t is the
> simplicity of the One who in Himself as Father, Son
> and Holy Ghost is love, who in Himself does not
> merely exist but co-exists, who in Himself has life . . .
> It is this God, who is not poor in Himself, but rich,
> who works together with the creature. He does not do
> it uniformly or monotonously or without
> differentiation, for He is not uniform or monotonous
> or undifferentiated in Himself. If he were to do it in
> this way He would be doing violence to his own
> nature; He would not be God (*CD* III/3, 138).

The significance of this second general point about human
agency is that the human act of constructing theology
presupposes a broader context, not just of the creature 'working
together' with the Creator, but an account of the relationship of

205

human and divine agency which envisages an intersection of human and divine *diversity*.

In now turning to the more specific point about human linguistic events, I begin with Barth's warnings, expounded in 'The People of God in World Occurrence', against what he calls an 'ecclesiological Docetism'. Insisting that the church's relationship with the world involves the former's total dependence upon and total freedom towards the latter (*CD* IV/3, 721-751), Barth declares that the church is a 'thoroughly worldly element participating in worldly occurrence' (*CD* IV/3, 723).

Consequently, the church 'does not have its own language in which to impart' its message. It can, says Barth, 'only adopt the modes of thought and speech of its spatial and temporal environment more near or distant, more ancient or modern . . . [and] when it speaks it stands on common ground with the world around' (*CD* IV/3, 735). In short, The church 'has no vocabulary of its own' (*CD* IV/3, 735) and there is 'no sacral speech peculiar to' (*CD* IV/3, 736) the Christian community. Barth places no limit on the sources from which the church might draw its language:

> The whole sphere of human speech and wealth of its possibilities is open to [the people of God], so that as they go to different men they can use their own modes of speech, simple in the case of the simple and complicated in the case of the complicated, to declare to them what the community has to declare as the witness of God and His work and Word (*CD* IV/3, 738).

None of this, of course, eliminates the divine agency in the event of proclamation. Nor does Barth surrender the *priority* of the divine agency in this act of church proclamation. God 'disposes . . . of the speech' of the people of His community. 'He puts His Word on their lips, . . . He sanctifies their profane language, . . . He gives them the power and freedom to speak of Him in their humanly secular words and expressions and sentences' (CD IV/3, 737). Nevertheless, in his account of the church 'adopting' language from the world (an account exactly mirrored a few pages later in the treatment of the church's sociological structure[29]) we see a clear example of the principle of active, obedient and authentic human agency which corresponds to the prior divine act of self-revelation.

These reflections by Barth on the church creatively and judiciously 'borrowing' from the world's language are brief and conceptually undeveloped. To the extent, however, that they provide some insight into some dimensions of the task of expanding theological discourse, they display important continuities with the above general points about human agency. Firstly, theological discourse which proceeds on this basis is able to understand itself as a human act which freely and actively corresponds to the divine initiative. Secondly, as such a human act, it allows theological discourse to reflect the particularities of the times and places in which it takes place—particularities which need not be levelled out but for which there is room in the intersection of divine and human diversity.

Perhaps the most significant issue here is the explicit manner in which the problematic idea of divine *conscription* of language is accompanied by the corresponding human act of *borrowing*. Attention to the correspondence of divine conscription and human borrowing can, I suggest, help deflect some of the criticisms levelled at the conscription claim. Recently that claim has been judged by Jay Wesley Richards as involving a violation of the normal semantic context of words.[30] To some extent, that is entirely correct. Nevertheless, the scandal of this position might be alleviated by the acknowledgment that words occupy constantly changing semantic contexts. In a response to Richards, Stephanus F Du Toit has pointed out that any appeal to analogy—including

---

29. See CD IV/3, 739-742.
30. Richards, *op cit*, 255-259.

Barth's—involves a rejection of univocity and an awareness that the meaning of words is 'the fluid and flexible product of relations within which these words operate'. What these mutual acts of *conscription* and *borrowing* can be understood to achieve is the placing of certain words in the semantic field of the reality which is God's covenant with humanity. It is this new context which, says Du Toit, 'could certainly open radically new semantic possibilities'.[31]

In the present context the preceding considerations suggest that there is a human linguistic event which corresponds to the divine conscription of language. As an act of corresponding obedience—an intersection of human and divine diversity—the church is truly and genuinely free to construct diverse, contingent, contextual languages which, with divine permission and empowerment, communicate its message to the world. This does not depend on any putatively transcendental character of language, but on the creative and obedient use of languages that are themselves human artifacts.

Conclusion

According to Barth, our language for God must change and be renewed, our lines and concepts continually break apart, not primarily because of any property of language, but because this triune God reveals himself in a history of revelation which consists of an infinite variety of particular events. Within the framework of Barth's theology this allows for a free human linguistic response that allows for the expansion of theological discourse. This study has suggested that assessments of Barth's contribution to contemporary discussions of language and divine mystery must not confine themselves to his explicit treatment of those issues. Instead, any such assessment must attend to the wide network of ideas which inform his

---

31. Du Toit, *op cit*, 13.

understanding of the nature and specific purposes of the divine act.

Implied in this network of ideas is a hint that the church's use of its various contextualised languages involves a certain 'negotiation of a variety of images'. I take this phrase from Willie James Jennings, but want to use it positively where he uses it negatively. It emerges in a discussion of apophaticism.

> The beauty of Apophatism is its power to challenge theological arrogance and pride in the ways we often presumed to speak of God while at the same time it offers us a pathway to worship that humbles us before God's own self-revealing. Unfortunately, most current apophatic approaches, shaped as they are by enlightenment dogmatism have banished God to a sphere of unknowing, leaving us with only the negotiation of a variety of images and metaphors for theological reflection. [32]

Where Jennings laments this state of affairs, because of God's banishment to a sphere of unknowing, Barth's theology could be seen as a resource for dealing constructively with it. Drawing on Barth, the need for negotiation arises not because of some idealist, Kantian sphere of unknowing, but a profoundly realist account of the promise of correspondence between the differentiated work of this God and the articulation of that work in the linguistic response of the community of faith.

---

[32] W J Jennings, '"He Became Truly Human": Incarnation, Emancipation and Authentic Humanity', *Modern Theology* 12 (1996): 242.

Barth on Divine Simplicity: Some Implications for Life in a Complex World

Stephen Pickard

The Imperative of Simplicity

Few words seem to offer so many complexities as does *simplicitas*.[1] In the biblical tradition simplicity *(haplotes)* is associated with singleness and undividedness of heart for God, and personal integrity and straightforwardness in all relationships as befits those of the Kingdom of God. This evangelical *simplicitas* is linked to that humility, poverty and childlike innocence in which Jesus rejoices: "I thank you, Father, Lord of heaven and earth, for you have hidden these things from the wise and understanding and revealed them to babes" *(nepiois)*, [Matthew 11:25; cf Luke 10:21]. The ethical, moral and religious dimensions of this evangelical *simpliticas* find their deepest theological rationale in the simple God who is wholly and undividedly trustworthy and faithful, and who accordingly calls forth similar trust and simplicity in life.

Throughout the history of the Christian tradition the simplicity of this God has been heavily influenced by a Neo-Platonic metaphysic of the absolute simplicity of the divine

---

1. See eg 'Simplicity' in C Brown (gen ed), *The New International Dictionary of New Testament Theology* (Grand Rapids: Zondervan, 1986), Vol 3, 571f; W Hill, 'Simplicity of God' in *New Catholic Encyclopedia of Theology*, Staff Catholic University of America, (eds), (Washington & NY: McGraw Hill, 1967), Vol 13, 229-232; S Payne, 'Simplicity' in M Downey (ed), *The New Dictionary of Catholic Spirituality* (The Liturgical Press, 1993), 885-889.

being entirely free from all composition.[2] However, preoccupation with the ontological status of simplicity has, under the pressure of an Enlightenment rationalism, given way to epistemological concerns. Here simplicity assumes primary significance as a parameter invoked, whether consciously or not, as a criterion in the structuring of knowledge.[3] In this respect the philosopher of science, Elliott Sober, has noted that the desire for theories in science, 'in large measures reduces to a desire for simplicity'.[4] He further notes the 'chaos of opinion' concerning simplicity and comments that

> diversity of our intuitions about simplicity is matched only by the tenacity with which these intuitions refuse to yield to formal characterisation. Our intuitions seem unanimous in favour of sparse ontologies, smooth curves, homogeneous universes, invariant equators and impoverished assumptions.[5]

These remarks suggest that the appeal of simplicity involves aesthetic as well as ontological and epistemological considerations. They also point to the elusiveness and, it seems, the inherently controversial nature of simplicity. Indeed, another philosopher of science, Mario Bunge, refers to the 'myth' of simplicity, arguing that the concept, though useful at some stages in the structuring of knowledge, fails as a reliable criterion of truth.[6] Bunge thus reverses the scholastic dictum, *simplex sigillum veri* (simplicity is the seal of truth). From this perspective simplicity as conceptual economy is thus a sign of transitoriness; of falsity being superseded by a lesser falsity. Simplicity may have aesthetic appeal but have little ontological weight.

---

2 See eg Karl Barth's lucid discussion in *CD* II/1, 322-350 & 440-461.

3 N Rescher, *Cognitive Systematization* (Oxford: Blackwell, 1979), Chapter 1.

4 E Sober, *Simplicity* (Oxford: Clarendon Press, 1975), 168.

5 *Ibid*, Preface.

6 M Bunge, *The Myth of Simplicity: Problems of Scientific Philosophy* (Englewood Cliffs, N J: Prentice-Hall, Inc, 1963).

This suggests that consideration of the ontological status of simplicity seems a highly problematic exercise. For a start it seems counter-intuitive given the fact that increasing penetration of reality discloses increasingly higher degrees of complexity. There is, as indicated earlier, a certain resistance to this recognition. As one theologian has noted, 'We are too fond of simplicities and the comfort they bring to face how deeply complexity reaches into the issues which we discuss'.[7] It seems that the sciences of the twenty-first century will be developed on the basis that we are 'part of an ever-changing, interlocking, nonlinear, kaleidoscopic world'.[8] The supposition of such an inner complexity which cannot be known without similar complexities in the structuring of knowledge[9] suggests that theology must divest itself of the simplicity ideal, except perhaps as a purely pragmatic strategy. On this account simplicity is a purely human construct, of some heuristic value in the ordering of knowledge but, as noted earlier, deserving of distrust as a measure of truth. Nevertheless the appeal of simplicity exercises a powerful and enduring attraction. Indeed, as Alfred North Whitehead recognised in his famous maxim—'seek simplicity and distrust it'—the appeal of simplicity seems to be an enduring preoccupation of the human spirit in its search for understanding and meaning.

Today, this search is undertaken in conditions of high risk and danger; the modern world has taken on a decidedly 'menacing appearance'.[10] Issues to do with trust, personal

---

7.   See the essay by D Hardy 'The Future of Theology in a Complex World', in H Regan & A Torrance (eds), *Christ and Context: The Confrontation between Gospel and Culture* (Edinburgh: T&T Clark, 1993), 22.

8.   M Waldrop, *Complexity: The Emerging Science at the Edge of Order and Chaos* (London: Viking, 1993), 333.

9.   See D Hardy, 'Rationality, The Sciences and Theology' in G Wainwright (ed), *Keeping the Faith: Essays to Mark the Centenary of Lux Mundi* (London: SPCK, 1989), 282.

10   See A Giddens, *The Consequences of Modernity* (Oxford: Polity

relations and identity have to be renegotiated within the context of abstract systems of security. The possibility of achieving some degree of personal and social harmony (control?) amidst the complexities and chaotic eruptions of modern life seems daunting. Risk of failure in these 'local projects' is intensified given other potential global catastrophes which 'provide an unnerving horizon of dangers for everyone'.[11] It's no surprise that simplicity in life and thought exercises a powerful attraction in such an environment and assumes something of the status of a foundational axiom of modern efforts to recover wholeness and integrity within a divided and complex world. This general social and cultural importance of the appeal of simplicity gives added force to what Joseph O'Leary refers to as the 'imperative of simplicity'. O'Leary notes that this 'thirst for first hand contact with the heart of the matter'[12] occurs in any radical questioning after religious identity. The force of this simplicity imperative has long been recognised as a feature of the Christian tradition as such. However, the attempt to grasp 'the heart of the matter' through recovery of a 'primordial simplicity'—developed historically, existentially or through some form of naturalism—is understandable but full of pitfalls. Primarily it disregards the radically contingent nature of Christian identity and its corollary ie, that 'the path to the simple' is never simple. It seems that distrusting simplicity may be good advice. However, as Karl Barth noted, a deeper problem concerns the originating impulse to seek the simple: 'It is very understandable, that complex as he (sic) is and suffering from his own complexity as he does, man would like to be different, ie, simple' (*CD* II/1, 449). Barth viewed the free and unfettered fulfillment of this drive for the simple as generative

---

Press, 1990), Chapter 4 for the following discussion.

11   *Ibid*, 125.

12   J O'Leary, *Questioning Back: The Overcoming of Metaphysics in Christian Tradition* (Minneapolis, Minnesota: Winston Press Inc, 1985), 205 and more generally 204-212.

of human idolatry and sin. His own discussion of simplicity, and in particular Divine simplicity, is important in its own right and also because it offers some clues for the practice of Christian discipleship in the complexities of modern life.

Divine Simplicity in the Tradition

Barth's discussion of simplicity occurs within the long tradition of reflection on the nature of the Divine simplicity. Indeed, as indicated earlier, the concept of God as absolute simplicity has exercised a significant impact on the development of the Christian doctrine of God from early in the tradition.[13] The roots of the doctrine of divine simplicity can be traced to Greek metaphysics where the supposition that ultimate reality is simple has been articulated within Neoplatonic and Aristotelian frameworks. According to Plato everything composite—ie, made up of parts—was necessarily divisible and consequently mutable or destructible. As Wolfhart Pannenberg points out, the Platonic doctrine of God as the ultimate and hence immutable origin (first cause) leads to the supposition of the absolute simplicity of God's essence; without qualities or properties.[14] The correlate to absolute simplicity is the radical incomprehensibility of the divine being.

Given the axiomatic strength of the doctrine of divine simplicity in Patristic theology it was clear that any reconstruction of the doctrine of God in light of the Christian revelation would present significant difficulties. Indeed, William Hill suggests that the early centuries of trinitarian and

---

13 See, for example W Pannenberg, *Basic Questions in Theology* (London: SCM, 1971), vol 2, 165-173. For a recent discussion on divine simplicity in philosophy see T Morris, *Our Idea of God: An Introduction to Philosophical Theology* (Notre Dame: University of Notre Dame Press, 1991), 113-118.

14. *Ibid*, 167.

christological reflection can be understood as an attempt in Christian theology to show how 'neither the Incarnation of the Word nor the real distinction of the divine persons is in any wise injurious to God's simplicity'.[15] On Hill's account the controlling question is clear: How might the Christian revelation be understood *within* the received doctrine of divine simplicity? Such an approach was full of danger. Thus when Arius distinguished between Christ as 'creature' and the divine 'Ungenerated One' his real mistake was not so much in lowering the status of the Son but rather inappropriately exalting the Father over the Son.[16] In doing so, Arius preserved the absolute simplicity of God at the price of displacing or nullifying an emerging Christian consciousness in respect of the doctrine of God. The Arian controversy could, from this perspective, be understood as an attempt to think through the received doctrine of divine simplicity in the light of the Christian gospel of God. In this respect the Nicene creed's affirmation of the *homoousion* of the Father and the Son suggested a quite radical and novel reconstitution of the simplicity of God; for the sake of the ontological coherence of the Gospel.[17] On this account affirmation of God's simplicity entailed less a denial of composition and division and more a recognition of God's rich and integral wholeness. Such a conception belonged to the evangelical significance of the *homoousion*. Barth recognised this when he spoke of the Church clarifying its mind about the simplicity of God by reference to the *homoousion* of the Son and Holy Spirit with the Father and the unity of the divine with human nature in Jesus Christ (*CD* II/1, 446).

However, developments in trinitarian theology indicated the difficulty, if not the impossibility, of satisfying the demands of

---

15. Hill, *op cit*, 230.
16. See F Young, *From Nicea to Chalcedon* (London: SCM, 1983), 63f.
17. See the discussion of *homoousion* by T Torrance, *The Trinitarian Faith* (Edinburgh: T&T Clark, 1988), 132-145.

the doctrine of divine simplicity and at the same time doing justice to the surprising novelty introduced in the doctrine of God through the life, death and resurrection of Jesus Christ in the power of the Holy Spirit. In the West this tension between the biblical tradition of the simplicity of God and an alien metaphysic of divine simplicity can be discerned in Augustine and traced through the Medieval tradition as expressed in, among others, Anselm, Aquinas and Ockham.[18] This tension remains in Barth's own illuminating discussion to which we now turn.

Barth on Divine Simplicity

Barth considered divine simplicity in the context of his inquiry into the perfections of God in volume two of the *Church Dogmatics*.[19] In this insightful discussion two kinds of simplicity emerge: a false simplicity that takes its cue from a general idea of simplicity and a genuine divine simplicity determined by the revelation of the Lord of Glory (*CD* II/1, 327ff, 449f). In the context of his discussion of the perfections of Divine freedom Barth considers the natural human tendency to absolutise the uniqueness of God. Whilst 'we must say that God is the absolutely One . . . we cannot say that the absolutely one is God' (*CD* II/1, 448). This latter and very natural human tendency evidences itself in monotheism, 'an idea which can be directly divined or logically and mathematically constructed without God' (*CD* II/1, 448). For Barth monothesim is 'the religious glorification of the number 'one', the absolutising of the idea of

---

18   See R La Croix, 'Augustine on the Simplicity of God', *The New Scholasticism* 51 (1977): 453-469; M Adams, *William Ockham*, 2 Vols, (Notre Dame: University of Notre Dame Press, 1987) Vol 2, Chapter 21; C Hughes, *On a Complex Theory of a Simple God: An Investigation in Aquinas' Philosophical Theology* (Ithaca & London: Cornell University Press, 1989) 166-170.

19   See above footnote 2.

uniqueness' (*ibid*). Thus in Barth's view there is a great gulf between the way in which Islam and Christianity proclaim that there is only one God.

In precisely the same way that it is quite false to say that the absolutely one is God so too with the notion of the simplicity of God: 'the assertion of the simplicity of God is not reversible in the sense that it could equally well be said that the simple is God' (*CD* II/1, 449). He notes that whenever human beings have 'begun to worship the unique as a deity, they have always more or less consistently tried to describe it as the simple as well' (*CD* II/1, 449). However, when the simple is equated with God this generates a natural yet mistaken understanding of divine simplicity (derived from the metaphysics of Ancient Stoicism and Neo-Platonism) and made determinative for Christian theology (*CD* II/1, 329). It leads to a view of the simple as 'an utterly unmoved being, remote from this world altogether, incapable of sound or action, influence on or relation to anything else' (*CD* II/1, 449). Such a view of the simple, abstracted from all that is complex, is correlated to a world that is necessarily autonomous and over which the absolutely simple has no 'mastery'. Alternatively, a relation between the simple (unconditioned) and the world (conditioned) is posited such that the latter becomes essential to the former thus generating a dialectical identity of the two. This leads to the abandonment of the absolute simplicity of the 'would-be-simple' and with it 'that in which we were seeking the divinity of God' (*CD* II/1, 449). This, in Barth's view, was the fate of the orthodox doctrine of God as it developed in the early church, and in medieval theology through to Hegel and Schleiermacher, at least 'to the extent that its basis was the concept of the *ens simplicissimum*' (*CD* II/1, 449). An 'absolutised idea of simplicity' thus leads to either a god no longer sovereign over and free for the world, or a god so co-mixed with the world that genuine simplicity is forfeited.

This false track on simplicity evidenced itself in the traditional discussion of the attributes of God. Under the

217

pressure of a strict nominalism all predications of the being of God (eg Ockham's 'attributal perfections') constitute mental constructs and descriptions to which there is no corresponding reality in God who is 'pure simplicity'. In a milder form the multiplicity of perfections attributed to God are expressive of a vision of God necessarily constrained by the limits of human existence. This could lead to the 'accommodation' view of Calvin in which the enumeration of God's perfections did not describe God's inner life 'but in relation to us, on order that our acknowledgment of him may be more a vivid actual impression than empty visual speculation'.[20] However, full recognition of God's perfections was continually thwarted or undermined by the 'alien proposition that the being of God meant at bottom God's *nuda essentia* whose simplicity must be conceptually the first and last and real thing' (*CD* II/1, 329). The properties of God inevitably assume a purely secondary significance. By beginning from a generalised notion of God, 'the idea of the divine simplicity was necessarily exalted to the all-controlling principal, the idol, . . . devouring everything concrete . . . [Accordingly] when we speak of God, we must mean essentially only the simplicity and not the richness, at best the simplicity of richness, but at bottom only the simplicity' (*CD* II/1, 329).

The false track on simplicity was, in Barth's view, symptomatic of the 'fundamental error of the whole earlier doctrine of God' (*CD* II/1, 348) which began first with God's being in general and then considered God's triune nature.[21] By beginning with the revelation of the personal Triune God, Barth argued that the notion of God's simple being is given its proper foundation. Formally this means that whilst God is absolutely simple, this simplicity 'can only be God Himself—and not "God Himself" interpreted by the idea of the absolutely simple, but

---

20 Calvin, *Institutes*, I x.2.
21. Cf J Moltmann, *The Trinity and the Kingdom of God* (London:SCM, 1981), 16ff.

God Himself in His self-interpretation' (*CD* II/1, 457). Thus, Barth characteristically points to God's self revelation attested in Scripture as the absolutely simple One, uncomposed and indivisible. Breaking the idolatrous simplicity of human imagining requires the recognition that 'the simplicity of God *is His own simplicity*' (*CD* II/1, 458; my italics). Barth's discussion of divine simplicity belongs to his inquiry into the revelation of the being of God as the one who loves in freedom. The utterly simple God is thus to be located precisely in the place in which the prophets and apostles found and were found by God—'in God's self-demonstration given by Him in His Word and work' (*CD* II/1, 459). Materially God's Word and work throughout the Bible are self demonstrations of God's trustworthiness, truthfulness and fidelity. God's simplicity consists in this, for God 'is trustworthy in His essence, in the inmost core of the His being. And this is His simplicity' (*CD* II/1, 459). As such God's simplicity is both foundational for life and known only by faith in the God who is trustworthy. God's trustworthiness and faithfulness converge and concentrate in Jesus Christ in whom 'is the Yea and the Amen of the one God' (*CD* II/1, 460). Ultimately, then, God is trustworthy and true because Jesus Christ is the true and faithful one of God. The simplicity of God thus reveals its inner grounding in the God of the doctrine of the Trinity and Christology: 'the unity of the triune God and of the Son of God with man in Jesus Christ is itself the simplicity of God' (*CD* II/1, 446).

Divine Simplicity Under Two Forms: God's Love and Freedom

Clearly for Barth, to speak of the divine simplicity is not to posit an abstract, impersonal absolute; rather the true and genuine simplicity of God—God's indivisible, indissoluble and inflexible being—is the implicate of the being of the God who loves in freedom. God's simplicity is demonstrated and confirmed in God's covenant of loving faithfulness with the creature. God's essence, revealed in God's act, is trustworthy; this is God's simpleness. The fulfilment of the covenant of love in Jesus Christ reveals the nature of God's simple being; 'indivisible' (whole and integral), 'indissoluble' (secure and indestructible) and 'inflexible' (unrelenting and unyielding) in faithfulness and truth. The simplicity of God is, in this way, transposed from bare essence to dynamic act; from the realm of metaphysics to implicate of revelation. God loves and so reveals who God is; the absolutely simple one. The ontological status of the simplicity of God is confirmed but only through particular concrete personal acts of love. Accordingly for Barth divine simplicity is above all else an ethical category.

Precisely because God loves *in freedom*, the simplicity of divine love has its necessary correlate in God's freedom. Being simple—wholly and undividedly God—in all distinctions, even in God's triunity, entails not only God's essential oneness and uniqueness but also designates God as 'incomparably free, sovereign and majestic' (*CD* II/1, 445). Accordingly, God's simplicity is God's Lordship; even in the triune life and 'the whole real wealth of His being' God remains 'unconditionally One'. Barth is quite clear: *'for every distinction of His being and working is simply a repetition and corroboration of the one being'* (*CD* II/1, 445; my italics). The implication of such simplicity is that God's relation to the world cannot entail any 'combination, amalgamation or identification'; nothing must be so interpreted 'not even the incarnation of the Son of God in Jesus Christ'. Even in the oneness of God with the creature in Jesus Christ 'God does not cease for a moment or in any regard to be the one, true God' (*CD* II/1, 446).

In Barth the simplicity of God is thus manifest from two perspectives; God's love and God's freedom. Formally of course simplicity as indivisibility is relevant in both domains. However, it is far from clear how the strong christological and ethical grounding for simplicity as faithfulness—'the real meaning and basis' of God's simplicity—informs the simplicity by which God is incomparably free, sovereign and one through all multiplicity. Perhaps a tension can be discerned here between a true and genuine basis for divine simplicity—one conducive to a rich trinitarian simplicity - and a remnant of another alien simplicity doctrine that informs Barth's strong assertion of the freedom and aseity of God? Might not Barth's discussion and deployment of the simplicity postulate evidence an ambiguity that has been discerned in the monist tendencies of this doctrine of the Trinity? This is hardly surprising, for Barth himself recognised that the "battle for the recognition of the simplicity of God was the same as for the recognition of the Trinity and of the relation between the divine and human natures in Jesus Christ" (*CD* II/1, 446). And again; 'the unity of the triune God and the Son of God with man in Jesus Christ *is itself* the simplicity of God' (*CD* II/1, 446; my italics). Problems in one area will necessarily manifest themselves in different guise in other related areas.

To Follow the Simple God

Our brief excursus of this major area of Christian theology as developed by Karl Barth highlighted both the importance and the difficulty of breaking through to a rich and adequate understanding of the true simplicity of God. Christian theology still struggles to cope with the fecundity, sheer novelty and complexity of the God of the Gospel. Insofar as Barth's point holds good, that 'the unity of the triune God and of the Son of God with man in Jesus Christ is itself the simplicity of God', it is possible to formulate a concept of God as *a being of maximal economy*, whose simplicity is concentration of plenitude.[22] This

---

22. Cf Sober, *op cit*, who proposes a notion of simplicity as relative informativeness. That which requires the minimum extra information, *i.e.*, that which is maximally informative is the most simple. High quality simplicity signifies maximal concentration.

seems to accord with Barth's own best intentions as evidenced in his remarkable discourse on the perfections of God. God does not merely possess the 'wealth' of his perfections—their multiplicity, individuality and diversity—God 'is this wealth'. The conclusion Barth draws from this is critical: God is '*in essence* not only one, but multiple, individual and diverse' (*CD* II/1, 331). His concern is to break the 'undialectical understanding' of the inner being of the *simplicitas Dei* which results in an 'empty and unreal' divine simplicity. For Barth, the simple being of God 'transcends the contrast of *simplicitas* and *multiplicitas*, including and reconciling both. We can only accept and interpret God's *simplicitas* and *multiplicitas* in such a way as to imply that they are not mutually exclusive but inclusive, or rather that they are both included in God Himself' (*CD* II/1, 333). The discussion of divine perfections reveals itself at this point as a search by Barth for that harmonious dynamic of God's dialectical simplicity (*CD* II/1, 348). Clearly on this account simplicity and plenitude (rich complexity) are correlated, a point expressed eloquently by Barth when he noted that: 'Consideration of the divine attributes can but move in circles around the one but infinitely rich being of God whose simplicity is abundance itself and whose abundance is simplicity itself' (*CD* II/1, 406). Barth was in no doubt, the doctrine of the Trinity, as plenitude in simplicity, was the Christian doctrine of God.

The project envisaged by Barth, of reconceiving the triune simplicity of God, remains on the theological agenda. Precisely because it is the truth of God's simple being that is sought, simplicities that offer genuine epistemological insight and possibilities for godly discipleship ideally engender a dynamic in Christian life and thought that befits God's own trinitarian simplicity. The supposition here is that the nature and dynamic of the simplicity of God is generative of a correspondence at the level of Christian discipleship. Here, in the face of the 'menacing appearance' of the modern world, the appeal of simplicity easily succumbs to precisely the same danger as observed in the doctrine of God. The barren simplicity of an impersonal deity is transferred into forms of discipleship that are similarly barren and impersonal. The monist drive in the doctrine of God re-emerges in forms of discipleship that 'succeed' through domination or self-enclosure. A more genuine and therefore radical Christian discipleship entails a prizing open of new possibilities amidst the complexities and confusions of modernity; of so willing the one thing that one is willing for anything for the sake of Jesus Christ. There is a richness to this kind of discipleship which cannot be reduced to a singular form but which is constrained only by the gospel of God's triune simplicity. To find a simplicity of life in correspondence with the simpleness of such a God is the other project that remains on the ecclesial agenda at the beginning of the third millennium.

Part Four

Theology After Barth and Beyond Modernity

Postliberal Theology and the Charge of Incorrigibility: A Misplaced Allegation?

Bruce Barber

Much contemporary theological conversation has been likened to that of a public speaker who is unable to begin because of continual need to clear the throat. That is to say, the important and extremely interesting matters of method do not seem so far to have led to much in the way of specific theological formulations. Thus Karl Rahner's pertinent observation of an earlier day that 'they are continually sharpening knives, and no longer have anything to cut'[1] continues to hold good. That could never be said of the one whose name this conference is honouring and to whose legacy this paper is indebted. For Barth above all, it was always the case that prolegomena or introductory matters were never what must be said *before* but always what must be said *first*.

As one attempts to make one's way through the contemporary methodological thicket occasioned by conversations between the so-called Chicago School[2] and Yale school[3], it becomes clear how questions of method are still unresolved in the arbitrary, even ideological, terminology being employed by the respective practitioners. We have correlationists and anti-correlationists, post-moderns and anti-moderns, deconstructive postmoderns and eliminative postmoderns, and now more recently, post-postmoderns; there

---

1. Referred to but not identified in H Thielicke, *The Evangelical Faith* Vol 1 (Grand Rapids: Eerdmans, 1974), 53.
2. Exemplified by the Catholic theologian, David Tracy.
3. Exemplified by the Lutheran theologian, George Lindbeck.

Bruce Barber

are constructive, revisionary, transformative or renewal theologies; neo-conservative, restorationist, retrievalist or postliberal theologies. We have foundationalists, non-foundationalists, anti-foundationalists, post-foundationalists; Barth called for a foundational non-foundation;[4] Colin Gunton, for a non-foundational foundation.[5]

Sometimes these designations are employed by advocates, sometimes by antagonists: in either case, never innocent of either tacit approval or disapproval. Further, just when we might imagine that we are getting these categorisations straight, suddenly confusion begins all over again. For example, David Tracy in a highly eirenic and nuanced essay advocates a correlative theology, but allows within this for instances of non-identity. 'No theologian' he says 'can decide before the actual enquiry whether identity or nonidentity or identity in difference (dialectical theology) or similarity in difference (analogical theology) should obtain'.[6] It is difficult to escape the conclusion that correlation as non-identity now means anti-correlation. And further, what is the nature of the 'actual enquiry'? When are the theologians about to display their wares? It is an open question as to how helpful all such categorisations ultimately are, delineating as they do some Procrustean bed which the theological enterprise is required to fit. Indeed, the game does appear to turn somewhat abrasive when naked value judgments are brought into play as, for example, with respect to Postliberal theology when it is repeatedly charged with being, amongst other negativities: relativistic, fideistic, isolationist, sectarian, tribalistic, imperialistic, totalitarian, triumphalist, obscurantist. Considerable heat, if not light, is engendered in this plethora of

---

4. See *CD* I/2, 868.
5. C Gunton, *The One, the Three and the Many* (Cambridge: Cambridge University Press, 1993), 132f.
6. D Tracy, 'The Uneasy Alliance Reconceived: Catholic Theological Method and Modernity', *Theological Studies* 50 (1989): 563.

adjectives, notwithstanding the fact that lively controversy and strong convictions have a long tradition in theology, as in other human enterprises.[7]

I wish in the remainder of this paper to restrict myself to consideration of one claim only: that proposed by intertextualists that intratextualists are guilty of incorrigibility in the sense that intratextual theology makes itself exempt from external correction and critique, and thus makes itself vulnerable to just the epithets exemplified above. Since my major concern is to identify key theological doctrines that might rebut such a charge, I will summarise briefly the main outlines of Postliberal theology, and the substance of the case brought against it.

Citing George Lindbeck as representative of Postliberal theology, three major tenets of Postliberal theology may be identified.[8] (i) the Christian faith is best described as a 'cultural linguistic' system, that is, as primarily neither propositions to be believed nor experiences to be expressed. (ii) Postliberal theology understands the canonical texts of scripture as being at the heart of this cultural linguistic system. (iii) Christian doctrine is primarily the regulative grammar governing the practice of Christian faith, in the sense of its being communally authoritative rules of discourse, attitude and action.

I understand Lindbeck's concern to be an identification of God in the text, not that of an intratextually defined God who subsequently has to be shown to be relevant to other texts.[9]

---

7. In earlier times (but much the same issue?) similar descriptions arose, if not between Barth and Bultmann themselves, at least between the Barthians and the Bultmannians. And what of the controversy between Kierkegaard and Hegel, Luther and Erasmus, Aquinas and Anselm, Clement and Irenaeus?

8. G Lindbeck, *The Nature of Doctrine: Religion and Theology in a Post Liberal Age* (Philadelphia: Westminster Press, 1984), *passim* but especially 17-19.

9. Robert Jenson has succinctly stated the problem: 'Were God identified *by* Israel's Exodus or Jesus' Resurrection, without being

This subtle distinction is crucial for clarifying the object of theological understanding: intratextuality seeks a textual identification labelled God; intertextuality seeks the reality of God identified but not confined by the text.[10] However, the issue may be better described as not so much one of a cultural linguistic specificity versus none, as of two such specificities each claiming pre-eminence.

Two criticisms of intratextuality have emerged.[11] The first is that the Bible or the gospel is not, and cannot be, the only text which determines the semiotic system of the Christian community. That community, it is claimed, is internally plural in that it has always had a multiplicity of canons and texts in which textual interpretation takes place. It has always been not a single 'acted document' but a set of "enacted texts". It is somewhat puzzling why this is regarded as being a significant criticism. Given the structure of Lindbeck's proposal, the text that 'absorbs the world' is not the biblical text *simpliciter* but 'the Christian text', which includes the grammar of doctrine and worship. The question therefore arises: is this criticism another illustration of the necessity to choose in formal terms the ostensive many rather than the one which embraces the many? Could it be that the intertextualists might in the final analysis be described as 'lapsed fundamentalists', either of text or tradition, who are now as preoccupied by the phenomenon of an

---

identified *with* them, the identification would be a revelation ontologically other than God himself. The revealing events would be our *clues* to God, but would not *be* God . . . It is precisely this distinction between the god and its revelation that the biblical critique of religion attacks' (*Systematic Theology Vol 1, The Triune God* (New York: Oxford University Press, 1997), 59).

10.   S L Stell, 'Hermeneutics in Theology and the Theology of Hermeneutics', *Journal of American Academy of Religion* 61 (1993): 691.

11.   S Kendall ,'Intratextual Theology in a Postmodern World': T W Tilley (ed), *Postmodern Theologies* (Maryknoll, NY: Orbis, 1995), 104.

undeniable plurality as they might formerly have been with a simplistic homogeneity?

The second criticism directed at Lindbeck is that pure intratextuality is a practical impossibility; that the *worlds* in which we live are internally plural. The claim is that the same sort of argument undermines the distinction between the pure intratextual and the intertextual as does that between the identical collapse of the anthropologists' distinctions between the intracultural and the intercultural. Here the one and the many problem identified in the first criticism is replaced by the requirement to conform to an internal/external categorization that, in the light of Christian doctrine itself, I shall argue is gratuitous.

In particular, two aspects to the charge of incorrigibility may be identified. The first is that of isolationism, the second that of imperialism.[12] The charge of isolationism is predicated on a view that the modern fragmentation of life is normative, and that because most of us live in a variety of contexts, the Christian claim will be found to be competitive with other claims. Thus, Postliberal theology is accused of making commensurability impossible. The second accusation of imperialism is thus near at hand; if, as Lindbeck asserts, the text absorbs the world, how can the Christian faith be anything but imperialistically incorrigible?

The issue at the heart of these accusations is that of how one can conceptualise any critique of the intratextual proposal, specifically with regard to the adequacy of the truth claims of the Christian faith thus understood. Yet it may well be that the apparent reluctance actually to unfold the theological doctrinal enterprise is responsible for the methodological disagreements having the force that they appear to have. Thus the remainder

---

12 B Marshall, 'Absorbing the World: Christianity and the Universe of Truths' in *idem*, (ed), *Theology and Dialogue: Essays in Conversation with George Lindbeck* (Notre Dame: University of Notre Dame, Press, 1990), 85f.

of the paper will be an endeavour to offer an analysis of the text understood in Lindbeck's sense, by sketching how actual doctrinal reflection overcomes the hitherto schematic formal classification. The issue then becomes not so much that of intratextuality per se versus intertextuality, as it is of what might be called a *contextual intratextuality* .[13]

On the grounds that doctrine is as much a critical principle as a method, I propose to identify three Christian doctrines which inherently resist incorrigibility: Creation, Christology and Ecclesiology, in order to demonstrate how each doctrine attacks the apparently otherwise unassailable commitment to dualistic internal / external designations.

Creation

The doctrine of Creation at the very least makes recourse to the claim of incorrigibility extremely problematic. The assumptions of correlative theology, whether of the 'hard' or 'soft' variety, is that the necessary contingency or independence of creation is synonymous with externality. But in a world celebrated by the Creator as a 'good work', where would one go that could possibly qualify as an external? Are not all human activities and enterprises not even finally but fundamentally located within this 'overarching metanarrative that the Church tells about God's relationship with the world'?[14] So much for isolationism.

---

13. In this regard, John Milbank makes the perceptive comment: 'My worry is really that (Lindbeck) is still residually *liberal*. By failing to see the regulative textual dynamics in a more Catholic manner as being *at one* with developing tradition, he still allows "context" to remain external and autonomous. But it is also true that if he revised his post-modernism in this direction he would give more scope for a self-critical process within Christian tradition and this might answer some of the fears of the liberals': 'An Essay against Secular Order', *The Journal of Religious Ethics* 15 (1987): 221.

14. P D Kenneson, 'The Alleged Incorrigibility of Postliberal

But what of the incorrigibility of triumphalism? Langdon Gilkey long ago pointed out that the biblical narratives of Creation are an amalgam of prescientific 'science', pre-rational 'philosophy' and primitive (sic) theology of ancient man.[15] The prejudice that the theology is primitive (a modern Enlightenment classification?) must not be allowed to conceal the intertextual nature of the narrative of Genesis chapter 1, with its radical demythologising of another (genuinely?) primitive vision of the Babylonian ENUMA ELISH created to demonstrate that Babylon is the centre of the Universe. What, incidentally, could be more triumphant than that claim? That the Hebrews chose to preface their specifically redemption-constituting narratives with (to use Barth's language) the Creation sagas—where how humans stand before God is the question rather than how God can be made to serve us—continues to offer a reconciling therapeutic repudiation of all attempts to instantiate a bifurcated world of religious and non-religious spheres. The scientific and philosophical vehicles for this theological vision have undeniably undergone many changes since the C6 BC, but in its turn, the theological logic of the texts has brought to birth the possibility of the modern technological scientific world in the midst of which we now stand. A Marcionite disjunction hermetically sealing off a world of redemption, purportedly of 'intratextual' content, from a world of creation, purportedly of 'intertextual' necessity, is thus problematic both for establishing the integrity of the world and its truth claims, but equally for safeguarding the integrity of the theological disciplines. In contrast, Lindbeck's call for the text to absorb the world is nothing other than to honour the text's *already* existing claim.

Theology' in T R Phillips and D L Okholm (eds), *The Nature of Confession* (Downers Grove, Illinois: IVP, 1996), 102.

15   L Gilkey, *Maker of Heaven and Earth* (New York: Doubleday, 1965), 26.

Bruce Barber

Christology

If we turn secondly to Christology, how does the charge of isolationism read? It was the final vindication of Athanasius against Arius that what Jesus Christ did not assume, he did not heal. The subsequent conviction that all humanity is assumed in the humanity of the second person of the Trinity made flesh must at the very least make unconvincing all accusations of isolationism. Thus the credal confession of Jesus Christ's conception by the very Spirit of life, and his birth from the womb of Mary, makes curious a claim to externality, revealing as that does a sectarian framework which partializes the universality of the incarnation into a purported external/internal dualism. No-one, to my knowledge, has stated this so sharply and clearly as Dietrich Bonhoeffer:

> The place where the answer is given both to the question concerning the reality of God and to the question concerning the reality of the world, is designated solely and alone by the name Jesus Christ ... Henceforward one can speak neither of God nor of the world without speaking of Jesus Christ. All concepts of reality which do not take account of Him are abstractions . . . In Christ we are offered the possibility of partaking in the reality of God and in the reality of the world, but not in the one without the other. [16]

If this be true, then the issue is not how the Christian claim is subject to corrigibility, but rather how the much vaunted 'external' reality of the world might be corrigible in the light of this foundation.

But again, what of the charge of imperialism? Ernst Käsemann put the issue here most clearly, 'The resurrection' he said 'is one aspect of the message of the cross; not that the cross is simply one chapter in a book of resurrection dogmatics'.[17]

---

16. D Bonhoeffer, *Ethics* (London: SCM, 1955), 61.
17. E Käsemann, *Jesus Means Freedom* (London: SCM, 1969), 68.

The pertinence of this observation clarifies how it is that theologies of glory have frequently in the history of the church suppressed what is at the heart of the faith by leaving the Cross behind, or rather by treating it merely as a vehicle for resurrection faith. Contemporary theology across the traditions, not to speak of the experienced disempowering of established churches, can fairly be said to have put this imperialistic misunderstanding well in the past. Indeed, the baton of triumphalism could well be said to have passed from the church to culture generally. Where the crucified Christ had as ironic, intertextual (?) superscription over the place of his end, written in Hebrew, Latin, and Greek,[18] there is instantiated, at the very least, the *worldly* triumph of final incorrigibility.

Ecclesiology

If we turn, thirdly, to ecclesiology and the—admittedly—Lucan unfolding of the pentecostal birth of the church, it would be difficult to conceive of anything less isolating. Those who do not understand each other—Parthians, Medes, Elamites and the rest, all understand the point of it all in the language in which they were reared. The church thus appears as a community both of heterogeneity and universality.

> The Pentecost event not only removes individual experiences of isolation and separation, as well as their social consequences, as in Jesus' exorcisms. It produces a powerful public in which there is the possibility and the reality of diverse experiences of the removal of isolation and of individual and collective separation coupled with the preservation of cultural, historical and linguistic diversity.[19]

Thus the Christian church is not simply another sociological community, but the prefiguring of the restored creation.

---

18   John 19:20

19.   M Welker, *God the Spirit* (Minneapolis: Fortress Press, 1994), 235.

Perhaps it was just this ecclesial identity which enabled the church to become such a powerful cultural force in the phenomenon of Christendom. Caesaropapism and papal Caesarism are a heady combination, and triumphalism once tasted is hard to shake off, as contemporary ecclesial nostalgia testifies. Yet reform movements alert to this hegemony have marked the churches throughout their history. Those in the Reformed tradition have, for example, gathered around the doctrine of *ecclesia reformata et semper reformanda*, conscious of the capacity of a tradition to usurp a power of its own devising, and precisely to read alien texts as a form of self-justification and domination. Consequently, whatever may be the sins of contemporary churches, if ecclesiology is allowed a voice, imperialism is in principle repudiated, if not in practice.

Finally, it must be noted that the force of these three doctrines—Creation, Christology and Ecclesiology—to outflank the charges of incorrigibility by those advocating a correlational theology is confirmed when the eschatological horizon from which all worldly and ecclesial texts are to be read is allowed to demonstrate how penultimate and provisional all readings must be, whether from a so-called without or a within.

In conclusion, as we await the outcome of the success of the conversations between so-called intertextualists and intratextualists, at least two other considerations might be raised. First, to the extent that intertextualists are continuing, but making more complex, the paradigm inherited from modernity of the inescapability of the intertextual agenda, Thomas Oden's question may well be asked whether it is indeed 'not some theory but actual modern history that is killing the ideology of modernit'[20] for which the images of Auschwitz, Rwanda, Kosovo, cocaine babies and youth suicide are but some examples.

---

20. T Oden, *After Modernity — What?* (Grand Rapids: Academie Books, 1990), 51.

Second, insofar as it is the case that Australia is 'the most godless place under heaven',[21] in the face of which prevailing modern modes of intertextual *demonstration* have been found to be less than compelling, it may well be the case that the models of *persuasion* through the power of a language not simply to corroborate experience, but actually to provide genuinely new experiences of a world that ought to be, may make the intratextual agenda promising. It is the conviction that this endeavour is so promising that has motivated this paper.

---

21. This description is the title of a survey of two hundred years of Church History in Australia, I Breward, *The Most Godless Place under Heaven?* (Melbourne: Beacon Hill Books, 1988).

George Lindbeck's 'The Nature of Doctrine': Symptom or Cure?

Craig Thompson

Introduction

The general concern of this essay is the challenge of being Christian in a world in which the experience of cultural and religious difference is becoming increasingly stark. Our expanding cross-cultural experience and our growing awareness of difference even within our own cultures give rise to two related questions concerning Christian identity. The first question is this: in such a context, how Christian does one have to be? The answer to this will be assumed to be something to the effect of 'very!'. The second question follows on from this: *can* one be so radically Christian? If one is to be *that* Christian, what then of our relation to the rest of the world and its people? What are we to do with the historical particularity of the Christian faith? How can we be thoroughly and self-consciously Christian in a world of extreme historical difference without condemning the rest of the world, or withdrawing from it? This last requirement is an important one, and arises from the doctrine of creation: is the historical particularity of the Christian confession such that it alienates the church from the wider world, or does it allow the church to engage with the world?

I want to address these questions and the general theme of being in a world of difference by drawing on the model of doctrine, and of Christian existence more generally, proposed by George Lindbeck in his book, *The Nature of Doctrine.*[1] After

---

1. G Lindbeck, *The Nature of Doctrine: Religion and Theology in a Postliberal Age* (Philadelphia: Westminster, 1984). While the

briefly outlining his proposal, I will offer a critique and then attempt to 'stretch' the cultural-linguistic model theologically with a view to addressing the above concern and questions.

Lindbeck writes out of a concern to facilitate a better understanding of ecumenical difference, and of the church's confession in the world more generally. He notes that the common understanding of Christian doctrines as propositional truth statements quickly gets us into difficulties when we are confronted with the fact that doctrines apparently change through time, either in their formulation or in their meaning. Understanding doctrine as true-for-all-time propositions cannot account for such change, except to reject one or the other doctrine or meaning as erroneous.[2] On a propositional model of doctrine, doctrinal difference is a problem which drives dividing wedges between different denominations and confessions, or between different eras. One way of overcoming this difficulty is to propose that it is not the doctrinal *words* which are important, but the unmediated and private religious *experience* which is prior to them. First comes the religious experience, and then the expression of this experience in whatever religious language happens to be at hand.[3] Partly on

---

present study is part of a collection of reflections on the contemporary significance of the theology of Barth, no direct links will be made here to Barth although many observations have been made on the similarity of his theology and Lindbeck's notion of intratextuality. On Lindbeck's proposal in relation to Barth, cf G Lindbeck, 'Barth and Textuality', *Theology Today* 43 (1986): 361-376, and the response of R Thiemann, 'Response to George Lindbeck', *Theology Today* 43 (1986): 377-382; cf also H W Frei, 'George Lindbeck and *The Nature of Doctrine*', in B Marshall (ed), *Theology and Dialogue: Essays in Conversation with George Lindbeck* (Notre Dame, Indiana: University of Notre Dame Press, 1990), 275-282.

2. Lindbeck, *Nature of Doctrine*, 16.
3. *Ibid*, 16, 19-25.

scientific grounds, but also out of theological preference,[4] Lindbeck rejects this approach and draws on conclusions from contemporary philosophy, sociology and anthropology to propose a 'cultural-linguistic' model of doctrine. These sciences variously hold that one requires a language or a cultural and linguistic formation in order to have meaningful experiences of the world, including experiences of God.[5] The Christian confession can be understood to be just such a cultural-linguistic 'text'.[6] It is the *order* of language and experience which is important here. Lindbeck argues that religious experience is not private and immediate but public and mediated, and that this mediation occurs in the linguistic and ethical particularities of one religious cultural-linguistic system or another. For example, in the Christian confession, the word 'God' is qualified by its relation to the life, death and resurrection of Jesus of Nazareth, and cannot be assumed to have a direct relation to the 'same' word in a non-Christian context.[7] In order to experience the God of Christian confession,

---

4.   *Ibid*, 31-45.

5.   *Ibid*, 18f, 32ff.

6.   The precise sense of 'text' here is difficult, and is not given full exposition by Lindbeck. While it is sometimes used in the sense of 'book' (cf *Nature of Doctrine* 116, 120), Raynal notes that for Lindbeck 'the Christian text' denotes the biblical text within the total network of worship, doctrine and ethical commitment: 'the whole complex of Christian communication' (C Raynal, 'An Approach to Religion for Today's Needs', *Interpretation* 41/1 [1987]: 83). Elsewhere Lindbeck speaks of a text generally as 'fixed communicative patterns embedded in rites, myths and other oral and representational traditions' (G Lindbeck, 'Ecumenical Theology', in D Ford (ed), *The Modern Theologians: An Introduction to Christian Theology in the Twentieth Century* Vol 2, [Oxford: Basil Blackwell, 1989], 267). The assessment of Lindbeck's proposal could be seen as an assessment of the theological adequacy of the category of text.

7.   Cf Lindeck, *Nature of Doctrine* 91ff, where Lindbeck applies his

one must make reference to specifically Christian statements about God, and speak God out of an immersion in the logic, or the grammar, of those statements.

However, the logic of this understanding of the action of language extends further than this. It is not simply that the Christian cultural-linguistic text gives content to things *religious*, but rather that this text has the capacity to give meaning to the *whole* world—'religious' and 'non-religious'. A particular cultural-linguistic text has the capacity to 'absorb the world', which means that it gives meaning to the various new things which may assault our senses or encounter us from without.[8] Just as it is possible (and necessary) to encounter the world and develop our experience of it as an English-encultured man or Japanese-encultured woman or whatever, there is also a specifically Christian dimension to the experience of the world.[9]

Lindbeck's Solution: Symptom or Cure?

As Lindbeck's proposal is aimed at the experience of confessional difference, and since such experiences of difference are the concern of this study, the question can be put: is Lindbeck's proposal a cure for the ills inflicting the church's self-understanding in the post-Christendom era, or is it merely (if nevertheless *helpfully*) symptomatic of those ills? While *The Nature of Doctrine* is not specifically directed at the question of post-Christendom Christianity, it *is* symptomatic of our age

---

model to specific examples.

8   *Ibid*, 113ff.

9   It may be noted in passing, then, that the 'Christian' experience of the world is not to be understood to be *exclusive* of our Englishness or Japaneseness; insofar as the Christian text is a living language, it *must* be embodied, and so mesh with the characteristics of a person necessary to be human—including the natural language and culture of a particular time and place.

insofar as ours is a time of the breaking down of old cultural paradigms and self-understandings, and so a time in which we are becoming less certain about what we have in common with each other. It is not that difference has not always been there, and has not always been a source of difficulty. Yet, we are becoming increasingly aware that we are each differently formed by our respective cultures and languages and histories, and on account of *that* awareness we are increasingly uncertain about how to transcend those differences. Whereas it was at least the case that the older heretics and orthodox usually agreed that they had something to argue about, this is much less the case now.

We experience difference in a multitude of situations and at many levels. What does even the liberal Christian have to say any more to one who grew up in a permissive, secular society? How guilty is the paedophile who was himself repeatedly abused as a child, or the battered wife who bites back once, and fatally? How saved or damned are the millions who never even hear the name of Jesus, let alone reject him? Where is the Church among the many denominational churches? Lindbeck's proposal is symptomatic of such problematic experiences of difference in its addressing of the particular problems of denominational difference, and the differences between systems of thought more generally. Confronted with these various differences, he seeks to understand how we may be in positive relation to each other without thereby requiring that we all become the same. Yet, an important question is whether Lindbeck's proposal is at the same time a *cure* for what ails us: *difference as a problem or affliction*. If his proposal were such a cure, we might expect it to give us a vision of God, ourselves and the world which is able to comprehend the challenge of difference, without thereby homogenising everything.

However, there are two inadequacies in Lindbeck's model which suggest that, helpful as it is, it does not yet go far enough. The first problem is a one of a logical inconsistency in what he proposes. The inconsistency resides in a clash of the logic of the cultural-linguistic model of doctrine with Lindbeck's own arguments for such a model. In the cultural-linguistic model, the world is what our cultural-linguistic text has absorbed for us. This process of absorption is *fully comprehensive*: our cultural-linguistic text is the lens through which we see the world, and we have no other lens, and no other world. The logical difficulty is that while Lindbeck argues for the capacity of the Christian confession to give shape to *all* we encounter, this permission to absorb the world is granted to the 'Christian text' from without. It is effectively the confluent ideas of sociology, anthropology and philosophy which 'allow' the Christian text to do its own absorption of the world. This sets up a dualistic distinction between the Christian view of the world and the apparently larger view which sociology (etc.) has in its categorisation of the Christian faith as a 'culture-language'. This duality is in conflict with the logic of the understanding of language to which Lindbeck appeals, for the duality's effect is to deny the Christian cultural-linguistic text access to one piece of the world (the sociology), and so to deny its capacity to absorb the whole of reality.

It is here that the second problem with Lindbeck's proposal appears: relativism. Sociology tells us that there are worlds other than that of the specific Christian cultural-linguistic system, and so Lindbeck's proposal appears fideistic or sectarian. More sympathetically, the Christian text appears to be simply part of a bigger whole. Consequently, Christian faith fails to be comprehensive of the *whole* world in the way Lindbeck suggests, and we have to be something *more* than just Christian if we are to experience the whole world. This problem arises from a failure to take seriously the logic of the textual absorption of the world, and reflects a failure in Lindbeck's own argument from culture-language to Christian faith. The notion of such an absorption is an answer to my opening question, 'How Christian must one be?', and that answer is that we are to be radical, thoroughgoing Christians: all we encounter should be subjected to the specifically Christian experience of God, the world and ourselves as these are held together in the Christian confession, there being nothing outside the bounds of the Christian linguistic confession (*qua* linguistic).

However, Lindbeck's use of the sociology of knowledge suggests that we *cannot* be such radical Christians, because the sociology tells us that there are other cultural-linguistic worlds which are different from what we have in our 'Christian' worldview. The point of all this is not simply to note a logical inconsistency in Lindbeck's proposal, but to draw attention to the matter as being both an existential and a theological problem insofar as these dimensions are distinguishable. It is an *existential* problem, for the Christian, because the dependence of Lindbeck's model on the philosophy of language leaves us stuck with the question of how we are related to each other: we remain confronted with many worlds and many truths, and no real sense of the oneness which holds them together. This concern for the oneness embodies the *theological* problem, for the explicit content of the Christian confession is universal in scope: there is only *one* God who is sovereign over *one* world.

Most generally, these problems arise from Lindbeck's deliberate appeal to the sociology and philosophy of language as *non-theological* sources for the description of doctrines. Being non-theological, he supposes that their description of doctrine will be less controversial than any which is associated with a particular theological tradition.[10] Yet, it is the absence of explicit correspondence between the religiously neutral description of doctrine and the religiously loaded doctrines which sets up the contradictions between the model and the explicit content of the Christian confession. In Lindbeck's proposal, one cultural-linguistic text—that of modernity with its categories of religion, culture and language—*describes* another such system (in this case, Christianity), *without actually understanding itself to be participating in that described system*. This is the critical point: such *description without participation* sets up a

---

10   Cf Lindbeck, *Nature of Doctrine*, 8-12, 135.

duality which dis-establishes at least one of the parties. Here modernity and its sociological ordering of the world is apparently stable and fixed, and the Christian confession becomes one floating subtext among many others.

What happens here is a failure of language. This is not a failure of words to make the point (although perhaps that too!), but a failure to be thoroughly linguistic, or thoroughly *engaged* with our interlocutors. If we *describe* Christian existence as a language, then for it *actually to be* linguistic we must expect it to speak back to us in some way, so that we are drawn into a conversation with what we have described, or into a *participation* in that reality. It is this conversation which is lacking in Lindbeck's bare, non-theological model, and this deficiency underlies much of the criticism directed at it from both more liberal and more conservative quarters.[11] For a human, cultural-linguistic text to be truly comprehensive of the whole world, including the specific text of modernity which describes it as 'cultural-linguistic', it has to be such that it is *inherently* engaged with any reality it encounters.

It must be noted, however, that in a conversation such as I have just described, the categories of text and world, culture-language and reality begin to break down. The specificity of, for example, the Christian text, begins to blur around the edges. Precisely because it is a *linguistic* text it takes its definition by linguistic engagement internally and externally, and so begins

---

11. Lindbeck's proposal has generated a large volume of responsive material; most generally, see G Michalson Jr, 'The Response to Lindbeck', *Modern Theology* 4 (1988): 107-120; and B Marshall, *Theology and Dialogue: Essays in Conversation with George Lindbeck* (Notre Dame, Indiana: University of Notre Dame Press, 1990). Representatives of less sympathetic assessments include T Tilley, 'Incommensurability, Intratexuality, and Fideism', *Modern Theology* 5 (1989): 87-111; R Gascoigne, 'The Relation between Text and Experience in Narrative Theology of Revelation', *Pacifica* 5 (1992) 43-58; and J C Sommerville, 'Is Religion a Language Game?', *Theology Today* 51, (January 1995): 594-599.

to be less specifically 'Christian' and more universal as it makes more and more links with newly encountered realities. To the extent that such a reality as a particular human existence is described in terms of its linguistic character, the potential to absorb the whole world would reside in that reality's inherent inability or refusal to be silenced, or in an endless capacity to talk or engage with this or that person or reality as they are encountered.[12] 'Engagement'—here, in open linguistic encounters—is revealed to supersede or supplant the rather more static concept of 'text', if a cultural-linguistic text is to do what is claimed for it in Lindbeck's proposal.

This is a sketch in quite general terms of what such a text might look like, or how it might behave. At this level, any cultural-linguistic text might be capable of such achievements. As the concern in this discussion is with Christian faith in a world of difference, the next task is to consider this characteristic of a world-absorbing text in relation to the specific Christian confession. If a particular, historical human cultural-linguistic text were to be able to give sense to the *whole* world of difference we encounter in the way I have described, to what extent does the Christian confession qualify as such a text? Put differently, does the text inherited by Christians have the resources to enable me to be in a world of difference in such a way that I can be Christian to the core, and not thereby be intrinsically alienated from anything I might encounter? In what follows, I will go beyond anything Lindbeck suggests in an attempt to outline what it might be in the Christian text which enables it to achieve the world-absorption Lindbeck's proposal claims for it.

---

12 For this way of putting it (although without reference to Lindbeck), cf R Jenson, *Essays in Theology of Culture* (Grand Rapids: Eerdmans, 1995), 76-83 and 163-174.

The Christian 'Text'

Before coming to the Christian text itself, one more thing needs to be clarified. When we ask about the linguistic character of a text there enters the need for a further qualification: 'texts' don't possess language, *people* do. If a text is truly 'linguistic', then this linguistic character resides in those who are formed by it. These people instantiate the linguistic, or *linguifying*, character of such a text. A 'text' which is truly linguistic is a reality which enhances the language or the inter-humanity of its instantiating persons.

There is a further difficulty. In relation to the desire to consider the particular *Christian* confession as such a text, it needs also to be noted that *everyone* has a language and a corresponding ethic by which they relate to others. Yet whether the linguistic engagements are person to person, or more generally the subsumption of a new idea into an old system, they can be arbitrary and abusive, and deal violently with the stranger or the new thing. If such violent dealings are rejected as not accommodating difference in the way we here require, the question then becomes, what or where is *good, non-violent* language?

We are now at the stage of having to step out of the general analysis and take up a particular position on this. Such a step *does* seem to have an arbitrary and possibly violent character about it, for there is no way of establishing its validity other than it actually being the *right* step, and *justifying itself* in its effects according to its own criteria. To the extent that the right step is taken, the tables are turned on the analysis which Lindbeck offers, and which I have extended to this point in categories similar to his. The self-demonstrating, good, non-violent language chosen will become the test of the linguistic character of other 'putative' languages and so of the 'putative' persons who speak them.

My step will be into the specifically Christian confession, and will involve taking up the Christian concept of love. Love, of

247

course, is more than a concept. To the extent that we talk *about* love, just as to the extent that we talk *about* language, we miss the point. Love is not an idea, but a relational reality. It is not present for us as a *concept* but only in a *concrete situation*. For our purposes, it is the most fundamental characteristic of the Christian concept of love which is important: love is that by which each of us stands *as ourselves*. This most fundamental characteristic has its foundational instance in the standing of creation before God. Creation stands out of the love of God, and the promise that God's love will not diminish. God's love for the world is what *makes* the world creation, and makes it precisely as a reality distinct from God, and yet not separable from God.

It is this last point which is important for our purposes: creation is distinct, and yet not separable from God. If we return to Lindbeck's model, we find that modernity and its sociology is distinct from the Christian subtext, but it is also *separable*, at least in the formal way the description of the Christian subtext is set up. Since, on the modernist reading, Christianity can be described without actually engaging with it, it can also be cut away without real loss.[13] Love, however, cannot do this if it is to remain love, because nothing is lost to love if love is grounded in God's sure faithfulness to creation. Love is creative and sustaining, and not destructive. While things might be *changed*, and even *must* be changed, they are not lost if it is love which is active. This 'changing' corresponds to Lindbeck's notion of absorption. In the absorption of the world by a love-creating 'text', what is not already in love begins a process of en-loving transformation.

---

13   Questions of the diachronic relation between philosophical engagement with the interest of Christian faith in history and the rise of post-Enlightenment, secular interest in history (including social anthropology and the philosophy of language) are not immediately important here, but would have to be considered in a fuller account.

In relation to the problem of the experience of difference with which I began, the step taken here into the specifically Christian understanding of loving relation and perduring identity admittedly involves, at one level, a begging of the question. This 'deficiency', however, can be differently understood. The 'solution' to the problem offered here in terms of the logic of love Christianly conceived is not so much one which arises out of the analysis of the problem, but one which actually challenges the very experience of the problem (*qua* problem) in the first place. Difference ceases to be a problem if all we encounter ultimately arises out of God's loving and creative self-differentiation from the world, and God's communication of this differentiation to the world.[14] Difference is not of itself a problem, but our *experience* of difference can be.

Although the intention here is to be critical of his presentation of the cultural-linguistic model, Lindbeck's emphasis on the relative priority of language over experience remains helpful: the language of God-and-creation enables us to reconceive difference and differentiated identities as God's creative purpose, rather than as a challenge to God's reality. In his ecumenical concerns, the reason Lindbeck rejects the propositional understanding of doctrine is not that he is uncomfortable with a referential theory of truth *per se*, but that he wishes to affirm an ecumenical communion in difference. Propositional truth does not work here because it homogenises, and requires that all things be the same. The contradiction in Lindbeck's proposal would be overcome, and his basic concern to affirm difference accommodated, if what is designated the 'Christian cultural-linguistic text' were a self-particularising and other-particularising reality. The suggestion that the particular Christian text can absorb the whole world would be

---

14 This is a very dense summary of the doctrine of creation. For a fuller discussion of God as the legitimacy of difference and particularity, cf C Gunton, *The One, the Three and the Many* (Cambridge: Cambridge University Press, 1993).

249

valid if that text were able to give meaning to the many elements of the world without stripping them of their own individuality, except to render them 'good'—what they are intended to be in God's loving, creative purpose. This would be good, non-violent language in action. To the extent that 'love' is a useful summary term for the content and action of the Christian text, and to the extent that this love is constructively preservative of difference and identity, the Christian text is then arguably able to 'absorb' the world without the world thereby ceasing to be itself.

Conclusion

While it is highly evocative to suggest that Christian existence in the world is akin to absorbing the world through the categories of a language, this suggestion runs aground theologically on account of its deliberately non-theological character in Lindbeck's argument. Lindbeck's concern with difference and his category of text needs to be subject to the logic of the text *as linguistic*—inherently engaged with the realities around it. This means that while we may begin with 'language' as a useful analogy for the action of Christian categories on our experience of the world, we have then to speak a *particular* language—the particular Christian 'language', in Lindbeck's case. There will occur, consequently, a 'reading backwards' of the content of the Christian 'language' onto the theory of language Lindbeck uses.[15] I have attempted, all too briefly, to argue that in such a reading backwards the category of text is shown to be inadequate for describing the Christian

---

15. Such a 'reading backwards' could justifiably be called an 'eschatological reading', such as is quintessentially embodied in the scriptural exposition of the God-world relation in terms of the experience of Christ. Consider, as an example, the reassessment of Adam in relation to the 'solution' of Christ in the pauline literature.

confession while at the same time avoiding problems of dualism and relativism. From within the Christian text itself, if that text is adequately summarised in terms of its message of love and its en-loving action, difference may be preserved with reference to the particular and specific Christian text, and so preserved without the theologically neutral category of text.

The questions with which I began were specifically Christian questions, although from what I have attempted to argue they might also be more generally *human* questions. Nevertheless, an important consequence of Lindbeck's model of Christian existence, in the more theological form I have tried to give it, might be the reclaiming of the world for the church, although in a particular way.

Whatever the situation may have been in previous ages, the church has recently found itself dethroned in general culture, particularly in the West. This has taken place through our culture's effective silencing of the church by denying its public character and relegating it to the sphere of the private.[16] For the most part, the church has been anxiously hopping up and down ever since, trying to regain the ascendancy and so to prove to itself and to the world that it *is* important. Yet, it may be more to the point for the church not to attempt to reclaim the world by grasping at a 'visible' (non-theological!) relevance, but by effectively disappearing as an institution and 're-appearing' as never-quite-visible salt and light, loving and en-loving the world. This is what a 'text' does if it is *really* linguistic, rather than confinable to a particular time and space: it overflows limiting constraints, smudges the lines of its own identifiability and becomes harder to discern. The only difference (alterity) the church will experience in relation to the 'rest' of the world is then that created and creative difference which will enable the world and the church to become their true selves.

---

16. This is a theme Lesslie Newbigin has consistently stressed; cf L Newbigin, *The Gospel in a Pluralist Society* (Grand Rapids: Eerdmans, 1989), 15ff.

Craig Thompson

A theologically appropriate 'absorption' of the world by the Christian text is not a claim to ownership or lordship, or even a claim to identity 'in' the world, but a secret stewardship in which Christians exercise their faith in open response to the challenges they encounter. In this very linguistic, loving openness they both are passively transformed by, and actively transform, the things they encounter. From the church's own perspective its relevance for the world—in its difference from the world—is then less established in the world's recognition of the church as 'relevant' or as a valid 'text', and more established in the hidden process by which church and world are made new by the loving action of the church's 'text'.

With and Beyond Barth?: John Milbank's Postmodern Christian Socialism as an Alternative Modernity

Trevor Hogan

Theology and Politics

After a dull session at the Oxford Conference on Church and Society in 1937, R H Tawney, Christian Socialist, Anglican layman and Professor of Economic History, London School of Economics, reported that he had listened to a long dissertation on the doctrine of Trinity but 'the man did come down at the end in favour of nationalization'.[1] Tawney's ironic comment highlights a fraught, dichotomous relationship between theology and politics. To his first hearers, the presumed, unambiguous good at stake was the securing of a particular policy package, with or without theological justification. Even so, a large number of this century's foremost theologians not only involved themselves in politics but sought to explicate their reasons in theological terms. Moreover, many shared an elective affinity between Christianity and socialism.[2] On this front, Karl Barth is justly famous for his provocative theology of crisis. Over against the dominant bourgeois ideologies of his age his theology was rigorously theocentric. It was a publically- and socially-engaged theology that envisaged socialism as an

---

1. R Terrill, *R H Tawney and His Times: Socialism as Fellowship* (Cambridge, MA: Harvard University Press, 1973), 60.
2. See for example, J Cort, *Christian Socialism: An Informal History* (Maryknoll, NY: Orbis, 1988); G Dorrien, *Reconstructing the Common Good: Theology and the Social Order* (Maryknoll, NY: Orbis, 1990); C West, *Communism and the Theologians: Study of an Encounter* (London: SCM Press, 1958).

253

alternative modernity *vis à vis* liberal capitalism, Bolshevist collectivism and Fascist corporatism alike. Moreover, Barth's socialism was articulated in specifically and uncompromising Christian theological terms: 'theology is the ground of Barth's socialism'.[3] Although this translated into an explicit commitment to socialism only during the early stage of Barth's career, George Hunsinger reminds us that 'Barth's theological work cannot be appreciated at any stage apart from his socialist commitment'. [4]

Sixty years on, however, at the end of a tumultuous century of cold wars and catastrophes, the other side of 1989, Tawney's joke seems newly ironic. Nationalisation policies and socialisms seem everywhere discredited and in ruins. Whether one reads this century from the Left or the Right, the consensus is in: the titanic struggle between Communism and Capitalism is over ending in a comprehensive victory for the latter. In this context, theologians who have not embraced this trend in ideological terms[5] have retreated from the quest of thinking *cosmos, psyche* and *polis* so that long dissertations on the doctrine of the Trinity would be more welcome insofar as they eschew political and social theory, and public policymaking. Such a move however is simply to reinstate the dualisms implied by the separation of realms, theological and political.

John Milbank, Anglo-Catholic lay theologian, has emerged over the past two decades as a distinctive voice whose advocacy of Christian socialism in specifically theological terms is not without analogies to that of Karl Barth.[6] Yet, Milbank's

---

3. C Green, 'Introduction: Barth's Mature Theology' in *idem* (ed), *Karl Barth: Theologian of Freedom* (London: Collins, 1989), 43

4. G Hunsinger (ed), *Karl Barth and Radical Politics* (Philadelphia: The Westminster Press, 1976), 7.

5. G Dorrien, *The Neoconservative Mind: Politics, Culture, and the War of Ideology* (Philadelphia: Temple University Press, 1993).

6. J Milbank, *Theology and Social Theory: Beyond Secular Reason* (Oxford: Blackwell, 1990] and *The Word Made Strange: Theology,*

proposal has emerged in even less promising circumstances for socialism and Christianity alike than that of either the 'age of catastrophes' or the cold war of Barth's time.[7] Whereas Barth turned theology against its would-be proclaimers to expose their surreptitious hubris, Milbank pursues the theological task at a time where the very possibility of its articulation, particularly by Anglicans, seems remote:

> both socialist and Christian are bound now to ask themselves whether capitalism is not the *definitive* shape of secularity, whether community is not an intrinsically religious, mythical matter, so that with the demise of common belief, only a competitive market system in all spheres can organise and manage the resultant pursuit of remorseless self-interest by individuals and groups.[8]

This essay then is not about Karl Barth so much as about John Milbank after Barth, and the uncovering of connections between their respective concerns.[9] By using Milbank's critique of Barth

---

Language, Culture (Oxford: Blackwell, 1997).

7. To old Cold War intellectual warriors like Eric Hobsbawm, 1914 to 1989 marks the short twentieth century. Moreover, 1989 also marks the final terminus of the main alternative modern projects to capitalism: fascism, state socialisms, and social democracy alike. See E Hobsbawm, *The Age of Extremes: The Short Twentieth Century, 1914-1991* (London: Michael Joseph, 1994). To neo-conservative commentators, such as Francis Fukuyama, all societies are now finally converging on the one ideal type: liberal, democratic capitalism. Humankind has reached its true telos: the universal right to shop. See F Fukuyama, *The End of History and the Last Man* (NewYork: Free Press, 1992).

8. J Milbank, 'Socialism of the Gift, Socialism by Grace', *New Blackfriars* 77 (1996): 533.

9. As this paper is not in the first place about Barth but Milbank's theological project after Barth, I have not endeavoured to undertake a systematic evaluation of Milbank's critique of Barth by a return to Barth's primary writings. That is a task which belongs to another time and place.

Trevor Hogan

I hope to open up an optic that not only looks back to Barth but forward to explore the problematics of an explicitly Christian narrative of politics at the 'end of modernity'. As Milbank notes, the end of modernity 'is not accomplished, yet continues to arrive'.[10] In particular, I seek to clarify how and why Milbank's characterisation of Christian socialism in postmodern mode is neither a theological baptising of Tony Blair's Third Way New Labour nor a nostalgia-driven argument for pre-modern agrarian, patriarchal community.

With and Beyond Barth?: From Neo-Orthodoxy to Radical Orthodoxy

Barth is not a major interlocutor for Milbank but he is important to him nevertheless. The one and only reference to Barth in *Theology and Social Theory* is parenthetical but nonetheless highly significant. Barth is listed with Augustine and Aquinas as a theologian who 'speaks in modes beyond the point where dialectics leave off, namely in terms of the imaginative explication of texts, practices and beliefs'.[11] and who therefore enables theology to speak back to other metaphysical positions on equal grounds without reference to some purportedly neutral and universal meta-discourse. That Augustine and Aquinas loom large in Milbank's agenda and that Barth is the only modern theologian listed here is highly suggestive of Barth's importance to Milbank. The implications of Barth's place in Milbank's thought are teased out in two key chapters in *The Word Made Strange* ('A Critique of the Theology of Right') and *Radical Orthodoxy* ('Knowledge: The Theological Critique of Philosophy in Hamann and Jacobi') respectively.[12] It is in these

---

10   J Milbank, '"Postmodern Critical Augustinianism": A Short Summa in Forty Two Responses to Unasked Questions', *Modern Theology* 7 (1991): 225.

11.   Milbank, *Theology and Social Theory*, 328.

12   J Milbank, C Pickstock and G Ward (eds), *Radical Orthodoxy: A*

essays that he demonstrates why he wishes to both recover and extend Barth's initial problematic but also why he is deeply unhappy with Barth's solution.

While Barth is rightly celebrated for blowing the whistle on neo-Kantian liberalism in German Protestant theology, Milbank thinks Barth's critique and his attempted overcoming were insufficiently radical. While Milbank affirms Barth's critique of the reduction of Christian faith and life to a humanist ethic which baptises modern German bourgeois culture, he nevertheless claims that Barth's reassertion of the radical otherness of the hidden God simply leaves the Kantian dualistic metaphysics untouched. Instead Barth is accused of positing an undialectical fideist riposte to undialectical rationalism. To Kant's *Religion within the bounds of Reason Alone* we have Barth's *Epistle to the Romans*. Faith without reason or reason without faith—either way the dialectic of the enlightenment persists. This is why the larger part of Milbank's essay on 'A Critique of the Theology of Right' makes Kant his main target. For Milbank, Kant's three *Critiques* are best understood as a systematic inversion of Aquinas' *Summa*. Where Aquinas provides a clear account of the Being of God-in-Himself, Kant is entirely agnostic. Where Aquinas is agnostic about the conditions of our relation to God, Kant is entirely formalistic and asserts universal and categorical rules and imperatives of natural law and knowledge. The results are manifold as they are profound: the privileging of abstract forms and rules and of ethics over and against the good, the assertion of individual will, rights and property over and against the common good. These developments set up in turn the dualisms which mark modern social sciences and law: of morals and empirical content, validity and values, morality and method.[13] Milbank succinctly concludes: 'knowledge of God for Kant is

---

New Theology (London: Routledge, 1999).

13   On this point Milbank follows G Rose, *Hegel Contra Sociology* (London: Athlone Press, 1981), see especially Chapter 1.

confirmation of this world as it is, or else a "sublime" aspiration which is a content-less bad infinitude, unrelated to actual social behaviour'.[14] This is why Milbank argues that

> while the Barthian claim is that post-Kantian philosophy liberates theology to be theological, the inner truth of this theology is that by allowing legitimacy to a methodologically atheist philosophy, he finishes by construing God on the model, ironically, of man without God.[15]

The turn from Barth, or what Milbank calls Barthianism or 'neo-orthodoxy', to the proclamation of 'radical orthodoxy' is declared in the form of a *Radical Orthodoxy* manifesto by the emergent subculture of Cambridge Anglo-Catholic and Catholic theologians. With Barth, they assert orthodoxy in the most straightforward sense of commitment to creedal Christianity and the exemplary patristic matrix. It is argued further that a richer and more coherent Christianity is gradually lost from view after the Middle Ages, so that both Protestant biblicism and post-tridentine Catholic positivist authoritarianism 'are seen as aberrant results of theological distortions already dominant even before the early modern period'.[16] With Barth too, they proclaim that the orthodox site of theological reflection is in and for the church. Against Barth, however, they argue that his mode of asserting the positive autonomy of theology comes at the cost of reasserting a duality of reason and revelation such that neo-orthodoxy is not able to make a Christian difference in and for the world. Moreover, this substantial difference has a stylistic-aesthetic corollary, 'where Barthianism can tend to the ploddingly exegetical, radical orthodoxy mingles exegesis, cultural reflection and philosophy in a complex but coherently executed *collage'*.[17]

---

14   J Milbank, 'A Critique of the Theology of Right' in *The Word Made Strange*, 16.

15   *Ibid*, 22.

16.   *Ibid*, 2.

17.   *Ibid*.

With and Beyond Barth?

The difference then between neo-orthodoxy and radical orthodoxy is laid out before us, but what do Milbank *et al* mean by 'radical'? Here the manifesto states at least four senses of the term, which they wish to embrace, and which bear quotation in full:

> Radical, first of all, in the sense of a return to patristic and medieval roots, especially in the recovery of the Augustinian vision of all knowledge as divine illumination—a notion which transcends the modern bastard dualisms of faith and reason, grace and nature. Radical, second, in . . . seeking to deploy this recovered vision systematically to criticise modern society, culture, politics, art, science and philosophy with an unprecedented boldness. But radical in yet a third sense of realising that via such engagements we *do* have also to rethink the tradition . . . since the Enlightenment was in effect a critique of decadent early modern Christianity, it *is* sometimes possible to learn from it, though in the end the Enlightenment itself massively repeated the decadence. Fourth, the great Christian critics of the Enlightenment—Christopher Smart, Hamann, Jacobi, Kierkegaard, Péguy, Chesterton, and others—in different ways saw that what secularity had most ruined and actually denied were the very things it apparently celebrated: embodied life, self-expression, sexuality, aesthetic experience, human political community . . .only transcendence, which 'suspends' these things in the sense of interrupting them, 'suspends' them also in the other sense of upholding their relative worth over-against the void. Such radicalism indeed refuses the secular, but at the same time it does 're-envision' a Christianity which *never* sufficiently valued the mediating participatory sphere which alone can lead us to God . . . once one has realised, . . . that sexual puritanism, political disciplinarianism and abuse of the poor are the result of the *refusal* of true Christianity . . . one is led to

259

articulate a more incarnate, more participatory, more aesthetic, more erotic, more socialised, even 'more Platonic' Christianity.[18]

An Alternative Version of Modernity?

Barth, then, for Milbank, is important, a rare modern theologian who 'thinks as a theologian'[19]—a theologian who pits modern theology over and against the self-avowed autonomy of modern philosophy. Nevertheless, to Milbank, Barth also becomes part of the problem to be overcome, for Barth has only half-pinned the secular tiger. Worse still in Milbank's eyes, Barth's own construal of the history of eighteenth and nineteenth century theology misleads his readers and interpreters into believing that 'an era of treacherously humanistic theology was brought to an end only with his own endeavours'.[20] This is not an accusation of hubris but rather of a faulty historical narration which fails to uncover a subterranean but highly significant alternative modern tradition, one which posits a theory of knowledge by faith alone. In *Radical Orthodoxy*, Milbank recuperates the so called German radical pietists, Hamann, Jacobi, Wizenmann, and Herder.[21] In individual articles he undertakes a similar service for Coleridge and Kiekergaard.[22] In various footnotes, he also

---

18. J Milbank, C Pickstock and G Ward, 'Introduction. Suspending the Material: The Turn of Radical Theology' in Milbank *et al.* (eds), *Radical Orthodoxy*, 2f.

19. Eberhard Jüngel, *The Doctrine of the Trinity: God's Being is in Becoming* (Grand Rapids: Eerdmans, 1976), xix.

20. J Milbank, 'Knowledge: The Theological Critique of Philosophy in Hamann and Jacobi' in Milbank *et al*, *Radical Orthodoxy*, 22.

21. *Ibid.*

22. See J Milbank, 'Divine Logos and Human Communication: A Recuperation of Coleridge', *Neue Zeitschrift fur Systematische Theologie und Religionsphilosophie* 29 (1987): 56-73 and 'The Sublime

contests Barth's negative portrait of Schleiermacher as a romantic individualist subjectivist, counter-suggesting that Schleiermacher recovers the Aristotelian project of an ethic of virtue, and has an ecclesio-centric sense of Christian community as the locus of this ethic.[23] Together these thinkers are trumpeted as representing a force for shaping modern philosophy on such issues as 'the priority of existence over thought', 'the primacy of language', 'the ecstatic character of time', 'the historicity of reason', 'the dialogical principle', 'the suspension of the ethical' and 'the ontological difference' and most importantly the thematisation of the concept of nihilism.[24]

Against this background, Milbank's own aim in developing an 'alternative version of modernity'[25] is twofold: to allow a critical space for the creativity of all human culture and the development of human history after the Fall; and to re-imagine the distinctive difference of Christian narrative of humanity under God that makes a critical and ultimate difference to how we both conceive of history and of our participation in it. To do this Milbank appeals above all to Giambattista Vico. For Milbank, Vico affirms that culture is a *factum*, a human product and not simply a fact of God's natural order. He avoids the

---

in Kierkegaard', *The Heythrop Journal* 37 (1996): 298-321.

23. See for example J Milbank, 'The Name of Jesus: Incarnation, Atonement, Ecclesiology', *Modern Theology* 7 (1991): 330f.

24. Milbank, 'Knowledge', 23f.

25. This expression is the heading of the conclusion to Volume One of *The Religious Dimension of the Thought of Giambattista Vico* (Lewiston, NY: Edwin Mellen, 1992). This two volumed work, originally Milbank's doctoral thesis, provides a good insight into a consistent refrain in Milbank's writings. More importantly, it clarifies why accusations of hermeticism and pre-modernism in his thought are at best misleading and worse grievously unjust. For such criticisms see A Nichols OP, "'Non Tali Auxilio': John Milbank's Suasion to Orthodoxy', *New Blackfriars* 73 (1992): 326-332; P Lakeland, '(En)countering the (Post)modern', *The Month*, February, 1993: 63-70.

dominant modern turn of reducing human autonomy to instrumental reason but instead posits cultural creativity as a matter of complex, contingent (therefore, free) and inter-personal works. This means that human work is a continuing sign of God's *creatio ex nihilo*, as blessing and not derivative of the Fall, which is but a contingency of creation. The fact of production is not placed over and against our human participation in the production of the good life and the common good. The freedom to create is integral to the progressive unfolding of meaning in and through our culture making.[26] *Contra* Kant, therefore, knowledge cannot be secured transcendentally in abstract, ahistorical and *apriori* terms but rather words and things are constituted together in and through their expression—poetically. Vico is a linguistic idealist/constructivist, in that because humans actively participate in divine creativity, so too the creation of knowledge is divinely mediated in language, so that our words are 'the expressivity of God's Word'.[27] *Contra* Hegel, this does not mean

---

[26] I know of only one contemporary social theorist who outlines a similar theory of human culture so as to overcome the moribund dichotomies that blight most sociological discussions, those of freedom and necessity, agency and structure, and system and life-world; namely, the post-Marxist, romantic modernist, Cornelius Castoriadis (d 1998), see especially his *The Imaginary Institution of Society* (Cambridge, MA: MIT Press, 1987).

[27] It is perhaps no coincidence that Graham Ward, one of the authors of *Radical Orthodoxy*, is responsible for drawing out these themes of language in Barth, bringing him back into conversation with the linguistic turn of deconstruction in the writings of Jacques Derrida. See G Ward's *Barth, Derrida and the Language of Theology* (Cambridge: Cambridge University Press, 1995). See the paper by Geoff Thompson in this volume which contests Ward's reading of Barth. Milbank's writings on these themes not already mentioned include: 'Theology Without Substance: Christianity, Signs, Origins: Parts One and Two', *Journal of Literature and Theology* 2 (1988): 1-17 and 131-152; 'William Warburton: An

that human history has an immanent telos, but rather the processes of human production of knowledge and culture and technologies are "the immanent pressure of a transcendent reality which, as infinite, is the totality and coherence of difference, an eminent 'inclusion' of things, but at the same time absolute Unity". 'The Christian vision' then in this account of human poetical-cultural history, is 'the apotheosis, rather than the cancellation, of creative figuration'.[28]

In this recuperation of Vico, Milbank's alternative version of modernity simultaneously half-affirms modern reason and the postmodern sense of creative flux (which it sees as modernity's consequence), but seeks to twist the immanent nihilism of postmodernism back to a vision, narration and practice of peaceable difference. Milbank has come to call this visionary, poetic and historicist practice, the 'discourse of participated perfections'.[29] It is possible to admire the scope and depth of his vision yet still might it be too little, too late to save the world? Should we concede that his *Theology and Social Theory*, for example, is the late modern equivalent of Dante's medieval *Divina Commedia* but that all such attempts must perforce fail in the face of the tragic trajectory of human history this century?[30] Marx once misquoted Hegel as claiming that history repeats, first as tragedy, then as farce. Such is the extirpating power of the universalising logics of capital and the state and of the sovereign individual seeking self-emancipation through and in property over against others that it is difficult not to be pessimistic about a Christian alternative except expressed as

---

Eighteenth Century Anglican Bishop Fallen Among Post-Structuralists, I and II', *New Blackfriars*, 64 (1983): 315-324 and 64 (1983): 374-383.

28 Milbank, *The Religious Dimension in the Thought of Giambattista Vico*, 335.

29 Milbank, *The Word Made Strange*, 25.

30 For this insight see G Ward, 'John Milbank's Divina Commedia', *New Blackfriars* 73 (1992): 311-318.

Trevor Hogan

'suffering and forbearance'.[31] Milbank does not wish to concede ontological power to tragedy but he is a pragmatist about late modernity as an epoch marked by tragic outcomes. Even as he argues that the 'use-value of the order of forgiveness derives from a "different" human commencement' he is acutely aware of the historical reality of an already prior inscription of tragedy. Can we only hope for: 'honour amongst thieves, love in the brothels, wisdom in the councils of state, Utopia constructed on the ravaged hunting-grounds of Indians'?[32]

Postmodern Christian Socialism: Imagining Peaceable Difference in Complex Space

Milbank faces these issues squarely: socialism like Christianity before it has 'assumed a spectral reality in the modern secularised world' after 1989, ceasing to 'appear either as plausible or rational' and consigned instead to the 'realm of faith'.[33] And yet, both continue to haunt the west 'by their excellence' and because 'nothing has emerged to replace' them: '. . . just as the story of a compassionate God who became man was the 'final religion', so also, the hope of a universal fraternity based on sharing was 'the final politics'.[34] The task of still actually existing Christian socialists in this era of spectral hauntings is to give an adequate account of this faith, of the possibility of living in and out of the 'discourse of participated perfections'. We return then to where we began on the possibility of connecting theology and politics from the side of theology and to the explicit commendation of socialism in both the writings of Barth and Milbank. What is the content of their

---

31 J Milbank, 'An Essay Against Secular Order', *The Journal of Religious Ethics* 15 (1987): 221.
32 *Ibid*, and also J Milbank,'Enclaves, or Where is the Church?', *New Blackfriars*, 73 (1992): 352.
33 Milbank, 'Socialism of the Gift, Socialism by Grace', 532.
34 *Ibid.*

respective faith commitments? (Given that their politics have been as controversial as their theology). Or to return to Milbank's claim that 'every social theory contains a theology and every theology contains a social theory', what then are their respective social theories contained in their theological visions and narratives?

For a man who spent the larger part of his life in his study, Barth's socialist praxis is indisputably impressive. Out of the detritus of his humanist liberal Protestant training the young Barth extracted a radical sense of the pressing social question of industrial capitalism and the exploitation of the working class, and his equation of the Kingdom of God with socialism: 'Jesus *is* the movement for social justice, and the movement for social justice is Jesus in the present'.[35] From his first hand exposure to these processes in his parish at Safenwil, his forming of two labour unions and joining the German Social Democratic Party through to his many public addresses and sermons on political, economic and social matters, the Barth of the crisis of World War was not only responsive to contemporary concerns but a partisan activist on the side of socialism. The failure of international socialism in the face of rival nationalisms in World War One, the fragile nature of the Weimar Republic, and the rise of Bolshevism in the Russian revolution, tempered Barth's revolutionary politics and prompted a shift from the madness of modern Europe to a restatement of socialism from the side of the Christian God.[36] Barth had come to the view that the redemptive carrier of history was neither the proletariat as

---

35 K Barth, 'Jesus Christ and the Movement for Social Justice' in C Green (ed), *Karl Barth: Theologian of Freedom* (London: Collins, 1989), 98-114.

36 H Gollwitzer, 'Kingdom of God and Socialism in the Theology of Karl Barth' in Hunsinger, *op cit*, 79f. See also B McCormack, *Karl Barth's Critically Realistic Dialectical Theology* (Oxford: Oxford University Press, 1995), Chapter 2: 'Socialism and Religious Socialism in Safenwil'.

Marx had hoped, nor the better selves of the enlightened bourgeois protestant culture as his theological teachers had preached; it was neither the vanguard party and commanding heights of the state as Lenin was practising, nor could it ever be the mythic *volk*, blood and soil of the nation that the young Hitler and his brownshirts were promoting. In his second, revised edition of his *Epistle to the Romans*, Barth transposed and transformed his socialism to Christian praxis, seeking to renew the church's consciousness of 'the Christian gospel's explosive contents' by writing a 'non-modernist, radical and Biblical sermon'.[37] Barth was no longer a pastoral and political activist but he remained throughout his life a moral political agitator whether that be in stiffening the Confessional Church's repudiation of the irrationalism of the Nazi regime, the critique of Bolshevist centralism, or the struggle against nuclear weapons and West German rearmament after World War Two.

Barth's Christian socialism was largely a matter of confessional difference, of viewing prophetically the spiritual issues in an age of global ideological warfare. The limits of Barth's socialism can therefore be outlined along three lines. First, his early socialism is second International Marxism, conducted through an intellectual dialogue on three fronts: with the Swiss Religious socialists, with the writings of Karl Kautsky and the German Social Democratic Party, and with the writings of Lenin, as well as through practical involvement in parochial activism.

Second, his dialectical theology of the twenties hides the political dimensions of his radicalism from his readers and followers because of the concentrated transposition of his thought from immanental history to salvation history, from class politics to the theology of Christian community. This shift helps us to make sense of his scathing critique of the Swiss religious socialists who had so inspired him in the first place and the reaction of disillusionment by his crisis theological

---

37. Gollwitzer, *op cit*, 82.

comrade in arms, Paul Tillich.[38] More important, however, this transposition inserts an unbridgeable chasm, 'an infinite qualitative difference' between 'the kingdom of God as the true socialism' and the ongoing political struggles of socialist movements of his time. This might enable the opening up of an autonomous space for critique but offers no mediating point of conversation across and between rival arguments and discourses.

Third, and most problematically, Barth's take on Marxism was largely anthropological (with his emphasis on the expropriation of the labourer's contribution to the wealth of capitalists and his Hegelian emphasis on the dehumanising dependency of workers on their masters) and political in its interests. He lacked a critique of political economy and his mature studies of politics smuggle in Weberian ideal types ('state', 'community', 'civil society', 'civilization', etc), in order to engage in a comparative analysis of Soviet Communism and American liberal democracy as competing ideological world views.[39] His attempt at positing a third way for the Christian church between the two world powers frustrated otherwise empathetic colleagues such as Reinhold Niebuhr. To Niebuhr and others there was no third way between totalitarianism and the defence of liberal and social democratic systems. Barth seemed perilously indifferent to careful discussions of the limits of rival economic systems, and to detailing the forms of political oppression and surveillance undertaken in totalitarian states (not to mention the death camps and pogroms). Ideology

---

38   See Cort, *op cit*, 207-213; Green, *op cit*, 11-45.

39.   See Karl Barth, 'The Christian Community and the Civil Community' (1946) in Green (ed), *op cit*, 265-296. For a more sympathetic account of Barth's later political ideas see Milbank's own teacher's article, Rowan Williams, 'Barth, War and the State' in Nigel Biggar (ed), *Reckoning with Barth* (London: Mowbray, 1988), 170-190.

critique and moral ideal types are inadequate vehicles for such debates, theoretical and empirical.[40]

Whereas Barth lived in the height of the cold war, we live in the time of socialism's manifold defeats. Command economics, market socialism and communism of every ideological hue no longer offer a viable politics let alone coherent theories of modernity. Even social democracy seems distinctly fragile in Western Europe and Scandinavia. The crisis of socialism is both intellectual and political and in this sense mimicks the fate of Christianity. Milbank's challenge, as it is for all Christians who believe that salvation is more—and certainly not less—than social, is to re-narrate socialism.

Cornelius Castoriadis has argued that the modern world revolves around three imaginaries: 'the market', 'the strato-bureaucratic society', and 'the autonomous society' (radical democracy).[41] Milbank endeavours to re-narrate Christian socialism as the outright rejection of the former two in the name of a modified valuation of democracy, redefined as associative democracy with a commitment to just living and the common good (*bonum*). Milbank's discourse of participated perfections and peaceable difference starts with the objective of imagining how communities (free-associations) might flourish in the production of complex spaces for the good of all.

Given that Milbank has already ruled out the possibility of a foundationalist account of socialism,[42] it follows that arguments for socialism, like Christianity before it, can only be a 'baseless suspicion' of the inadequacy and ultimate lack of a world order which propagates and projects 'a future of infinite

---

40. See Gollwitzer, in Hunsinger, *op cit*, 103.
41. Castoriadis, *op cit*; see also John Rundell, *Origins of Modernity* (Cambridge: Polity, 1987), 200.
42. For example, viewing socialism as the dialectical completion of class conflict, as evolutionary progress, as humanist or liberal idealism, as the logical outcome of the progressive emancipation of humanity from religion, nature and/or government, etc.)

utilitarian calculation by individuals, states and transnational companies, of the possible gains and losses, the greater and the lesser risks'.[43] Milbank refuses to grant capitalism any universal purchase beyond that of the creative capacities of human participation in the production of human culture and systems across time and space. In spite of capitalism's apparent universal character as a global system it is nevertheless neither anything more nor less than a humanly produced system that embodies the sedimentation of socially unjust practices and perpetuates traditions of social injustice. It institutes a social imaginary that separates the regulation of society from social, political, aesthetic and moral norms, and the possibility of consensus on these values. Consequently, 'the critique of capitalism is a moral critique or else it is no critique at all'.[44] Moreover, 'socialism is not right because it is "rational" but because it is just', or at least offers the possibility and the vision of human excellence in just community.[45] The argument for socialism, likewise for Christianity, is an exercise of the 'contingent imagination' for a certain kinds of possibilities in the future ordering of human societies: partial utopias 'composed out of fragments of past justice' and the self-reflexive 'critique of past social and ecclesial error'.[46]

Socialism, in Milbank's terms, is synonymous with community which, in turn, he argues is a singularly Christian concept, practice, narrative, norm and aesthetic.[47] Community

---

[43] Milbank, 'Socialism of the Gift, Socialism by Grace', 532.

[44] J Milbank, 'On Baseless Suspicion: Christianity and the Crisis of Socialism', *New Blackfriars* 69 (1988): 4.

[45] *Ibid.*

[46] *Ibid*, 6. In addition to Milbank's discussion of Marx, Marxism and Christian Marxism and liberation theology in Theology and Social Theory, see an earlier essay, 'The Body by Love Possessed: Christianity and Late Capitalism in Britain', *Modern Theology* 3 (1986): 35-65.

[47] Shades of Barth's discussion of Christian community in *Church Dogmatics* here, a connection worthy of detailed comparison and

qua community is 'actually performed, ideally imagined, and in both aspects, contemplated'.[48] The task of Christian theology is the explication of Christian practice, which is nothing more than reflection of the singularity of Christian norms of community; these in turn give the content of God-speak, articulating 'God' not just through words, but also in images and bodily actions.[49] The Christian church then is paradoxically a 'nomad city' that cannot draw boundaries to exclude the stranger and the outsider, but is rather more like an 'asylum' and a 'hospital' than an 'enclave'.[50] The church lives inside the discourse of participated perfections, on the site of the Eucharist, which is 'nowhere—yet . . . Everywhere'.[51]

So what does this community look like? Milbank defines it as 'socialism of the gift, socialism by grace', and highlights what he means by it with reference to contemporary debates between liberals and communitarians especially with relation to various European experiments in 'New Labour' and democratic socialism on the one hand and on the other over and against the incipient organicist corporatism of Papal social teachings.

Tony Blair's much trumpeted Third Way politics of New Labour in no way endeavours to contest the logic of capitalism and liberal market economics and repudiates the older tradition of Labour politics in government, nationalisation, high income taxes, employment schemes and the welfare state. Rather, Third Way politics is about the rediscovery of civil society, a neo-Durkheimian social policy of helping social institutions to modernise so as to catch up to the rapid economic changes

---

study.
48   Milbank, 'Postmodern Critical Augustinianism', 229.
49.   *Ibid*, 228f.
50   Here Milbank is using the pre-modern, Christian senses of the terms 'asylum' and 'hospital' rather than the highly policed bureaucracies of the modern epoch.
51.   Milbank, 'Enclaves, or Where is the Church?', 352 .

brought about by information and communication technology revolutions and the globalization of finance capitalism.

Community, in Milbank's argument, is not a totalising monad (family, locality, nation) because the community as monad contains and is modelled on the same logic of self-government which too easily leads to exclusion and scapegoating of difference and strangers. It is neither the interpellation of like with like (for community needs difference for true encounter to take place), nor a matter of networking or stake holding politics (that is, association for a predetermined, ulterior purpose). Rather it cannot exist apart from exchange of and between differences; community needs strangers who in the gift of endless exchanges are our neighbours: 'to value community is to value encounter'.[52]

In what is essentially a re-configuration, this time in political terms, of Milbank's theological and philosophical arguments for a Vichian view of human creativity and culture making that I have summarised above, Milbank outlines four positive constructive proposals for a postmodern Christian socialism of the gift, by grace. First, there is the ideal, practice and discourse of the free-association, the relational unity which is achieved in relations of the gift exchange and yet bound to others in a consensus of the common good. The historic traces and fragments of free associations are to be glimpsed in the urban work and trade guilds, monasteries, and universities of medieval Europe, and of the various experiments in mutualism and co-operativism as they have emerged during and since the nineteenth century. As Milbank acerbically observes, the end of the Middle ages and this principle of free association is occurring only now in our universities!

---

52   Milbank, 'Socialism of the Gift, Socialism by Grace', 539. We need to hear more from Milbank on 'associative democracy' in relation to his indebtedness to the radical wing of Anglo-Catholic socialism from W G Ward to J N Figgis and R H Tawney through to David Nicholls.

Second, the principle of community in exchange demands that we seek to 'socialise the markets' wherever possible even as this must take place on 'a global scale and must often work within businesses': 'In every exchange, something other than calculation of profit and loss must enter, we must at every turn, at every specific point . . . negotiate concerning what here, in this place, must be justice, what here might be a space of shared benefit'.[53]

Third, this instilling of a new ethos might encourage the recovery of a Platonic idea of education as wisdom, such as through the promotion of the professionalisation of the gift exchange in multiple forms and in every place of what might constitute human social good.[54] Here also, Milbank addresses the tension between democratic and aristocratic notions of politics, between the ideal of participation and the problem of propaganda, manipulation and corruption, and the place of authority, pastoral oversight (such as modelled on non-coercive educative ideal of teachers and students; bishops and priests, parents and their children, etc.) and institutional legitimation.

Finally, a postmodern Christian socialism "makes festivity central", of celebration, worship and expenditure (instead of capitalist accumulation), of mutual giving and showing, of the Eucharist.[55] How though does this differ from the universal right to shop? Does not the Christian centrality of festivity make it a functional fit with consumer capitalism's orgiastic excess of

---

53 Milbank, 'Socialism of the Gift, Socialism by Grace', 544. Note that Milbank is not advocating socialisation in the Marxist sense of communism of property but more a Ruskinian ethic as outlined most famously in John Ruskin's four essays first published in 1861, *Unto this Last*, and discussed in *Theology and Social Theory*.

54 *Ibid*. This understanding of the place of the professional ethos in modern welfare state societies has been a feature of Weberian historical sociology such has been practised by H Perkin, *The Rise of Professional Society: England since 1880* (London: Routledge, 1989).

55 *Ibid*.

the endless carnival?[56] Indeed it could do so, but Milbank is careful to differentiate nihilism from Christianity in several ways. Love of the other and mutual giving cannot be reconciled with an 'impersonal, meaningless process of nature'.[57] Moreover, consumer and stakeholder capitalism is romantic individualism *writ large*, whereby substantive content is made everywhere subordinate to form, and ends are reduced to means. The individual is proclaimed a consumer and a stakeholder over and against his/her value as a person, citizen or worker but these choices as consumers and investors are already predetermined by abstract and technologically dissimulated markets. These processes are taking place concurrently with the strategic and systematic dismantling of social forms of solidarity instituted by trade unions, co-operatives and mutualist organisations and associations.

It should be clearer now that when Nichols, Lakeland and others accuse Milbank of turning back to theocracy and *Gemeinschaft*, they have missed entirely the theological centrality of gift exchange economy in his thinking. It is perhaps ironic that Milbank's critics on this point are both Roman Catholics, for Milbank goes to some pains to show why it is that this re-narration of socialism cannot be equated with pre-modern corporatism found in the Papal social teachings. Here again Milbank's discussion is marked by ambivalence.[58] On the one hand, he wishes to recognise the important and positive contribution of Papal social doctrine to the distinctive difference of Christian socialism in its persistent emphasis on space, and not the messianic temporal emphases which more frequently has informed modern socialist and communist social

---

56. Here Milbank's 'festivity' motif perhaps surprisingly recalls Harvey Cox's *Feast of Fools: A Theological Essay on Festivity and Fantasy* (Cambridge, MA: Harvard University Press, 1969).
57. Milbank, 'Socialism of the Gift, Socialism by Grace', 544.
58. The following discussion is based on J Milbank, 'On Complex Space', in *The Word Made Strange*, Chapter 12.

imaginaries with such tragic consequences. In particular Milbank praises the Vatican's consistent emphasis on such concepts as personalism, solidarism, subsidiarity, household independence, free association and the balance between regions and rural and urban centres, as well as for the Popes' continuous praise of all forms of 'intermediate associations' between state and individual. These are good themes: put together, they represent the best of modern Christian social advocacy of complex space over the past two centuries. They contest the *chronotope* of the dialectic of enlightenment in its perpetuation of the simple space of the *saeculum*. Nevertheless, Milbank is also quick to criticise Papal social teaching for its fatal flaw in non-socialist corporatism, which he calls the falling into the *kitsch* and violence of fascism. The counter-modern logic of Papal critiques of capitalism is the belief that it represents a temporary and reversible falling away from a universal, trans-historical natural order. 'Turn back, turn back!' is the call of the Roman Church. But, says Milbank, the Papal teachings elide the embarrassing tragedies of actually-practised non-socialist corporatism.[59] Against this vision, Milbank argues that it is possible to uphold the reality of justice, the possibility of human harmony and community "without retreating to pre-modern contemplation of eternal positions and pre-given hierarchies" or resigning ourselves to the empty and violent formalism of the modern logics of capitalism and litigious individuals and bureaucracies.[60] Nevertheless, Christian socialism must take a wager on justice, living out of the gift, continuously given:

> Christians can have faith that things will, ontologically, arrive in the mode of beauty, of proper proportion which is also the mode of justice. And they can recognise, also, that the only possible road to the reception of this grace is to have the initial grace

---

[59.] *Ibid*, 283-285.
[60.] *Ibid*, 283.

to bear the cross, to endure it to the full, to realise
existentially the full horror of existing disharmony. In
this sense, socialism is now by grace alone.[61]

And we might add: or not at all?

---

61. Milbank, 'Socialism of the Gift, Socialism by Grace', 545. I am
grateful to friends and colleagues who freely gave of their time
and intelligence to converse with me on matters of mutual
interest, especially Andrew Dawson, Christopher Houston, and
Rowan Ireland.

275

Milbank and Barth:
A Catholic Perspective

Neil Ormerod

In a critical review essay entitled 'For and Against John Milbank' Canadian theologian Gregory Baum ponders the possibility that Milbank is 'Karl Barth *revivivus*' because he argues 'with Barthian vehemence that there is no good society, no valid ethics, and no true wisdom apart from the life and message of Jesus Christ'. However Baum notes specific differences between these two thinkers, in particular Milbank's insistence that it is 'the practice not the proclamation of God's approaching reign' which is foundational. This priority of praxis over kerygma leads Baum to conclude that Milbank is 'an Anabaptist or Mennonite Barth'.[1] This claim by Baum invites a more detailed comparison of these two to see what the points of contact between them might be.

My interest is primarily in Milbank and stems from his radical rejection of the role of the social sciences in theology, a stance which, though I do not accept it, has caused my to rethink and clarify my own stance on the relationship between them. So the comparison will be a modest one, more detailed on the Milbank side than the Barth side, but one which I hope brings out the similarities and differences between them.

My starting point will be a quick review of the various references that Milbank makes to Barth in his two books, *Theology and Social Theory*[2] and the more recent work, *The Word*

---

1.   G Baum, *Essays in Critical Theory* (Kansas: Sheed & Ward, 1994), 52.

2   J Milbank, *Theology and Social Theory: Beyond Secular Reason* (Oxford: Blackwell, 1990).

Made Strange.[3] I will then bring a third party into the dialogue, Catholic theologian Bernard Lonergan.

The first point to note is that despite the parallels drawn between them by Baum, Milbank himself makes scant reference to the work of Barth. In *Theology and Social Theory*, the work on which Baum was commenting, there is only one explicit mention of Barth, quite a minor one, where he is lumped together with Augustine and Aquinas, as a theologian who 'speaks in modes beyond the point where dialectics leaves off, namely, in terms of the imaginative explication of texts, practices and beliefs'.[4] Still, the context of this comment is within Milbank's critique of MacIntyre, so the reference is really tangential.

There is however another reference which is not explicit, but which could be taken as Milbank's summary rejection of the Barthian project. In a chapter entitled "Policing the Sublime: A Critique of the Sociology of Religion", Milbank refers to "certain styles of neo-orthodoxy that insist on the absolute contrast between the revealed word of God and human 'religion'", which are happy to hand over to a reductive sociology the study of religions. However, he attacks this position most strongly seeing it as nothing more than a variant of liberal protestantism:

> a revealed word of God which speaks only of itself,
> which does not really penetrate the realm of human
> symbolic constructions without getting tainted and
> distorted, must continue to be without impact upon
> the world, and therefore remains locked in a category
> of the specifically religious, just as much as the liberal
> protestant notion of 'religious experience'.[5]

---

3. J Milbank, *The Word Made Strange: Theology, Language, Culture* (Oxford: Blackwell, 1997).

4. Milbank, *Theology and Social Theory*, 328.

5. Milbank, *Ibid*, 101. It should be noted that Milbank does not capitalise the 'p' of Protestant.

This it seems is Milbank's fundamental criticism of the neo-orthodox movement of which Barth was a champion. Like the extrinsicism which dominated Catholic theology at least since the Council of Trent, the religious realm, for the neo-orthodox, remains locked out of any real contact with the world of human history and society. Indeed Milbank shows far more interest in the Catholic debate on this issue and the ensuing controversy surrounding the *nouvelle theologie*, devoting an entire chapter to it, than he does to the position of Barth and other neo-orthodox writers. Thus while one could take this as a reference to Barth, it is not a central part of Milbank's project.

The references in his second work, *The Word Made Strange*, are more numerous, though not necessarily less summary. There are two references where he compares Barth and von Balthasar as two theologians seeking to develop an theological aesthetics,[6] and two references where Milbank criticises the Hegelian influence on Barth, one in which Milbank claims that the ontological difference between God and humanity is stressed to the neglect of the 'tragic' difference created by the fall,[7] and the other in which he criticises the Hegelian 'gnostic ontology' present in Barth's soteriology which obscures a fuller treatment of the atonement. (This is similar to the criticism made of Barth by Alister McGrath[8] and highlights the difference noted by Baum between these two thinkers, between proclamation and praxis.) Then there is a brief comparison with Jean-Luc Marion, to the effect that 'compared with Marion, the

---

6.   Milbank, *The Word Made Strange*, 123, 162f.

7.   *Ibid*, 132.

8.   A McGrath, *The Making of Modern German Christology 1750-1990* (Grand Rapids: Zondervan, 1994), 136: 'Barth's Christology seems to be located within precisely the same framework as that of the Enlightenment . . . namely a concern for a "right knowledge" of our situation . . . For Barth, Christ's incarnation, passion, death and resurrection cannot in any way be said to *change* the relationship between God and us; they merely *disclose* the Christologically determined situation to us.'

ambition of a Barth is as nothing, for it is as if, so to speak . . . Marion seeks to be both Barth and Heidegger at once'.[9]

Finally there is a perhaps more programatic statement in the early part of the book where Milbank is setting his own theological agenda. Here Milbank argues for the fact that moral virtues can only be legitimated within a 'narrative framework', a conclusion which he states 'is now inescapable'. Further this historicist approach is preferable 'to a more purely "Barthian" one which thinks of the Christian moral narrative too schematically as presenting to us plots and goals provided by "revelation", reflecting a revealed "story of God"'.[10] Milbank goes on to argue that one can develop this historicist perspective to advance a 'specifically Christian metaphysics' or a 'theological ontology'—not, one might note, an ontological theology; just as von Balthasar develops a theological aesthetics, not an aesthetical theology.[11] This would open up the possibility 'of the transformation of specifically Greek metaphysics . . . through its subsumption into Christian tradition'. He concludes that such an 'ecclesiological mediation might then finally allow the *analogia entis* and the *analogia Christi* to come together'.[12]

Here Milbank clearly spells out a program which stands in some sort of dialectical relationship to that of Barth. Milbank envisages the possibility of overcoming the great Barthian opposition between the *analogia entis* and the *analogia fidei* through an ecclesiological mediation. However, this new sublation of philosophy within theology will not be of the type found in the work of Aquinas, for Milbank gives priority to language, 'because language does not stand for ideas, as Aquinas thought, but constitutes ideas and 'expresses' things in

---

9. Milbank, *The Word Made Strange*, 36f.
10. *Ibid*, 28f.
11. H U von Balthasar, *The Glory of the Lord: A Theological Aesthetics I: Seeing the Form* (Edinburgh: T&T Clark, 1982), especially 79-116.
12. Milbank, *The Word Made Strange*, 28f.

their disclosure of truth for us'. And language is, of course, 'always particular and traditioned'.[13]

This difference between Milbank and Barth has its parallels in the way each views the social sciences. Overall it seems Barth is as dismissive of the social sciences playing a role in theology as he is of philosophy. Both are the product of a corrupted human reason. In discussing the task of the Christian community Barth refuses to allow

> any general or special anthropology to intervene with its supposedly normative suggestions. We cannot be helped to our goal by any definition of man projected from the sphere occupied by a biological, sociological, psychological or ethical conception. Common to all such anthropologies is the fact that their pictures of man are all products of the same human self-understanding . . . no help is to be found even in the most penetrating analyses of what in any given age . . . is called 'modern' man. (CD IV/3, 803.)

Similarly Milbank rejects any contribution from the social sciences to theology. This is because 'there can be no sociology in the sense of a universally "rational" account of the "social" character of all societies'.[14] Following MacIntyre, who argues for an interrelationship between ethics and sociology,[15] Milbank contends that Christianity is a distinctive ethical practice which requires its own distinctive social theory. To quote:

> The theory, therefore, is first and foremost an *ecclesiology*, and only an account of other human societies to the extent that the Church defines itself, in its practice, as in continuity and discontinuity with these societies. As the Church is *already*, necessarily,

---

13 *Ibid*, 29.
14 Milbank, *Theology and Social Theory*, 380f.
15 A MacIntyre, *After Virtue, a Study in Moral Theory* 2nd Ed (Notre Dame: University of Notre Dame Press, 1984), 23: 'A moral philosophy . . . characteristically presupposes a sociology'.

by virtue of its institution, a 'reading' of other human societies, it becomes possible to consider ecclesiology as also a 'sociology'.[16]

Talk of a 'Christian sociology' makes sense precisely because there is no universal sociology, only the narratives of particular societies such as the church. According to Milbank it should not be that theology adds to itself a new competence to make 'social pronouncements', rather, 'all theology has to reconceive itself as a kind of "Christian sociology"'.[17] Just as Milbank envisages a mediation between Greek philosophy and Christian tradition so too he conceives of that theology as constituting its own social science, so as to develop what could be called a 'theological sociology'. One might add however that in his earlier work, he seem less likely to envisage a constructive mutuality between theology and existing social sciences, whereas his later work seems to suggest a more constructive dialogue between philosophy and theology.

This brief comparison highlights at least two areas of agreement between Milbank and Barth. Both reject the notion of autonomous reason, either in the sphere of philosophy or the human sciences, as providing a reliable touchstone to weight against the apparent claims of faith. Both assert the absolute priority of revelation. Nevertheless, Milbank envisages, in a way he discounts as impossible for Barth, the possibility that Christian revelation creates, sustains and prolongs its own tradition of rationality which can ground a Christian theological philosophy and social science (ecclesiology). However, unlike the self-understanding of the classical Christian philosophical tradition, for Milbank this tradition is based in the historical particularity of the Christ-event and as such is a contingent and "unfounded mythos", as are all traditions of rationality such as that of instrumental rationality propounded by modernity. Thus this tradition makes no claim to being a universal reason,

---

16. Milbank, *Theology and Social Theory*, 380.
17. *Ibid*, 381.

281

but is accessible only in and through Christian revelation and praxis. In this way Milbank seeks to overcome his criticism of neo-orthodoxy, that it conceives of revelation as leaving the world unchanged. On his view revelation enters into the fabric of human history to create a new society which mediates the Christ-event to the world through the on-going praxis of the church.

It is beyond the expertise of the present author to judge the validity of Milbank's summary account as an accurate portrayal of Barth or neo-orthodoxy on this point. On the Catholic side Hugo Meynell describes Barth's understanding of justification as 'so heavenly that it makes no earthly difference'.[18] A more sympathetic analysis is provided by Ingolf Dalferth. He describes Barth's approach as a 'theological perspective of universal inclusiveness which incorporates and reconstructs the shared and public reality of our world within theology'. Barth 'does not deny the secularity of the world but reinterprets it theologically in the light of the presence of Christ'.[19] Milbank's own engagement with Barth's writings is so minimal as to say that at best his account would require further substantiation.

Thus we conclude that Milbank is more than willing to draw deeply from the wells of the Christian engagement with philosophical reason, while remaining more distant from the possibility of such a mutual engagement with sociological reason. It sould be noted however that this is a very selective drawing which contains two fundamental options from within that tradition. The first is a preference for the stream of Platonic-Augustinian idealism over and against that of Aristotelian-Thomistic realism. Indeed Milbank's first book, *Theology and Social Theory* is replete with Augustinian themes—knowledge

---

18 H Meynell, *Grace Versus Nature, Studies in Karl Barth's Dogmatics* (London: Sheed and Ward, 1965), 261.

19 I Dalferth, 'Karl Barth's eschatological realism' in *Karl Barth: Centenary Essays* S W Sykes (ed), (Cambridge: Cambridge University Press, 1989), 30.

through illumination; emanations from the divine; the virtues of pagans are vices in disguise; the two cities, of God and of humanity and so on. The second is his preference for conceptualism over the dynamic intellectualism of Aquinas. Thus, to return to the passage already quoted, Milbank identifies Aquinas' 'error' in these terms: 'language does not stand for ideas, as Aquinas thought, but constitutes ideas and 'expresses' things in their disclosure of truth for us'.[20] These two preferences combine to form what Milbank himself identifies as 'linguistic idealism'.[21]

The first point to make about these preferences is that it is difficult to see how they could be justified on the basis of revelation alone. Indeed one could argue that the idealism of Augustine produced unresolved and unresolvable tensions in his theological synthesis of revelation, particularly in the area of the theology of grace and original sin. These tensions were resolved in quite different directions by Aquinas in the twelfth century, through the introduction of the grace-nature distinction, and the Reformers in the sixteenth century, with the notion of the total corruption of fallen humanity. Milbank is quite dismissive of both these options. Indeed Aquinas' solution involving the introduction of a theoretical construct identified as "nature" is seen by Milbank as the beginning of the end of Christendom and the starting point of modern secularism.[22] Similarly the Reformers are blamed for the privatisation of religion and its retreat into the realm of interiority.[23] Yet it is not clear to this reader that Milbank overcomes the tensions in the Augustinian synthesis or is even aware of them.

---

20 Milbank, *The Word Made Strange*, 29.

21 Milbank, *Theology and Social Theory*, 343.

22 *Ibid*, 407. Aquinas' theology of grace-nature allows for 'the idea of a permanent political sphere concerned with the positive goals of finite well-being, and clearly distinguished as a 'natural' institution, from the Church as a 'supernatural' one' (*Ibid*).

23 *Ibid*, 17f.

In a similar vein it is difficult to see how the option for conceptualism over the dynamic intellectualism of Aquinas can be justified on the basis of revelation alone. Indeed it would seem to me to do violence to the literary forms of the biblical texts to have them settle such a precise philosophical issue as this. To adopt this option would require going beyond the Scriptures and entering into the tradition of dialogue between philosophy and theology initiated in the patristic era and prolonged into the scholastic era. Within that tradition Milbank's linguistic turn has more in common with the conceptualism of Duns Scotus and the nominalism of Ockham than other competing strands; yet these too are thinkers who feel his rejection.[24]

The starting point for conceptualism is the priority of concepts or language over understanding. In taking this path Milbank not only departs from Aquinas, but also from Augustine for whom the inner 'word' is a 'nonlinguistic utterance of truth'.[25] As Catholic theologian Bernard Lonergan notes, Augustine 'begged his readers to look within themselves and there to discover the speech of spirit within spirit, an inner *verbum* prior to any use of language'.[26] On the other hand Scotus' inversion of this relationship between understanding and language led eventually to the neglect and even suspicion

---

24 *Ibid*, 14: 'In the thought of the nominalists, following Duns Scotus, the Trinity loses its significance as a prime location for discussing will and understanding in God and the relationship of God to the world. No longer is the world participatorily enfolded within the divine expressive *logos*, but instead a bare divine unity starkly confronts the other distinct unities which he has ordained'. See also page 376 where Milbank speaks of the Scotist God as 'only singular in its solitary arbitrariness'.

25 B Lonergan, *Verbum: Word and idea in Aquinas*, Collected Works of *Bernard Lonergan* Vol 2 (Toronto: University of Toronto Press, 1997), 7. Lonergan refers his readers to Augustine's *De Trinitate*, XV, xii, 22.

26 Lonergan, *Verbum*, 6.

of understanding altogether, as in the nominalism of Ockham. Only the names remain, and of course, individual existents in their concrete particularity. The parallels with post-modern thought are evident.

The second point is that there is another way of reading the Christian tradition which would call into questions Milbank's option for a linguistic idealism. Lonergan has argued in relation to the process of religious conversion, that:

> First there is God's gift of his love. Next, the eye of this love reveals values in their splendour, while the strength of this love brings about their realization, and that is moral conversion. Finally, among the values discerned by the eye of love is the value of believing the truths taught by the religious tradition, and in such tradition and belief are the seeds of intellectual conversion.[27]

Note that as with Milbank and Barth, Lonergan holds for the priority of divine action, the gift of God's love. Like Milbank, Lonergan argues that this divine action grounds an ongoing moral and intellectual tradition, identified in terms of a religious tradition evoking moral and intellectual conversion. But the fruit of this tradition is not a linguistic idealism, but what Lonergan calls 'intellectual conversion' or what he also identifies as 'critical realism'. By critical realism Lonergan means the philosophical position, grounded in an analysis of interiority, which holds that reality is known in objective judgments. He distinguishes critical realism from various forms of naive realism where reality is considered to be grasped in some prior act of extroverted consciousness, such as looking.[28] Lonergan scholar Robert Doran, in reflecting on Lonergan's

---

27. Bernard Lonergan, *Method in Theology* (London: DLT, 1972), 243.
28. For a good summary of these positions see, Bernard Lonergan, 'Cognitional Structures' in *Collection, Collected Works of Bernard Lonergan* Vol 4, (Toronto: University of Toronto Press, 1988), 205-221, and 'The Subject' in *A Second Collection* (Philadelphia: Westminster Press, 1974), 69-86.

analysis, surmises, 'perhaps only a Christian theologian could have articulated critical realism'.[29] Thus, Lonergan's position can also be interpreted along the lines of Milbank's desire for an ecclesiological mediation between the *analogia entis* and the *analogia Christi*. Yet the conclusion of this mediation is an intellectualist realism, not a linguistic idealism.[30]

According to Dalferth, Barth can also be counted among those who hold to a realist position. Like the early Councils of the church, Barth's stance is a dogmatic realism, one grounded in the belief that Christian doctrines assert a truth about real objects which are intrinsically intelligible.[31] As Dalferth states it, for Barth 'Christian discourse is reality-depicting'.[32] This position is far removed from Milbank's idealism. Nonetheless there are differences between the realism of Barth and that of Lonergan. Like Milbank, Barth rejects the notion of autonomous reason. Lonergan, on the other hand, while arguing that Christian tradition contains the seeds of intellectual conversion, would also hold that this same realism can be arrived at

---

29. R Doran, *Theology and the Dialectic of History* (Toronto: University of Toronto Press, 1991), 165.

30. In passing I will note that the promotion of a philosophical realism can be found in the latest encyclical of John Paul II, *Fides et Ratio*. While recognising the fragility of reason due to human sin, still 'illumined by faith, reason is set free from the fragility and limitations deriving from the disobedience of sin and finds strength required to rise to the knowledge of the Triune God' (n 43). Further, John Paul II, stresses that 'human reason is by its nature oriented to truth and is equipped moreover with the means necessary to arrive at truth' (n49). He encourages philosophers 'to trust in the power of human reason and not to set themselves goals that are too modest in their philosophising' (n56).

31. On the dogmatic realism of the early Councils see B Lonergan, 'The Origins of Christian Realism', *Second Collection* (Philadelphia: Westminster Press, 1974), 239-262.

32. Dalferth, *op cit*, 23.

independently of that particular tradition, though with considerable difficulty. Reason is perhaps 'relatively' autonomous in this regard. This differences precisely mirror differing understandings of the grace-nature debate, a point also picked up by Dalferth in his analysis of Barth's realism.[33]

Further comparison between these two thinkers, Milbank and Lonergan, raises a third point touched on above. Milbank marks the beginning of the end of Christendom in the grace-nature distinction introduced by Phillip the Chancellor and exploited systematically by Aquinas. The grace-nature distinction, according to Milbank, created the needed space for the creation of the secular and the eventual marginalisation and privatisation of religion. Milbank's own preference is for a 'supernaturalising of the natural', so that only a Christian society is a true society, only Christian theology (in the form of ecclesiology) provides a true account of society. Lonergan on the other hand conceives of Aquinas' adoption of the grace-nature distinction as the major theoretical advance which allows for the resolution of the difficulties within the Augustinian inheritance and a movement towards a fully systematic theological position.[34] This position also allows for a real contribution to theology from the social sciences which enjoy a real if relative autonomy from theology.[35] For Lonergan

---

33 This is evident where Dalferth describes reality, according to Barth, as made real 'through judgement and grace', *Ibid*, 28. From a Catholic perspective such as Lonergan's, this blurs the distinction between grace and nature.

34 See for example, B Lonergan, *Grace and Freedom: Operative Grace in the Thought of St Thomas Aquinas* (London: DLT, 1970).

35 Lonergan, *Insight: A Study of Human Understanding, Collected Works of Bernard Lonergan* Vol 3 (Toronto: University of Toronto Press, 1992), 767: 'Grace perfects nature, both in the sense that it adds a perfection beyond nature and in the sense that it confers on nature the effective freedom to attain its own perfection. But grace is not a substitute for nature, and theology is not a substitute for empirical human science'.

the roots of the decline of modernity lie not in the grace-nature distinction, as Milbank opines, but in the conceptualism of Scotus and the nominalism of Ockham[36] (a position also echoed by Hans Urs von Balthasar,[37] Alasdair MacIntyre[38] and by John Paul II[39]). Conceptualism marks a philosophical "flight from understanding", a flight which in modernity has reduced reason to instrumentality and introduced a pall of suspicion over the powers of intelligence. From this perspective Milbank's option for 'linguistic idealism' and the thorough-going historicism of post-modernity represent not a solution to the problems posed by modernity but more the final stages of decline and dissolution of a longer cycle of decline initiated by the emergence and dominance of conceptualism since the time of Duns Scotus.

At this stage I have introduced a third character into the comparison between Barth and Milbank. It would be interesting to prolong this dialogue to other points of comparison, for example, the stance of each towards the psychological analogy of the Trinity. Barth's rejection of such 'natural theology' is well known, and does not need to be recapitulated. Again the issue of conceptualism divides the approaches of Milbank and

---

36. For example, Lonergan, *Insight*, 396f: 'Five hundred years separate Hegel from Scotus . . . that notable interval of time was largely devoted to working out in a variety of manners the possibilities of the assumption that knowing consists in taking a look. The ultimate conclusion was that it did not and could not'.

37. In his article, 'Bernard Lonergan and the Functions of Systematic Theology', *Theological Studies* 59 (1998), Lonergan scholar Robert Doran refers to the 'scattered references' to Scotus to be found in von Balthasar's *The Glory of the Lord 5: The Realm of Metaphysics in the Modern World* (San Francisco: Ignatius, 1991) for von Balthasar's critique of Duns Scotus, n46.

38. Cf A MacIntyre, *Three Rival Versions of Moral Enquiry: Encyclopaedia, Genealogy and Tradition* (Notre Dame: University of Notre Dame Press, 1990), 152ff.

39. *Fides et Ratio*, n45.

Lonergan on this question. Milbank offers a very compressed and barely intelligible paragraph rejecting Lonergan's classical interpretation of Aquinas' psychological analogy in his work, *Verbum: Word and Idea in Aquinas*, a work which encapsulates Lonergan's own rejection of the conceptualist tradition which had overtaken Thomistic studies.[40] One could also explore in more detail a comparison of these three on the question of grace, in particular on the grace-nature distinction. But this would take us too far afield in the space allowed.

To conclude by a return to the original direction of this paper, let me recall the comments made by Baum which initiated my investigation. Is Milbank Barth *revivivus*? Certainly there are similarities in that both take their stand on a Christo-centric revelation which is not to be judged by any other standards extrinsic to itself. And in his earlier work, *Theology and Social Theory* there is a strong rejection of the possibility that human reason in the form of the social sciences have any contribution to make to Christian theologising. Still in his later work, *The Word Made Strange*, Milbank seems to envisage a far more catholic mediating position between theology and philosophy. However, his post-modern commitments put him at odds with the more dominant realist stance of the Christian tradition, as exemplified by both Barth and Lonergan. From that stance Milbank's post-modernism is a capitulation to the forces of decline evident within modernity. From this same realist stance one might also conclude that Barth's neo-orthodoxy is far more consistent in its rejection of these forces than Milbank.

---

40 Milbank, *The Word Made Strange*, 92f. An investigation of Milbank's rejection of Lonergan is the subject of my forthcoming paper, 'It is easy to see—the footnotes of John Milbank', *Philosophy and Theology*.

Epilogue

Wes Campbell

Contrary passions are aroused by the name Karl Barth. Contrary passions are also aroused by the term *postmodern*.[1] Both have passionate supporters and virulent detractors. To bring the two together in a conference appears to be the height of absurdity.

Karl Barth: A Future for Postmodern Theology? What do the *colon* and the *question mark* in the conference title signify? Does the *colon* denote relatedness or separation? What is the effect of the *question mark*? Does the interrogative question the future of Karl Barth's approach to theology, make a claim for Barth as a *postmodern theologian*, or challenge the notion of postmodern *theology* altogether? Does the claim that Karl Barth is 'the *initiator* of . . . a '*postmodern paradigm in theology*' but 'not the perfecter of such a paradigm'[2] clarify the issue?

The preceding papers do not definitively answer that question. Nor can they. Indeed, they pose even more sharply the question of how the name *Karl Barth* and the term *postmodern* relate. Or, more pointedly, how or whether *theology* as understood and practised by Barth and self-declared

---

1. See for example: P Beilharz, *Postmodern Socialism: Romanticism, City and State* (Melbourne: Melbourne University Press, 1994), 7-22; D Harvey, *The Condition of Postmodernity: An Enquiry into the Origins of Cultural Change* (Oxford: Blackwell, 1989), Chapter 3. On postmodernism as a form of relativism or nihilism: E Gellner, *Postmodernism, Reason and Religion* (London and New York: Routledge 1992), 70; G Steiner, *Real Presences* (London and Boston: Faber & Faber, 1989), 229.

2. H Küng, *Theology for the Third Millennium: An Ecumenical View* (New York, London, Toronto, Sydney, Auckland: Anchor Books and Doubleday, 1990), 271.

postmodern theology have anything to do with each other at all. In placing *Karl Barth* and *postmodern* together, the conference took a risk in seeming to set up what post/moderns oppose: *binary opposites*. An attempt to link Barth and the postmodern could be regarded as a futile attempt to combine the modern with its critical successor, for the 'neo-orthodox dogmatician' must surely be counted among the modern opponents of the *postmodern project*. The absurdity of such an attempt is heightened if, as some of Barth's critics believe, he attempts a return to the *premodern*! Even playful postmodern theorists, who applaud plurality and agree that any two items in a sentence are linked merely by being placed in one sentence, will be given pause by the title linking such obvious opposites. Theological *Barthians*, of course, may well agree with such opposition. Ignoring cultural and philosophical questions as uninteresting or irrelevant to the main theological task, they would be tempted to dismiss postmodern thinking as another passing fad or fancy. Here theologians would form alliances with social theorists yet to be convinced that the 'postmodern' is itself something other than another form of the 'modern'. [3]

Karl Barth: A future for Postmodern Theology? Does the *colon*, then, hold Barth and the postmodern together, or does it separate them, even in aggressive opposition? Could the title even suggest that Barth *is the future*? And more, the future *of postmodern theology*! Alternatively, it might question whether Barth, in postmodern days, has a future at all. Again, it may claim that Barth charts a way for theology in the post/modern situation; or that Barth's way of doing theology provides *the* way of doing postmodern theology. The conference papers demonstrated that all such interpretations are possible.

More than one paper takes the *colon* as a reason to report on Barth's theological enterprise as approaching apologetics and questions of cultural engagement with a certain disinterest. Describing Barth's approach as both playful and serious because of its single minded attention to its subject matter,

---

3   Beilharz, *op cit*, 7ff.

namely the triune God revealed in Jesus Christ, John Webster reports that Barth sought to do theology 'as if nothing had happened'. At the *colon*, a wedge appears to be driven between Barth and the postmodern. In making a claim for a 'disinterested' theology, Webster's approach seeks to echo Barth's. He takes up the diversity of terms *postmodern, postmodernity, postmodernism, postmodern theology* as a means of introducing the conference to Barth's characteristic theological method. The assertion that Barth is 'disinterested' may, sadly, give Barth's detractors further grounds to agree that his theological approach is of no interest. That would mean the question mark is read against Barth: a future for postmodern theology, yes, but not as Barth attempted it.

Would that response do justice to either Barth or Webster? Barth, a 'child of the nineteenth century', engaged modernity, asking theological questions of it, and listening to the critique its proponents exercised against the church and Christian theology. In spite of Webster's unease with postmodernism, he does indeed engage main themes of postmodern thought: *the removal of teleology, abolition of grand narratives, the relationship of the particular to the universal,* and *narrative* itself. Under the rubric of 'severe postmodernity' Webster examines postmodern claims concerning the 'death of the subject' and Barth's 'the-anthropology'. These themes are taken up in relationship to the subject matter of Christian theology. They *are* taken up! What is the relationship here? How does that *colon* hold these two together? Webster brings the two together in order to retrieve the main intent of Barth's work, a subject matter which is not controlled by any cultural period or human fashion but by the 'grand narrative of Jesus Christ' in which the triune God is known.

The tension detected in Webster's reading of Barth and his interpretation of postmodernity can be seen to have its source in Barth's own approach. Barth's assertion of *disinterest* must be understood *polemically* against those forms of theological work

Epilogue

he opposes.[4] If an exposition of Barth's method insists on a lack
of relationship, rather than a transformation of that relationship,
the breadth and integrity of Barth's project risks being
diminished. Moreover, like Barth's own work, Webster
demonstrates a difference between what is *said* and what is
done. Barth may have *said* that his intention was to do theology
as if nothing happened. He did *in fact* engage contemporary
philosophers and ideologues in his work. His dogmatic work
did give rise directly to ecclesial and ethical implications. Barth
rejected certain forms of science, yet, as Mostert reminds us in
his paper, his theology was constructed as a *Gotteswissenschaft*.
His theological work led to the composition of the *Barmen
Declaration* and the formation of the Confessing Church. Later
than Bonhoeffer, but even so, he came to the Jewish question
and the relationship of the church and Israel as the primary
ecumenical question. His theology led to pronouncements
against the splitting of the atom and atomic bombs, to extended
discussion of warfare (and his own participation in the Swiss
defence forces), even to a newspaper article on God as the
'upholder and avenger' of the rights of the poor.[5] In contrast to
his opposition to Nazism, Barth refused to condemn the Soviet
Union and took steps to form alliances with church leaders in
the Eastern bloc. The 'red pastor' of Safenwil did not entirely
disappear. The final fragment of the *Church Dogmatics*, *The
Christian Life*, addressed human life in society, as did his early
Tambach lecture.[6]

What, then, is the relationship between a theology which
attends single-mindedly to Jesus Christ and the contemporary
setting of the theologian? Hendrikus Berkhof accused Barth of

4. K Barth, *The Humanity of God* (London & Glasgow:
Fontana/Collins, 1971), 34f.
5. K Barth, 'Poverty', in *Against the Stream: Shorter Post-War Writings
1946-52* (London: SCM, 1954), 244.
6. K Barth, 'The Christian's Place in Society', in *The Word of God and
the Word of Man* (New York and Evanston: Harper & Row, 1957),
322.

concealing his own theological path and thus the relationship under discussion here.[7] Moltmann, against Barth's claim that his theology is centred on one point alone, insists that all theology is 'mediating theology'.[8] Newbigin is correct in his observation that the gospel is never naked word but comes clothed in the language of the speaker.[9] So it is with theology. Certainly, Barth's whole attempt is to insist that the *subject matter* of Christian theology is that which must control its work and not any other factor, such as the subjectivity of the theologian, or the relativity of the culture, or any other prior matter. Barth, a student of liberal Protestant theology, understands the radical relativity of all culture. He knows Christian theology is a human work which will never be finished. In this regard, he seeks a 'genuine understanding' of the biblical text.[10]

Thus, even if the relationship of Barth's theology to postmodernity—and *certainly* postmodernism—is constituted negatively, a relationship does exist. The *colon* is there. But, is the *negative* the entire story? If Barth approached modernity (Feuerbach, for example) so as to listen to its critique against the church and Protestant theology,[11] might there not be an analogous listening to postmodernity and the proponents of *postmodernism*? Certainly Barth was open to recognising in

---

7. H Berkhof, *Two Hundred Years of Theology: Report of a Personal Journey* (Grand Rapids: Eerdmans, 1989), 307.

8. J Moltmann, *Theology Today: Two Contributions Towards Making Theology Present* (London: SCM, 1988), 53.

9. L. Newbigin, *Foolishness to the Greeks* (Geneva: World Council of Churches Publications, 1986), 4.

10. K Barth, *The Epistle to the Romans* (London: Oxford University Press, 1933, 1968), 7.

11. K Barth, 'Evangelical Theology', in *The Humanity of God* (Collins: London, 1961), 32; and his *Protestant Theology in the Nineteenth Century* (London: SCM, 1972), especially Chapter 1.

culture a self-witness of Jesus Christ.[12] None of this is to seek to
fit Barth into a schema he so powerfully rejected: some form of
foundationalism or correlative system. In his late reflections,
The Humanity of God, Barth smiled somewhat self-mockingly at
his early *diastasis*.[13] He did not wish to further that. Nor should
we. Indeed, Barth details the path that led him to his theological
breakthrough. Insisting that the theological motivations were
primary, Barth nevertheless acknowledges the elements of crisis
and breakdown in European culture in the second decade of
this century, including new encounters with the strangeness of
the biblical world and its eschatology.

So, do the conference papers assist in bringing the figure and
work of the theologian Karl Barth into creative engagement
with the *postmodern condition* and, more, into dialogue with that
elusive creature *postmodern theology*? Certainly, the effect of the
colon is visible in the way the conference papers actually
demonstrate the dilemma which runs through contemporary
theology: theology's subject matter is approached either
through the work of a particular theologian or by way of a
contemporary question. Is that a covert form of the
theory/practice (*praxis*) divide? Is it a result of theological
curricula which have developed 'systematic theology' as one of
a number of disciplines, separated from biblical, church history
and pastoral specialisations? A number of conference papers
provide an exposition of theologians and their work. A number
of the papers take a main theme in Barth or compare Barth with
another theologian. In that, of course, they are implicitly
addressing the culture and questions posed; the shape, style
and method of the theologian Barth is to the fore. Alternatively,
papers take up a contemporary question, provoked by
theological or cultural considerations, addressing Barth only by
implication, taking their bearing from present issues.

---

12   See, for example, the discussion of the modern world: *CD* IV/3,
     21ff; and the discussion of other lights, *ibid*, 160ff.

13   K Barth, 'The Humanity of God', in *The Humanity of God* (London:
     Collins, 1961), 38ff.

An interest in theology's subject matter is found in the papers in Part Two. Chris Mostert engages Barth in critical conversation with Wolfhart Pannenberg, whose concern is the science of the mystery of God who is revealed. Barth's work, like that of Pannenberg, is a response to the challenge of modernity. The difference between them turns on *verification*. John Capper draws the reader to a neglected theme in Barth's work: the joy and the beauty of God, as the expression of God's love. Here a new way is offered for the apprehending of the character of God. Mark Lindsay takes up the disputed and continuing role of dialectic in Barth's later work with the express purpose of displaying Barth's treatment of Israel. Lindsay reports that the doctrine of election was developed at the time when Nazi propaganda was deifying the German *Volk* as the new chosen race, and electing Jews for death. and permitted Barth to refuse to separate church and Israel, to exercise a church-critique while affirming present day Jews. He observes that Barth's language must be revised in the light of the *Shoah*. It is clear in Lindsay's treatment that Barth's doctrinal work was written in a specific political and ideological context and must be read critically in the light of the genocide which later came to light (which Bonhoeffer and others at the time already appreciated). Contemporary questions put to Barth are most explicitly addressed in Part Three, in which Preece, Victorin-Vangerud, Thompson and Pickard bring contemporary questions to bear on Barth's work. There is a clear response to the failures and consequences of modernity at play. Barth as the 'disinterested' theologian is absent here. Themes engaged by postmodern theorists are engaged. It remains clear that even here Barth as theologian must be engaged for the sake of the triune God who is known in the suffering outsider and breaks up our language. The final four papers which constitute Part Four seek to chart a theological way through the new waters of a *postmodern* environment. They depend upon the Barthian legacy and engage theology critically after Barth and beyond modernity. Two papers address the post-liberal quest with reference or affinity to Lindbeck; the other two papers take up Milbank whose references to Barth are few but, like Pannenberg, depends upon Barth's preceding work. Each requires the reader to begin learning a new theological language (especially when confronted with Milbank's prose!). As contemporary readers we are pressed to acknowledge the power of Barth's legacy in present theology. It is clear that those who have been provoked to theology by Barth, being faithful to his intent, will seek to do the work he has initiated, only better.

Thus, the conference papers provide evidence of a rich discussion concerning the theological task in post/modernity and Barth's role there. Based on the survey of the papers in this volume, there can be little ground for a reading of Barth as neo-orthodox, committed to the repristination of a premodern form of theology. Barth is far more a dogmatic theologian who, though schooled in modernity, sought a way out of modernity's impasses by attending single-mindedly to Christian theology's own subject matter, listening to the whole theological history of Christian thought. The claim is contentious and problematic. He attends to that subject matter by refusing any foundation for Christian theology other than Jesus Christ.

Barth's treatment of the theme, *Baptism as the Foundation of the Christian Life*, in CD IV/4 demonstrates his commitment to, and represents his final account of, the way in which Christian existence is shaped by the ground upon which it stands. The term 'foundation' or *Grund* appears repeatedly in this text as Barth excludes all foundationalist thinking. There we may detect Barth's common cause with postmodern thinking, refusing the *foundational strategy* so common in modernity.[14] Equally, however, against a postmodern rejection of any ground or foundation, Barth stakes Christian knowledge of and faith in God upon the one foundation, Jesus Christ, according to Scripture, achieved, according to the editors of that volume,

---

14 Cf J Thiel, *Nonfoundationalism: Guides to Theological Inquiry* (Minneapolis: Fortress Press, 1994); Barth, 'Evangelical Theology', 18-20.

only with 'unwearied and relentless questioning, with enthralling intellectual passion, with the self-less objectivity that is born of complete commitment to the subject-matter' (*CD* IV/4,vi).

Lest the vast quantity of Barth's work suggest that his is a stolid and immobile lump, producing only indigestion in already overloaded minds, we may be relieved to be reminded by Eberhard Busch that Barth himself did not expect that every reader would read all his work. Moreover, as Busch also indicates, even Barth's insistence on a serious engagement with his work did not prevent him from sitting somewhat lightly to it himself:

> Barth did not expect that everyone should read all . . . volumes . . . . . But Barth hoped that his readers would not only read his work but also understand it—though they might not necessarily agree. 'We are not here to agree with one another and to pass compliments. If there are 'Barthians', I myself am not among them. We are here to learn from one another, and to make the best of the literary works we present to one another. After that we go our way—not into a theological school but into the church—and we go it alone. Precisely because of that we must understand one another.' [15]

Barth's invitation, like the conference papers, show that the *colon* of the conference title leaves neither Barth nor postmodern theology in splendid isolation. Instead, the colon brings both Barth the theologian and contemporary culture and theological work into close proximity, seeking mutual understanding. Such proximity does not remove the question mark, for the nature of that relationship is still open. It serves neither mere repristination of a past church thinker, nor adulation of the latest intellectual fashion. Both, as the conference was often

---

15. E Busch, *Karl Barth: His Life from Letters and Autobiographical Texts* (London: SCM, 1976), 375f, quoted from O Weber, *Karl Barth's Church Dogmatics* (London: Lutterworth Press, 1953), 10.

reminded, are to be engaged in the task of interpreting and understanding the subject matter to which theologians are responsible. Barth's own description of that responsibility is contained in his *Epistle to the Romans* and gives a clue to the relationship posed by both the colon and the question mark.

> By genuine understanding and interpretation I mean that creative energy which Luther exercised with intuitive certainty in his exegesis; which understanding underlies the sympathetic interpretation of Calvin . . . how energetically Calvin, having first established what stands in the text, sets himself to re-think the whole material and wrestle with it, till the walls which separate the sixteenth century from the first become transparent! Paul speaks, and the man of the sixteenth century hears. The conversation between the original record and the reader moves around the subject matter, until a distinction between yesterday and to-day becomes impossible.[16]

As for text and exegete, so for Barth and postmodern theology: both are held together by that colon, as by the cross and resurrection of Jesus Christ, to the glory of the triune God.

---

[16]   Barth, *The Epistle to the Romans*, 7.

Author Index

302

Subject Index

CPSIA information can be obtained
at www.ICGtesting.com
Printed in the USA
JSHW031647120320
4695JS00001B/84